YOUR 15-MONTH CANDID,
COMPLETE AND INDIVIDUAL FORECAST

ARIES
March 21 - April 20

1989
SUPER HOROSCOPE

ARROW BOOKS LIMITED
62-65 Chandos Place
London WC2N 4NW

CONTENTS

THE PUBLISHERS REGRET THAT THEY CANNOT ANSWER INDIVIDUAL LETTERS
REQUESTING PERSONAL HOROSCOPE INFORMATION.

FIRST PUBLISHED IN GREAT BRITAIN BY ARROW BOOKS 1988
© GROSSET & DUNLAP, INC., 1974, 1978, 1979, 1980, 1981, 1982
© CHARTER COMMUNICATIONS, INC., 1983, 1984, 1985
COPYRIGHT © 1986, 1987, 1988 THE BERKLEY PUBLISHING GROUP
THIS EDITION PUBLISHED BY AGREEMENT WITH THE BERKLEY PUBLISHING
GROUP

PRINTED IN GREAT BRITAIN BY
GUERNSEY PRESS CO. LTD
GUERNSEY C.I.
ISBN 0 09 954480 6

NOTE TO THE CUSP-BORN

First find the year of your birth, and then find the sign under which you were born according to your day of birth. Thus, you can determine if you are a true Aries (or Pisces or Taurus), according to the variations of the dates of the Zodiac. (See also page 7.)

Are you *really* an Aries? If your birthday falls during the fourth week of March, at the beginning of Aries, will you still retain the traits of Pisces, the sign of the Zodiac before Aries? And what if you were born late in April—are you more Taurus than Aries? Many people born at the edge, or cusp, of a sign have difficulty determining exactly what sign they are. If you are one of these people, here's how you can figure it out, once and for all.

Consult the following table. It will tell you the precise days on which the Sun entered and left your sign for the year of your birth. If you were born at the beginning or end of Aries, yours is a lifetime reflecting a process of subtle transformation. Your life on Earth will symbolize a significant change in consciousness, for you are either about to enter a whole new way of living or are leaving one behind.

If your birthday falls at the end of March, you may want to read the horoscope book for Pisces as well as Aries, for Pisces holds the keys to many of your hidden uncertainties, past guilts, weaknesses, sorrows, unspoken wishes, and your cosmic unfoldment.

You are eager to start living, and possess, in a way, the secret of eternal youth. Obstacles enrage you but never beat you, for you usually feel you have sacrificed more than your share. In some way (after waiting) you will assert yourself and your right to make your own decisions.

However, you are often drawn back through Pisces into a sense of responsibility, a duty to others, a selflessness that at times eats away at your confidence and undermines your character. Honor and the vitality of life are your gifts.

If you were born late in April, you may want to read the horoscope book for Taurus as well as Aries. The investment could be revealing and profitable, for Taurus is often your means of putting your talents to practical use and turning your ideas into actual, tangible rewards.

You are headstrong and determined; you have a sense of independence and fight that nothing can destroy. Sometimes you can vacillate and be worried and negative, but you never give up. You have the earthy sense of all your needs to meet responsibilities, do your duties, build, acquire, and collect. You are attracted to all you possess, and the more you possess, the more permanent your life. You are thus less able to simply pick up and go back to zero; what you start you must try to finish.

DATES SUN ENTERS ARIES
(LEAVES PISCES)

March 20 every year from 1900 to 2000, except for the following:

March 21:

1901	1911	1923	1938	1955
02	13	26	39	59
03	14	27	42	63
05	15	30	43	67
06	18	31	46	71
07	19	34	47	75
09	22	35	51	79
10				

DATES SUN LEAVES ARIES
(ENTERS TAURUS)

April 20 every year from 1900 to 2000, except for the following:

April 19:			April 21:
1948	1972	1988	1903
52	76	89	07
56	80	92	11
60	81	93	19
64	84	96	
68	85	97	

HISTORY AND USES
OF ASTROLOGY

Does astrology have a place in the fast-moving, ultra-scientific world we live in today? Can it be justified in a sophisticated society whose outriders are already preparing to step off the moon into the deep space of the planets themselves? Or is it just a hangover of ancient superstition, a psychological dummy for neurotics and dreamers of every historical age?

These are the kind of questions that any inquiring person can be expected to ask when they approach a subject like astrology which goes beyond, but never excludes, the materialistic side of life.

The simple, single answer is that astrology works. It works for tens of millions of people in the western world alone. In the United States there are 10 million followers and in Europe, an estimated 25 million. America has more than 4000 practicing astrologers, Europe nearly three times as many. Even down-under Australia has its hundreds of thousands of adherents. The importance of such vast numbers of people from diverse backgrounds and cultures is recognized by the world's biggest newspapers and magazines who probably devote more of their space to this subject in a year than to any other. In the eastern countries, astrology has enormous followings, again, because it has been proved to work. In countries like India, brides and grooms for centuries have been chosen on the basis of astrological compatibility. The low divorce rate there, despite today's heavy westernizing influence, is attributed largely to this practice.

In the western world, astrology today is more vital than ever before; more practicable because it needs a sophisticated society like ours to understand and develop its contribution to the full; more valid because science itself is confirming the precepts of astrological knowledge with every new exciting step. The ordinary person who daily applies astrology intelligently does not have to wonder whether it is true nor believe in it blindly. He can see it working for himself. And, if he can use it—and this book is designed to help the reader to do just that—he can make living a far richer experience, and become a more developed personality and a better person.

Astrology is the science of relationships. It is not just a study of planetary influences on man and his environment. It is the study of man himself.

We are at the center of our personal universe, of all our relationships. And our happiness or sadness depends on how we act, how we relate to the people and things that surround us. The emotions that we generate have a distinct affect—for better or worse—on the world around us. Our friends and our enemies will confirm this. Just look in the mirror the next time you are angry. In other words, each of us is a kind of sun or planet or star and our influence on our personal universe, whether loving, helpful or destructive, varies with our changing moods, expressed through our individual character.

And to an extent that includes the entire galaxy, this is true of the planetary bodies. Their radiations affect each other, including the earth and all the things on it. And in comparatively recent years, giant constellations called "quasars" have been discovered. These exist far beyond the night stars that we can observe, and science says these quasars are emitting radiating influences more powerful and different than ever recorded on earth. Their effect on man from an astrological point of view is under deep study. Compared with these inter-stellar forces, our personal "radiations" are negligible on the planetary scale. But ours are just as potent in the way they affect our moods, and our ability to control them. To this extent they determine much of the happiness and satisfaction in our lives. For instance, if we were bound and gagged and had to hold some strong emotion within us without being able to move, we would soon start to feel very uncomfortable. We are obviously pretty powerful radiators inside, in our own way. But usually, we are able to throw off our emotion in some sort of action—we have a good cry, walk it off, or tell someone our troubles—before it can build up too far and make us physically ill. Astrology helps us to understand the universal forces working on us, and through this understanding, we can become more properly adjusted to our surroundings and find ourselves coping where others may flounder.

Closely related to our emotions is the "other side" of our personal universe, our physical welfare. Our body, of course, is largely influenced by things around us over which we have very little control. The phone rings, we hear it. The train runs late. We snag our stocking or cut our face shaving. Our body is under a constant bombardment of events that influence our lives to varying degrees.

The question that arises from all this is, what makes each of us act so that we have to involve other people and keep the ball of activity and evolution rolling? This is the question that both science and astrology are involved with. The scientists have attacked it from different angles: anthropology, the study of human evolution as body, mind and response to environment; anatomy, the study of bodily structure; psychology, the science of the human mind; and so on. These studies have produced very impressive classifications and valuable information, but because the approach to the problem is fragmented, so is the result. They remain "branches" of science. Science generally studies effects. It keeps turning up wonderful answers but no lasting solutions. Astrology, on the other hand approaches the question from the broader viewpoint. Astrology began its inquiry with the totality of human experience and saw it as an effect. It then looked to find the cause, or at least the prime movers, and during thousands of years of observation of man and his *universal* environment, came up with the extraordinary principle of planetary influence—or astrology, which, from the Greek, means the science of the stars.

Modern science, as we shall see, has confirmed much of astrology's foundations—most of it unintentionally, some of it reluctantly, but still, indisputably.

It is not difficult to imagine that there must be a connection between outer space and the earth. Even today, scientists are not too sure how our earth was created, but it is generally agreed that it is only a tiny part of the universe. And as a part of the universe, people on earth see and feel the influence of heavenly bodies in almost every aspect of our existence. There is no doubt that the sun has the greatest influence on life on this planet. Without it there would be no life, for without it there would be no warmth, no division into day and night, no cycles of time or season at all. This is clear and easy to see. The influence of the moon, on the other hand, is more subtle, though no less definite.

There are many ways in which the influence of the moon manifests itself here on earth, both on human and animal life. It is a well-known fact, for instance, that the large movements of water on our planet—that is the ebb and flow of the tides—are caused by the moon's gravitational pull. Since this is so, it follows that these water movements do not occur only in the oceans, but that all bodies of water are affected, even down to the tiniest puddle.

The human body, too, which consists of about 70 percent water, falls within the scope of this lunar influence. For example the menstrual cycle of most women corresponds to the lunar month; the period of pregnancy in humans is 273 days, or equal to nine lunar months. Similarly, many illnesses reach a crisis at the change of the moon, and statistics in many countries have shown that the crime rate is highest at the time of the full moon. Even human sexual desire has been associated with the phases of the moon. But, it is in the movement of the tides that we get the clearest demonstration of planetary influence, and the irresistible correspondence between the so-called metaphysical and the physical.

Tide tables are prepared years in advance by calculating the future positions of the moon. Science has known for a long time that the moon is the main cause of tidal action. But only in the last few years has it begun to realize the possible extent of this influence on mankind. To begin with, the ocean tides do not rise and fall as we might imagine from our personal observations of them. The moon as it orbits around the earth, sets up a circular wave of attraction which pulls the oceans of the world after it, broadly in an east to west direction. This influence is like a phantom wave crest, a loop of power stretching from pole to pole which passes over and around the earth like an invisible shadow. It travels with equal effect across the land masses and, as scientists were recently amazed to observe, caused oysters placed in the dark in the middle of the United States where there is no sea, to open their shells to receive the non-existent tide. If the land-locked oysters react to this invisible signal, what effect does it have on us who not so long ago in evolutionary time, came out of the sea and still have its salt in our blood and sweat?

Less well known is the fact that the moon is also the primary force behind the circulation of blood in human beings and animals, and the movement of sap in trees and plants. Agriculturists have established that the moon has a distinct influence on crops, which explains why for centuries people have planted according to moon cycles. The habits of many animals, too, are directed by the movement of the moon. Migratory birds, for instance, depart only at or near the time of the full moon. Just as certain fish, eels in particular, move only in accordance with certain phases of the moon.

Know Thyself—Why?

In today's fast-changing world, everyone still longs to know what the future holds. It is the one thing that everyone has in common: rich and poor, famous and infamous, all are deeply concerned about tomorrow.

But the key to the future, as every historian knows, lies in the past. This is as true of individual people as it is of nations. You cannot understand your future without first understanding your past, which is simply another way of saying that you must first of all know yourself.

The motto "know thyself" seems obvious enough nowadays, but it was originally put forward as the foundation of wisdom by the ancient Greek philosophers. It was then adopted by the "mystery religions" of the ancient Middle East, Greece and Rome, and is still used in all genuine schools of mind training or mystical discipline, both in those of the East, based on yoga, and those of the West. So it is universally accepted now, and has been through the ages.

But how do you go about discovering what sort of person you are? The first step is usually classification into some sort of system of types. Astrology did this long before the birth of Christ. Psychology has also done it. So has modern medicine, in its way.

One system classifies men according to the source of the impulses they respond to most readily: the muscles, leading to direct bodily action; the digestive organs, resulting in emotion, or the brain and nerves. Another such system says that character is determined by the endocrine glands, and gives us labels like "pituitary," "thyroid" and "hyperthyroid" types. These different systems are neither contradictory nor mutually exclusive. In fact, they are very often different ways of saying the same thing.

Very popular and useful classifications were devised by Dr. C. G. Jung, the eminent disciple of Freud. Jung observed among the different faculties of the mind, four which have a predominant influence on character. These four faculties exist in all of us without exception, but not in perfect balance. So when we say, for instance, that a man is a "thinking type," it means that in any situation he tries to be rational. It follows that emotion, which some say is the opposite of thinking, will be his weakest function. This type can be sensible and reasonable, or calculating and unsympathetic. The emotional type, on the other hand, can often be recognized by exaggerated language—everything is either marvelous or terrible—and in extreme cases they even invent dramas and quarrels out of nothing just to make life more interesting.

The other two faculties are intuition and physical sensation. The sensation type does not only care for food and drink, nice clothes and furniture; he is also interested in all forms of physical experience. Many scientists are sensation types as are athletes and naturelovers. Like sensation, intuition is a form of perception and we all possess it. But it works through that part of the mind which is not under conscious control—consequently it sees meanings and connections which are not obvious to thought or emotion. Inventors and original thinkers are always intuitive, but so, too, are superstitious people who see meanings where none exist.

Thus, sensation tells us what is going on in the world, feeling (that is, emotion) tells us how important it is to ourselves, thinking enables us to interpret it and work out what we should do about it, and intuition tells us what it means to ourselves and others. All four faculties are essential, and all are present in every one of us. But some people are guided chiefly by one, others by another.

Besides these four types, Jung observed a division into extrovert and introvert, which cuts across them. By and large, the introvert is one who finds truth inside himself rather than outside. He is not, therefore, ideally suited to a religion or a political party which tells him what to believe. Original thinkers are almost necessarily introverts. The extrovert, on the other hand, finds truth coming to him from outside. He believes in experts and authorities, and wants to think that nature and the laws of nature really exists, that they are what they appear to be and not just generalities made by men.

A disadvantage of all these systems of classification, is that one cannot tell very easily where to place oneself. Some people are reluctant to admit that they act to please their emotions. So they deceive themselves for years by trying to belong to whichever type they think is the "best." Of course, there is no best; each has its faults and each has its good points.

The advantage of the signs of the Zodiac is that they simplify classification. Not only that, but your date of birth is personal—it is unarguably yours. What better way to know yourself than by going back as far as possible to the very moment of your birth? And this is precisely what your horoscope is all about.

What Is a Horoscope?

If you had been able to take a picture of the heavens at the moment of your birth, that photograph would be your horoscope. Lacking such a snapshot, it is still possible to recreate the picture—and this is at the basis of the astrologer's art. In other words, your horoscope is a representation of the skies with the planets in the exact positions they occupied at the time you were born.

This information, of course, is not enough for the astrologer. He has to have a background of significance to put the photograph on. You will get the idea if you imagine two balls—one inside the other. The inner one is transparent. In the center of both is the astrologer, able to look up, down and around in all directions. The outer sphere is the Zodiac which is divided into twelve approximately equal segments, like the segments of an orange. The inner ball is our photograph. It is transparent except for the images of the planets. Looking out from the center, the astrologer sees the planets in various segments of the Zodiac. These twelve segments are known as the signs or houses.

The position of the planets when each of us is born is always different. So the photograph is always different. But the Zodiac and its signs are fixed.

Now, where in all this are you, the subject of the horoscope?

You, or your character, is largely determined by the sign the sun is in. So that is where the astrologer looks first in your horoscope.

There are twelve signs in the Zodiac and the sun spends approximately one month in each. As the sun's motion is almost perfectly regular, the astrologers have been able to fix the dates governing each sign. There are not many people who do not know which sign of the Zodiac they were born under or who have not been amazed at some time or other at the accuracy of the description of their own character. Here are the twelve signs, the ancient zodiacal symbol, and their dates for the year 1989.*

ARIES	Ram	March 20–April 19
TAURUS	Bull	April 19–May 20
GEMINI	Twins	May 20–June 21
CANCER	Crab	June 21–July 22
LEO	Lion	July 22–August 22
VIRGO	Virgin	August 22–September 22
LIBRA	Scales	September 22–October 23
SCORPIO	Scorpion	October 23–November 22
SAGITTARIUS	Archer	November 22–December 21
CAPRICORN	Sea-Goat	December 21–January 19
AQUARIUS	Water-Bearer	January 19–February 18
PISCES	Fish	February 18–March 20

The time of birth—apart from the date—is important in advanced astrology because the planets travel at such great speed that the patterns they form change from minute to minute. For this reason, each person's horoscope is his and his alone. Further on we will see that the practicing astrologer has ways of determining and reading these minute time changes which dictate the finer character differences in us all.

However, it is still possible to draw significant conclusions and make meaningful predictions based simply on the sign of the Zodiac a person is born under. In a horoscope, the signs do not necessarily correspond with the divisions of the houses. It could be that a house begins halfway across a sign. It is the interpretation of such combinations of different influences that distinguishes the professional astrologer from the student and the follower.

However, to gain a workable understanding of astrology, it is not necessary to go into great detail. In fact, the beginner is likely to find himself confused if he attempts to absorb too much too quickly. It should be remembered that this is a science and to become proficient at it, and especially to grasp the tremendous scope of possibilities in man and his affairs and direct them into a worthwhile reading, takes a great deal of study and experience.

*These dates are fluid and change with the motion of the Earth from year to year.

If you do intend to pursue it seriously you will have to learn to figure the exact moment of birth against the degrees of longitude and latitude of the planets at that precise time. This involves adapting local time to Greenwich Mean Time (G.M.T.), reference to tables of houses to establish the Ascendant, as well as making calculations from Ephemeris—the tables of the planets' positions.

After reading this introduction, try drawing up a rough horoscope to get the "feel" of reading some elementary characteristics and natal influences.

Draw a circle with twelve equal segments. Write in counterclockwise the names of the signs—Aries, Taurus, Gemini etc.—one for each segment. Look up an ephemeris for the year of the person's birth and note down the sign each planet was in on the birthday. Do not worry about the number of degrees (although if a planet is on the edge of a sign its position obviously should be considered). Write the name of the planet in the segment/sign on your chart. Write the number 1 in the sign where the sun is. This is the first house. Number the rest of the houses, counterclockwise till you finish at 12. Now you can investigate the probable basic expectation of experience of the person concerned. This is done first of all by seeing what planet or planets is/are in what sign and house. (See also page 72.)

The 12 houses control these functions:

1st.	Individuality, body appearance, general outlook on life	(Personality house)
2nd.	Finance, business	(Money house)
3rd.	Relatives, education, correspondence	(Relatives house)
4th.	Family, neighbors	(Home house)
5th.	Pleasure, children, attempts, entertainment	(Pleasure house)
6th.	Health, employees	(Health house)
7th.	Marriage, partnerships	(Marriage house)
8th.	Death, secret deals, difficulties	(Death house)
9th.	Travel, intellectual affairs	(Travel house)
10th.	Ambition, social standing	(Business and Honor house)
11th.	Friendship, social life, luck	(Friends house)
12th.	Troubles, illness, loss	(Trouble house)

The characteristics of the planets modify the influence of the Sun according to their natures and strengths.

Sun: Source of life. Basic temperament according to sun sign. The will.
Moon: Superficial nature. Moods. Changeable. Adaptive. Mother.
Mercury: Communication. Intellect. Reasoning power. Curiosity. Short travels.
Venus: Love. Delight. Art. Beautiful possessions.
Mars: Energy. Initiative. War. Anger. Destruction. Impulse.
Jupiter: Good. Generous. Expansive. Opportunities. Protection.
Saturn: Jupiter's opposite. Contraction. Servant. Delay. Hardwork. Cold. Privation. Research. Lasting rewards after long struggle.
Uranus: Fashion. Electricity. Revolution. Sudden changes. Modern science.
Neptune: Sensationalism. Mass emotion. Devastation. Delusion.
Pluto: Creates and destroys. Lust for power. Strong obsessions.

Superimpose the characteristics of the planets on the functions of the house in which they appear. Express the result through the character of the birth (sun) sign, and you will get the basic idea of how astrology works.

Of course, many other considerations have been taken into account in producing the carefully worked out predictions in this book: The aspects of the planets to each other; their strength according to position and sign; whether they are in a house of exaltation or decline; whether they are natural enemies or not; whether a planet occupies his own sign; the position of a planet in relation to its own house or sign; whether the planet is male, female or neuter; whether the sign is a fire, earth, water or air sign. These are only a few of the colors on the astrologer's pallet which he must mix with the inspiration of the artist and the accuracy of the mathematician.

The Problem of Love

Love, of course, is never a problem. The problem lies in recognizing the difference between infatuation, emotion, sex and, sometimes, the downright deceit of the other person. Mankind, with its record of broken marriages, despair and disillusionment, is obviously not very good at making these distinctions.

Can astrology help?

Yes. In the same way that advance knowledge can usually help in any human situation. And there is probably no situation as human, as poignant, as pathetic and universal, as the failure of man's love.

Love, of course, is not just between man and woman. It involves love of children, parents, home and so on. But the big problems usually involve the choice of partner.

Astrology has established degrees of compatibility that exist between people born under the various signs of the Zodiac. Because people are individuals, there are numerous variations and modifications and the astrologer, when approached on mate and marriage matters makes allowances for them. But the fact remains that some groups of people are suited for each other and some are not and astrology has expressed this in terms of characteristics which all can study and use as a personal guide.

No matter how much enjoyment and pleasure we find in the different aspects of each other's character, if it is not an overall compatibility, the chances of our finding fulfillment or enduring happiness in each other are pretty hopeless. And astrology can help us to find someone compatible.

History of Astrology

The origins of astrology have been lost far back in history, but we do know that reference is made to it as far back as the first written records of the human race. It is not hard to see why. Even in primitive times, people must have looked for an explanation for the various happenings in their lives. They must have wanted to know why people were different from one to another. And in their search they turned to the regular movements of the sun, moon and stars to see if they could provide an answer.

It is interesting to note that as soon as man learned to use his tools in any type of design, or his mind in any kind of calculation, he turned his attention to the heavens. Ancient cave dwellings reveal dim crescents and circles representative of the sun and moon, rulers of day and night. Mesopotamia and the civilization of Chaldea, in itself the foundation of those of Babylonia and Assyria, show a complete picture of astronomical observation and well-developed astrological interpretation.

Humanity has a natural instinct for order. The study of anthropology reveals that primitive people—even as far back as prehistoric times—were striving to achieve a certain order in their lives. They tried to organize the apparent chaos of the universe. They had the desire to attach meaning to things. This demand for order has persisted throughout the history of man. So that observing the regularity of the heavenly bodies made it logical that primitive peoples should turn heavenwards in their search for an understanding of the world in which they found themselves so random and alone.

And they did find a significance in the movements of the stars. Shepherds tending their flocks, for instance, observed that when the cluster of stars now known as the constellation Aries was in sight, it was the time of fertility and they associated it with the Ram. And they noticed that the growth of plants and plant life corresponded with different phases of the moon, so that certain times were favorable for the planting of crops, and other times were not. In this way, there grew up a tradition of seasons and causes connected with the passage of the sun through the twelve signs of the Zodiac.

Astrology was valued so highly that the king was kept informed of the daily and monthly changes in the heavenly bodies, and the results of astrological studies regarding events of the future. Head astrologers were clearly men of great rank and position, and the office was said to be a hereditary one.

Omens were taken, not only from eclipses and conjunctions of the moon or sun with one of the planets, but also from storms and earthquakes. In the eastern civilizations, particularly, the reverence inspired by astrology appears to have remained unbroken since the very earliest days. In ancient China, astrology, astronomy and religion went hand in hand. The astrologer, who was also an astronomer, was part of the official government service and had his own corner in the Imperial Palace. The duties of the Imperial astrologer, whose office was one of the most important in the land, were clearly defined, as this extract from early records shows:

"This exalted gentleman must concern himself with the stars in the heavens, keeping a record of the changes and movements of the Planets, the Sun and the Moon, in order to examine the movements of the terrestial world with the object of prognosticating good and bad fortune. He divides the territories of the nine regions of the empire in accordance with their dependence on particular celestial bodies. All the fiefs and principalities are connected with the stars and from this their prosperity or misfortune should be ascertained. He makes prognostications according to the twelve years of the Jupiter cycle of good and evil of the terrestial world. From the colors of the five kinds of clouds, he determines the coming of floods or droughts, abundance or famine. From the twelve winds, he draws conclusions about the state of harmony of heaven and earth, and takes note of good and bad signs that result from their accord or disaccord. In general, he concerns himself with five kinds of phenomena so as to warn the Emperor to come to the aid of the government and to allow for variations in the ceremonies according to their circumstances."

The Chinese were also keen observers of the fixed stars, giving them such unusual names as Ghost Vehicle, Sun of Imperial Concubine, Imperial Prince, Pivot of Heaven, Twinkling Brilliance or Weaving Girl. But, great astrologers though they may have been, the Chinese lacked one aspect of mathematics that the Greeks applied to astrology—deductive geometry. Deductive geometry was the basis of much classical astrology in and after the time of the Greeks, and this explains the different methods of prognostication used in the East and West.

Down through the ages the astrologer's art has depended, not so much on the uncovering of new facts, though this is important, as on the interpretation of the facts already known. This is the essence of his skill. Obviously one cannot always tell how people will react (and this underlines the very important difference between astrology and predestination which will be discussed later on) but one can be prepared, be forewarned, to know what to expect.

But why should the signs of the zodiac have any effect at all on the formation of human character? It is easy to see why people thought they did, and even now we constantly use astrological expressions in our everyday speech. The thoughts of "lucky star," "ill-fated," "star-crossed," "mooning around," are interwoven into the very structure of our language.

In the same way that the earth has been created by influences from outside, there remains an indisputable togetherness in the working of the universe. The world, after all, is a coherent structure, for if it were not, it would be quite without order and we would never know what to expect. A dog could turn into an apple, or an elephant sprout wings and fly at any moment without so much as a by your leave. But nature, as we know, functions according to laws, not whims, and the laws of nature are certainly not subject to capricious exceptions.

This means that no part of the universe is ever arbitrarily cut off from any other part. Everything is therefore to some extent linked with everything else. The moon draws an imperceptible tide on every puddle; tiny and trivial events can be effected by outside forces (such as the fall of a feather by the faintest puff of wind). And so it is fair to think that the local events at any moment reflect to a very small extent the evolution of the world as a whole.

From this principle follows the possibility of divination, and also knowledge of events at a distance, provided one's mind were always as perfectly undisturbed, as ideally smooth, as a mirror or unruffled lake. Provided, in other words, that one did not confuse the picture with hopes, guesses, and expectations. When people try to foretell the future by cards or crystal ball gazing they find it much easier to confuse the picture with expectations than to reflect it clearly.

But the present does contain a good deal of the future to which it leads—not all, but a good deal. The diver halfway between bridge and water is going to make a splash; the train whizzing towards the station will pass through it unless interfered with; the burglar breaking a pane of glass has exposed himself to the possibility of a prison sentence. Yet this is not a doctrine of determinism, as was emphasized earlier. Clearly, there are forces already at work in the present, and any one of them could alter the situation in some way. Equally, a change of decision could alter the whole situation as well. So the future depends, not on an irresistible force, but on a small act of free will.

An individual's age, physique, and position on the earth's surface are remote consequences of his birth. Birth counts as the original cause for all that happens subsequently. The horoscope, in this case, means "this person represents the further evolution of the state of the universe pictured in this chart." Such a chart can apply equally to man or woman, dog, ship or even limited company.

If the evolution of an idea, or of a person, is to be understood as a totality, it must continue to evolve from its own beginnings, which is to say, in the terms in which it began. The brown-eyed person will be faithful to brown eyes all his life; the traitor is being faithful to some complex of ideas which has long been evolving in him; and the person born at sunset will always express, as he evolves, the psychological implications or analogies of the moment when the sun sinks out of sight.

This is the doctrine that an idea must continue to evolve in terms of its origin. It is a completely non-materialist doctrine, though it never fails to apply to material objects. And it implies, too, that the individual will continue to evolve in terms of his moment of origin, and therefore possibly of the sign of the Zodiac rising on the eastern horizon at his birth. It also implies that the signs of the Zodiac themselves will evolve in the collective mind of the human race in the same terms that they were first devised and not in the terms in which modern astrologers consciously think they ought to work.

For the human race, like every other kind of animal, has a collective mind, as Professor Jung discovered in his investigation of dreams. If no such collective mind existed, no infant could ever learn anything, for communication would be impossible. Furthermore, it is absurd to suggest that the conscious mind could be older than the "unconscious," for an infant's nervous system functions correctly before it has discovered the difference between "myself" and "something else" or discovered what eyes and hands are for. Indeed, the involuntary muscles function correctly even before birth, and will never be under conscious control. They are part of what we call the "unconscious" which is not really "unconscious" at all. To the contrary, it is totally aware of itself and everything else; it is merely that part of the mind that cannot be controlled by conscious effort.

And human experience, though it varies in detail with every individual, is basically the same for each one of us, consisting of sky and earth, day and night, waking and sleeping, man and woman, birth and death. So there is bound to be in the mind of the human race a very large number of inescapable ideas, which are called our natural archetypes.

There are also, however, artificial or cultural archetypes which are not universal or applicable to everyone, but are nevertheless inescapable within the limits of a given culture. Examples of these are the cross in Christianity, and the notion of "escape from the wheel of rebirth" in India. There was a time when these ideas did not exist. And there was a time, too, when the scheme of the Zodiac did not exist. One would not expect the Zodiac to have any influence on remote and primitive peoples, for example, who have never heard of it. If the Zodiac is only an archetype, their horoscopes probably would not work and it would not matter which sign they were born under.

But where the Zodiac is known, and the idea of it has become worked into the collective mind, then there it could well appear to have an influence, even if it has no physical existence. For ideas do not have a physical existence, anyway. No physical basis has yet been discovered for the telepathy that controls an anthill; young swallows migrate before, not after, their parents; and the weaver-bird builds its intricate nest without being taught. Materialists suppose, but cannot prove, that "instinct" (as it is called, for no one knows how it works) is controlled by nucleic acid in the chromosomes. This is not a genuine explanation, though, for it only pushes the mystery one stage further back.

Does this mean, then, that the human race, in whose civilization the idea of the twelve signs of the Zodiac has long been embedded, is divided into only twelve types? Can we honestly believe that it is really as simple as that? If so, there must be pretty wide ranges of variation within each type. And if, to explain the variation, we call in heredity and environment, experiences in early childhood, the thyroid and other glands, and also the four functions of the mind mentioned at the beginning of this introduction, and extroversion and introversion, then one begins to wonder if the original classification was worth making at all. No sensible person believes that his favorite system explains everything. But even so, he will not find it much use at all if it does not even save him the trouble of bothering with the others.

Under the Jungian system, everyone has not only a dominant or principal function, but also a secondary or subsidiary one, so that the four can be arranged in order of potency. In the intuitive type, sensation is always the most inefficient function, but the second most inefficient function can be either thinking (which tends to make original thinkers such as Jung himself) or else feeling (which tends to make artistic people). Therefore, allowing for introversion and extroversion, there are at least four kinds of intuitive types, and sixteen types in all. Furthermore, one can see how the sixteen types merge into each other, so that there are no unrealistic or unconvincingly rigid divisions.

In the same way, if we were to put every person under only one sign of the Zodiac, the system becomes too rigid and unlike life. Besides, it was never intended to be used like that. It may be convenient to have only twelve types, but we know that in practice there is every possible gradation between aggressiveness and timidity, or between conscientiousness and laziness. How, then, do we account for this?

The Tyrant and the Saint

Just as the thinking type of man is also influenced to some extent by sensation and intuition, but not very much by emotion, so a person born under Leo can be influenced to some extent by one or two (but not more) of the other signs. For instance, famous persons born under the sign of Gemini include Henry VIII, whom nothing and no-one could have induced to abdicate, and Edward VIII, who did just that. Obviously, then, the sign Gemini does not fully explain the complete character of either of them.

Again, under the opposite sign, Sagittarius, were both Stalin, who was totally consumed with the notion of power, and Charles V, who freely gave up an empire because he preferred to go into a monastery. And we find under Scorpio, many uncompromising characters such as Luther, de Gaulle, Indira Gandhi and Montgomery, but also Petain, a successful commander whose name later became synonymous with collaboration.

A single sign is therefore obviously inadequate to explain the differences between people; it can only explain resemblances, such as the combativeness of the Scorpio group, or the far-reaching devotion of Charles V and Stalin to their respective ideals—the Christian heaven and the Communist utopia.

But very few people are born under one sign only. As well as the month of birth, as was mentioned earlier, the day matters, and, even more, the hour, which ought, if possible, to be noted to the nearest minute. Without this, it is impossible to have an actual horoscope, for the word horoscope means literally, "a consideration of the hour."

The month of birth tells you only which sign of the Zodiac was occupied by the sun. The day and hour tell you what sign was occupied by the moon. And the minute tells you which sign was rising on the eastern horizon. This is called the Ascendant, and it is supposed to be the most important thing in the whole horoscope.

If you were born at midnight, the sun is then in an important position, although invisible. But at one o'clock in the morning the sun is not important, so the moment of birth will not matter much. The important thing then will be the Ascendant, and possibly one or two of the planets. At a given day and hour, say, dawn on January 1st, or 9:00 p.m. on the longest day, the Ascendant will always be the same at any given place. But the moon and planets alter from day to day, at different speeds and have to be looked up in an astronomical table.

The sun is said to signify one's heart, that is to say, one's deepest desires and inmost nature. This is quite different from the moon, which, as we have seen, signifies one's superficial way of behaving. When the ancient Romans referred to the Emperor Augustus as a Capricornian, they meant that he had the moon in Capricorn; they did not pay much attention to the sun, although he was born at sunrise. Or, to take another example, a modern astrologer would call Disraeli a Scorpion because he had Scorpio rising, but most people would call him Sagittarian because he had the sun there. The Romans would have called him Leo because his moon was in Leo.

The sun, as has already been pointed out, is important if one is born near sunrise, sunset, noon or midnight, but is otherwise not reckoned as the principal influence. So if one does not seem to fit one's birth month, it is always worthwhile reading the other signs, for one may have been born at a time when any of them were rising or occupied by the moon. It also seems to be the case that the influence of the sun develops as life goes on, so that the month of birth is easier to guess in people over the age of forty. The young are supposed to be influenced mainly by their Ascendant which characterizes the body and physical personality as a whole.

It should be clearly understood that it is nonsense to assume that all people born at a certain time will exhibit the same characteristics, or that they will even behave in the same manner. It is quite obvious that, from the very moment of its birth, a child is subject to the effects of its environment, and that this in turn will influence its character and heritage to a decisive extent. Also to be taken into account are education and economic conditions, which play a very important part in the formation of one's character as well.

However, it is clearly established that people born under one sign of the Zodiac do have certain basic traits in their character which are different from those born under other signs. It is obvious to every thinking person that certain events produce different reactions in various people. For instance, if a man slips on a banana skin and falls heavily on the pavement, one passer-by may laugh and find this extremely amusing, while another may just walk on, thinking: "What a fool falling down like that. He should look where he is going." A third might also walk away saying to himself: "It's none of my business—I'm glad it wasn't me." A fourth might walk past and think: "I'm sorry for that man, but I haven't the time to be bothered with helping him." And a fifth might stop to help the fallen man to his feet, comfort him and take him home. Here is just one event which could produce entirely different reactions in different people. And, obviously, there are many more. One that comes to mind immediately is the violently opposed views to events such as wars, industrial strikes, and so on. The fact that people have different attitudes to the same event is simply another way of saying that they have different characters. And this is not something that can be put down to background, for people of the same race, religion, or class, very often express quite different reactions to happenings or events. Similarly, it is often the case that members of the same family, where there is clearly uniform background of economic and social standing, education, race and religion, often argue bitterly among themselves over political and social issues.

People have, in general, certain character traits and qualities which, according to their environment, develop in either a positive or a negative manner. Therefore, selfishness (inherent selfishness, that is) might emerge as unselfishness; kindness and consideration as cruelty and lack of consideration towards others. In the same way, a naturally constructive person, may, through frustration, become destructive, and so on. The latent characteristics with which people are born can, therefore, through environment and good or bad training, become something that would appear to be its opposite, and so give the lie to the astrologer's description of their character. But this is not the case. The true character is still there, but it is buried deep beneath these external superficialities.

Careful study of the character traits of different signs can be immeasurable help, and can render beneficial service to the intelligent person. Undoubtedly, the reader will already have discovered that, while he is able to get on very well with some people, he just "cannot stand" others. The causes sometimes seem inexplicable. At times there is intense dislike, at other times immediate sympathy. And there is, too, the phenomenon of love at first sight, which is also apparently inexplicable. People appear to be either sympathetic or unsympathetic towards each other for no apparent reason.

Now if we look at this in the light of the Zodiac, we find that people born under different signs are either compatible or incompatible with each other. In other words, there are good and bad interrelating factors among the various signs. This does not, of course, mean that humanity can be divided into groups of hostile camps. It would be quite wrong to be hostile or indifferent toward people who happen to be born under an incompatible sign. There is no reason why everybody should not, or cannot, learn to control and adjust their feelings and actions, especially after they are aware of the positive qualities of other people by studying their character analyses, among other things.

Every person born under a certain sign has both positive and negative qualities, which are developed more or less according to his free will. Nobody is entirely good or entirely bad, and it is up to each one of us to learn to control himself on the one hand, and at the same time to endeavor to learn about himself and others.

It cannot be repeated often enough that, though the intrinsic nature of man and his basic character traits are born in him, nevertheless it is his own free will that determines whether he will make really good use of his talents and abilities—whether, in other words, he will overcome his vices or allow them to rule him. Most of us are born with at least a streak of laziness, irritability, or some other fault in our nature, and it is up to each one of us to see that we exert sufficient willpower to control our failings so that they do not harm ourselves or others.

Astrology can reveal our inclinations and tendencies. Our weaknesses should not be viewed as shortcomings that are impossible to change. The horoscope of a man may show him to have criminal leanings, for instance, but this does not mean he will definitely become a criminal.

The ordinary man usually finds it difficult to know himself. He is often bewildered. Astrology can frequently tell him more about himself than the different schools of psychology are able to do. Knowing his failings and shortcomings, he will do his best to overcome them, and make himself a better and more useful member of society and a helpmate to his family and friends. It can also save him a great deal of unhappiness and remorse.

And yet it may seem absurd that an ancient philosophy, something that is known as a "pseudo-science," could be a prop to the men and women of the twentieth century. But below the materialistic surface of modern life, there are hidden streams of feeling and thought. Symbology is reappearing as a study worthy of the scholar; the psychosomatic factor in illness has passed from the writings of the crank to those of the specialist; spiritual healing in all its forms is no longer a pious hope but an accepted phenomenon. And it is into this context that we consider astrology, in the sense that it is an analysis of human types.

Astrology and medicine had a long journey together, and only parted company a couple of centuries ago. There still remain in medical language such astrological terms as "saturnine," "choleric," and "mercurial," used in the diagnosis of physical tendencies. The herbalist, for long the handyman of the medical profession, has been dominated by astrology since the days of the Greeks. Certain herbs traditionally respond to certain planetary influences, and diseases must therefore be treated to ensure harmony between the medicine and the disease.

No one expects the most eccentric of modern doctors to go back to the practices of his predecessors. We have come a long way since the time when phases of the moon were studied in illness. Those days were a medical nightmare, with epidemics that were beyond control, and an explanation of the Black Death sought in conjunction with the planets. Nowadays, astrological diagnosis of disease has literally no parallel in modern life. And yet, age-old symbols of types and of the vulnerability of, say, the Saturnian to chronic diseases or the choleric to apoplexy and blood pressure and so on, are still applicable.

But the stars are expected to foretell and not only to diagnose. The astrological forecaster has a counterpart on a highly conventional level in the shape of the weather prophet, racing tipster and stock market forecaster, to name just three examples. All in their own way are aiming at the same result. They attempt to look a little further into the pattern of life and also try to determine future patterns accurately.

Astrological forecasting has been remarkably accurate, but often it is wide of the mark. The brave man who cares to predict world events takes dangerous chances. Individual forecasting is less clear cut; it can be a help or a disillusionment. Then welcome to the nagging question: if it is possible to foreknow, is it right to foretell? A complex point of ethics on which it is hard to pronounce judgment. The doctor faces the same dilemma if he finds that symptoms of a mortal disease are present in his patient and that he can only prognosticate a steady decline. How much to tell an individual in a crisis is a problem that has perplexed many distinguished scholars. Honest and conscientious astrologers in this modern world, where so many people are seeking guidance, face the same problem.

The ancient cults, the symbols of old religions, are eclipsed for the moment. They may return with their old force within a decade or two. But at present the outlook is dark. Human beings badly need assurance, as they did in the past, that all is not chaos. Somewhere, somehow, there is a pattern that must be worked out. As to the why and wherefore, the astrologer is not expected to give judgment. He is just someone who, by dint of talent and training, can gaze into the future.

Five hundred years ago it was customary to call in a learned man who was an astrologer who was probably also a doctor and a philosopher. By his knowledge of astrology, his study of planetary influences, he felt himself qualified to guide those in distress. The world has moved forward at a fantastic rate since then, and in this twentieth century speed has been the keyword everywhere. Tensions have increased, the spur of ambition has been applied indiscriminately. People are uncertain of themselves. At first sight it seems fantastic in the light of modern thinking that they turn to the most ancient of all studies, and get someone to calculate a horoscope for them. But is it *really* so fantastic if you take a second look? For astrology is concerned with tomorrow, with survival. And in a world such as ours, those two things are the keywords of the time in which we live.

HOW TO USE
THESE PREDICTIONS

A person reading the predictions in this book should understand that they are produced from the daily position of the planets for a group of people and are not, of course, individually specialized. To get the full benefit of them he should relate the predictions to his own character and circumstances, co-ordinate them, and draw his own conclusions from them.

If he is a serious observer of his own life he should find a definite pattern emerge that will be a helpful and reliable guide.

The point is that we always retain our free will. The stars indicate certain directional tendencies but we are not compelled to follow. We can do or not do, and wisdom must make the choice.

We all have our good and bad days. Sometimes they extend into cycles of weeks. It is therefore advisable to study daily predictions in a span ranging from the day before to several days ahead; also to re-read the monthly predictions for similar cycles.

Daily predictions should be taken very generally. The word "difficult" does not necessarily indicate a whole day of obstruction or inconvenience. It is a warning to you to be cautious. Your caution will often see you around the difficulty before you are involved. This is the correct use of astrology.

In another section, detailed information is given about the influence of the moon as it passes through the various signs of the Zodiac. It includes instructions on how to use the Moon Tables. This information should be used in conjunction with the daily forecasts to give a fuller picture of the astrological trends.

THE MOON

Moon is the nearest planet to the earth. It exerts more observable influence on us from day to day than any other planet. The effect is very personal, very intimate, and if we are not aware of how it works it can make us quite unstable in our ideas. And the annoying thing is that at these times we often see our own instability but can do nothing about it. A knowledge of what can be expected may help considerably. We can then be prepared to stand strong against the moon's negative influences and use its positive ones to help us to get ahead. Who has not heard of going with the tide?

Moon reflects, has no light of its own. It reflects the sun—the life giver—in the form of vital movement. Moon controls the tides, the blood rhythm, the movement of sap in trees and plants. Its nature is inconstancy and change so it signifies our moods, our superficial behavior—walking, talking and especially thinking. Being a true reflector of other forces, moon is cold, watery like the surface of a still lake, brilliant and scintillating at times, but easily ruffled and disturbed by the winds of change.

The moon takes 28½ days to circle the earth and the Zodiac. It spends just over 2¼ days in each sign. During that time it reflects the qualities, energies and characteristics of the sign and, to a degree, the planet which rules the sign. While the moon in its transit occupies a sign incompatible with our own birth sign, we can expect to feel a vague uneasiness, perhaps a touch of irritableness. We should not be discouraged nor let the feeling get us down, or, worse still, allow ourselves to take the discomfort out on others. Try to remember that the moon has to change signs within 55 hours and, provided you are not physically ill, your mood will probably change with it. It is amazing how frequently depression lifts with the shift in the moon's position. And, of course, when the moon is transiting a sign compatible or sympathetic to yours you will probably feel some sort of stimulation or just plain happy to be alive.

In the horoscope, the moon is such a powerful indicator that competent astrologers often use the sign it occupied at birth as the birth sign of the person. This is done particularly when the sun is on the cusp, or edge, of two signs. Most experienced astrologers, however, coordinate both sun and moon signs by reading and confirming from one to the other and secure a far more accurate and personalized analysis.

For these reasons, the moon tables which follow this section (see pages 28–35) are of great importance to the individual. They show the days and the exact times the moon will enter each sign of the Zodiac for the year. Remember, you have to adjust the indicated times to local time. The corrections, already calculated for most of the main cities, are at the beginning of the tables. What follows now is a guide to the influences that will be reflected to the earth by the moon while it transits each of the twelve signs. The influence is at its peak about 26 hours after the moon enters a sign.

MOON IN ARIES

This is a time for action, for reaching out beyond the usual self-imposed limitations and faint-hearted cautions. If you have plans in your head or on your desk, put them into practice. New ventures, applications, new jobs, new starts of any kind—all have a good chance of success. This is the period when original and dynamic impulses are being reflected onto the earth. The energies are extremely vital and favor the pursuit of pleasure and adventure in practically every form. Sick people should feel an improvement. Those who are well will probably find themselves exuding confidence and optimism. People fond of physical exercise should find their bodies growing with tone and well-being. Boldness, strength, determination should characterize most of your activities with a readiness to face up to old challenges. Yesterday's problems may seem petty and exaggerated—so deal with them. Strike out alone. Self-reliance will attract others to you. This is a good time for making friends. Business and marriage partners are more likely to be impressed with the man and woman of action. Opposition will be overcome or thrown aside with much less effort than usual. CAUTION: Be dominant but not domineering.

MOON IN TAURUS

The spontaneous, action-packed person of yesterday gives way to the cautious, diligent, hardworking "thinker." In this period ideas will probably be concentrated on ways of improving finances. A great deal of time may be spent figuring out and going over schemes and plans. It is the right time to be careful with detail. People will find themselves working longer than usual at their desks. Or devoting more time to serious thought about the future. A strong desire to put order into business and financial arrangements may cause extra work. Loved ones may complain of being neglected and may fail to appreciate that your efforts are for their ultimate benefit. Your desire for system may extend to criticism of arrangements in the home and lead to minor upsets. Health may be affected through overwork. Try to secure a reasonable amount of rest and relaxation, although the tendency will be to "keep going" despite good advice. Work done conscientiously in this period should result in a solid contribution to your future security. CAUTION: Try not to be as serious with people as the work you are engaged in.

MOON IN GEMINI

The humdrum of routine and too much work should suddenly end. You are likely to find yourself in an expansive, quicksilver world of change and self-expression. Urges to write, to paint, to experience the freedom of some sort of artistic outpouring, may be very strong. Take full advantage of them. You may find yourself finishing something you began and put aside long ago. Or embarking on something new which could easily be prompted by a chance meeting, a new acquaintance, or even an advertisement. There may be a yearning for a change of scenery, the feeling to visit another country (not too far away), or at least to get away for a few days. This may result in short, quick journeys. Or, if you are planning a single visit, there may be some unexpected changes or detours on the way. Familiar activities will seem to give little satisfaction unless they contain a fresh element of excitement or expectation. The inclination will be towards untried pursuits, particularly those that allow you to express your inner nature. The accent is on new faces, new places. CAUTION: Do not be too quick to commit yourself emotionally.

MOON IN CANCER

Feelings of uncertainty and vague insecurity are likely to cause problems while the moon is in Cancer. Thoughts may turn frequently to the warmth of the home and the comfort of loved ones. Nostalgic impulses could cause you to bring out old photographs and letters and reflect on the days when your life seemed to be much more rewarding and less demanding. The love and understanding of parents and family may be important, and, if it is not forthcoming you may have to fight against a bit of self-pity. The cordiality of friends and the thought of good times with them that are sure to be repeated will help to restore you to a happier frame of mind. The feeling to be alone may follow minor setbacks or rebuffs at this time, but solitude is unlikely to help. Better to get on the telephone or visit someone. This period often causes peculiar dreams and up-surges of imaginative thinking which can be very helpful to authors of occult and mystical works. Preoccupation with the more personal world of simple human needs should overshadow any material strivings. CAUTION: Do not spend too much time thinking—seek the company of loved ones or close friends.

MOON IN LEO

New horizons of exciting and rather extravagant activity open up. This is the time for exhilarating entertainment, glamorous and lavish parties, and expensive shopping sprees. Any merrymaking that relies upon your generosity as a host has every chance of being a spectacular success. You should find yourself right in the center of the fun, either as the life of the party or simply as a person whom happy people like to be with. Romance thrives in this heady atmosphere and friendships are likely to explode unexpectedly into serious attachments. Children and younger people should be attracted to you and you may find yourself organizing a picnic or a visit to a fun-fair, the cinema or the seaside. The sunny company and vitality of youthful companions should help you to find some unsuspected energy. In career, you could find an opening for promotion or advancement. This should be the time to make a direct approach. The period favors those engaged in original research. CAUTION: Bask in popularity but not in flattery.

MOON IN VIRGO

Off comes the party cap and out steps the busy, practical worker. He wants to get his personal affairs straight, to rearrange them, if necessary, for more efficiency, so he will have more time for more work. He clears up his correspondence, pays outstanding bills, makes numerous phone calls. He is likely to make inquiries, or sign up for some new insurance and put money into gilt-edged investment. Thoughts probably revolve around the need for future security—to tie up loose ends and clear the decks. There may be a tendency to be "finicky," to interfere in the routine of others, particularly friends and family members. The motive may be a genuine desire to help with suggestions for updating or streamlining their affairs, but these will probably not be welcomed. Sympathy may be felt for less fortunate sections of the community and a flurry of some sort of voluntary service is likely. This may be accompanied by strong feelings of responsibility on several fronts and health may suffer from extra efforts made. CAUTION: Everyone may not want your help or advice.

MOON IN LIBRA

These are days of harmony and agreement and you should find yourself at peace with most others. Relationships tend to be smooth and sweet-flowing. Friends may become closer and bonds deepen in mutual understanding. Hopes will be shared. Progress by cooperation could be the secret of success in every sphere. In business, established partnerships may flourish and new ones get off to a good start. Acquaintances could discover similar interests that lead to congenial discussions and rewarding exchanges of some sort. Love, as a unifying force, reaches its optimum. Marriage partners should find accord. Those who wed at this time face the prospect of a happy union. Cooperation and tolerance are felt to be stronger than dissension and impatience. The argumentative are not quite so loud in their bellowings, nor as inflexible in their attitudes. In the home, there should be a greater recognition of the other point of view and a readiness to put the wishes of the group before selfish insistence. This is a favorable time to join an art group. CAUTION: Do not be too independent—let others help you if they want to.

MOON IN SCORPIO

Driving impulses to make money and to economize are likely to cause upsets all round. No area of expenditure is likely to be spared the axe, including the household budget. This is a time when the desire to cut down on extravagance can become near fanatical. Care must be exercised to try to keep the aim in reasonable perspective. Others may not feel the same urgent need to save and may retaliate. There is a danger that possessions of sentimental value will be sold to realize cash for investment. Buying and selling of stock for quick profit is also likely. The attention may turn to having a good clean up round the home and at the office. Neglected jobs could suddenly be done with great bursts of energy. The desire for solitude may intervene. Self-searching thoughts could disturb. The sense of invisible and mysterious energies at work could cause some excitability. The reassurance of loves ones may help. CAUTION: Be kind to the people you love.

MOON IN SAGITTARIUS

These are days when you are likely to be stirred and elevated by discussions and reflections of a religious and philosophical nature. Ideas of far-away places may cause unusual response and excitement. A decision may be made to visit someone overseas, perhaps a person whose influence was important to your earlier character development. There could be a strong resolution to get away from present intellectual patterns, to learn new subjects and to meet more interesting people. The superficial may be rejected in all its forms. An impatience with old ideas and unimaginative contacts could lead to a change of companions and interests. There may be an upsurge of religious feeling and metaphysical inquiry. Even a new insight into the significance of astrology and other occult studies is likely under the curious stimulus of the moon in Sagittarius. Physically, you may express this need for fundamental change by spending more time outdoors: sports, gardening or going for long walks. CAUTION: Try to channel any restlessness into worthwhile study.

MOON IN CAPRICORN

Life in these hours may seem to pivot around the importance of gaining prestige and honor in the career, as well as maintaining a spotless reputation. Ambitious urges may be excessive and could be accompanied by quite acquisitive drives for money. Effort should be directed along strictly ethical lines where there is no possibility of reproach or scandal. All endeavors are likely to be characterized by great earnestness, and an air of authority and purpose which should impress those who are looking for leadership or reliability. The desire to conform to accepted standards may extend to sharp criticism of family members. Frivolity and unconventional actions are unlikely to amuse while the moon is in Capricorn. Moderation and seriousness are the orders of the day. Achievement and recognition in this period could come through community work or organizing for the benefit of some amateur group. CAUTION: Dignity and esteem are not always self-awarded.

MOON IN AQUARIUS

Moon in Aquarius is in the second last sign of the Zodiac where ideas can become disturbingly fine and subtle. The result is often a mental "no-man's land" where imagination cannot be trusted with the same certitude as other times. The dangers for the individual are the extremes of optimism and pessimism. Unless the imgination is held in check, situations are likely to be misread, and rosy conclusions drawn where they do not exist. Consequences for the unwary can be costly in career and business. Best to think twice and not speak or act until you think again. Pessimism can be a cruel self-inflicted penalty for delusion at this time. Between the two extremes are strange areas of self-deception which, for example, can make the selfish person think he is actually being generous. Eerie dreams which resemble the reality and even seem to continue into the waking state are also possible. CAUTION: Look for the fact and not just for the image in your mind.

MOON IN PISCES

Everything seems to come to the surface now. Memory may be crystal clear, throwing up long-forgotten information which could be valuable in the career or business. Flashes of clairvoyance and intuition are possible along with sudden realizations of one's own nature, which may be used for self-improvement. A talent, never before suspected, may be discovered. Qualities not evident before in friends and marriage partners are likely to be noticed. As this is a period in which the truth seems to emerge, the discovery of false characteristics is likely to lead to disenchantment or a shift in attachments. However, where qualities are realized it should lead to happiness and deeper feeling. Surprise solutions could bob up for old problems. There may be a public announcement of the solving of a crime or mystery. People with secrets may find someone has "guessed" correctly. The secrets of the soul or the inner self also tend to reveal themselves. Religious and philosophical groups may make some interesting discoveries. CAUTION: Not a time for activities that depend on secrecy.

MOON TABLES

TIME CORRECTIONS FOR
GREENWICH MOON TABLES

London, Glasgow, Dublin, Dakar...Same time

Vienna, Prague, Rome, Kinshasa, Frankfurt,
Stockholm, Brussels, Amsterdam, Warsaw,
Zurich..Add 1 hour

Bucharest, Istanbul, Beirut, Cairo, Johannesburg,
Athens, Cape Town, Helsinki, Tel Aviv............................Add 2 hours

Dhahran, Baghdad, Moscow, Leningrad, Nairobi,
Addis Ababa, Zanzibar...Add 3 hours

Delhi, Calcutta, Bombay, Colombo...................................Add 5 ½ hours

Rangoon..Add 6 ½ hours

Saigon, Bangkok, Chungking..Add 7 hours

Canton, Manila, Hong Kong, Shanghai, Peking...................Add 8 hours

Tokyo, Pusan, Seoul, Vladivostok, Yokohama.....................Add 9 hours

Sydney, Melbourne, Guam, Port Moresby...........................Add 10 hours

Azores, Reykjavik...Deduct 1 hour

Rio de Janeiro, Montevideo, Buenos Aires,
Sao Paulo, Recife...Deduct 3 hours

LaPaz, San Juan, Santiago, Bermuda, Caracas,
Halifax..Deduct 4 hours

New York, Washington, Boston, Detroit, Lima,
Havana, Miami, Bogota..Deduct 5 hours

Mexico, Chicago, New Orleans, Houston...........................Deduct 6 hours

San Francisco, Seattle, Los Angeles, Hollywood,
Ketchikan, Juneau..Deduct 8 hours

Honolulu, Fairbanks, Anchorage, Papeete.........................Deduct 10 hours

1989 MOON TABLES—GREENWICH TIME

JANUARY		FEBRUARY		MARCH	
Day Moon Enters		**Day Moon Enters**		**Day Moon Enters**	
1. Scorpio	9:27 pm	1. Sagitt.		1. Sagitt.	
2. Scorpio		2. Capric.	11:31 pm	2. Capric.	8:53 am
3. Scorpio		3. Capric.		3. Capric.	
4. Sagitt.	7:26 am	4. Capric.		4. Aquar.	1:31 pm
5. Sagitt.		5. Aquar.	2:40 am	5. Aquar.	
6. Capric.	1:24 pm	6. Aquar.		6. Pisces	2:26 pm
7. Capric.		7. Pisces	3:54 am	7. Pisces	
8. Aquar.	4:44 pm	8. Pisces		8. Aries	2:13 pm
9. Aquar.		9. Aries	4:26 am	9. Aries	
10. Pisces	6:40 pm	10. Aries		10. Taurus	2:09 pm
11. Pisces		11. Taurus	5:45 am	11. Taurus	
12. Aries	8:58 pm	12. Taurus		12. Gemini	4:21 pm
13. Aries		13. Gemini	9:30 am	13. Gemini	
14. Taurus	11:34 pm	14. Gemini		14. Cancer	9:42 pm
15. Taurus		15. Cancer	4:08 pm	15. Cancer	
16. Taurus		16. Cancer		16. Cancer	
17. Gemini	4:03 am	17. Cancer		17. Leo	6:43 am
18. Gemini		18. Leo	0:52 am	18. Leo	
19. Cancer	9:50 am	19. Leo		19. Virgo	6:00 pm
20. Cancer		20. Virgo	11:48 am	20. Virgo	
21. Leo	6:10 pm	21. Virgo		21. Virgo	
22. Leo		22. Libra	11:42 pm	22. Libra	6:25 am
23. Leo		23. Libra		23. Libra	
24. Virgo	4:31 am	24. Libra		24. Scorpio	6:52 pm
25. Virgo		25. Scorpio	0:48 pm	25. Scorpio	
26. Libra	4:39 pm	26. Scorpio		26. Scorpio	
27. Libra		27. Scorpio		27. Sagitt.	7:01 am
28. Libra		28. Sagitt.	0:24 am	28. Sagitt.	
29. Scorpio	5:33 am			29. Capric.	4:49 pm
30. Scorpio				30. Capric.	
31. Sagitt.	4:21 pm			31. Aquar.	10:46 pm

Summer time to be considered were applicable.

1989 MOON TABLES—GREENWICH TIME

APRIL		MAY		JUNE	
Day Moon Enters		**Day Moon Enters**		**Day Moon Enters**	
1. Aquar.		1. Pisces		1. Taurus	
2. Aquar.		2. Aries	11:41 am	2. Gemini	9:56 pm
3. Pisces	1:13 am	3. Aries		3. Gemini	
4. Pisces		4. Taurus	11:22 am	4. Gemini	
5. Aries	1:15 am	5. Taurus		5. Cancer	0:26 am
6. Aries		6. Gemini	11:41 am	6. Cancer	
7. Taurus	0:49 am	7. Gemini		7. Leo	5:36 am
8. Taurus		8. Cancer	2:18 pm	8. Leo	
9. Gemini	1:35 am	9. Cancer		9. Virgo	2:13 pm
10. Gemini		10. Leo	8:31 pm	10. Virgo	
11. Cancer	5:07 am	11. Leo		11. Virgo	
12. Cancer		12. Leo		12. Libra	2:54 am
13. Leo	0:47 pm	13. Virgo	6:27 am	13. Libra	
14. Leo		14. Virgo		14. Scorpio	3:14 pm
15. Leo		15. Libra	7:20 pm	15. Scorpio	
16. Virgo	0:13 am	16. Libra		16. Scorpio	
17. Virgo		17. Libra		17. Sagitt.	2:18 am
18. Libra	0:48 pm	18. Scorpio	7:39 am	18. Sagitt.	
19. Libra		19. Scorpio		19. Capric.	10:43 am
20. Libra		20. Sagitt.	6:59 pm	20. Capric.	
21. Scorpio	1:19 am	21. Sagitt.		21. Aquar.	5:08 pm
22. Scorpio		22. Sagitt.		22. Aquar.	
23. Sagitt.	0:36 pm	23. Capric.	4:04 am	23. Pisces	9:44 pm
24. Sagitt.		24. Capric.		24. Pisces	
25. Capric.	10:35 pm	25. Aquar.	11:18 am	25. Pisces	
26. Capric.		26. Aquar.		26. Aries	1:18 am
27. Capric.		27. Pisces	4:31 pm	27. Aries	
28. Aquar.	6:09 am	28. Pisces		28. Taurus	3:50 am
29. Aquar.		29. Aries	7:30 pm	29. Taurus	
30. Pisces	10:10 am	30. Aries		30. Gemini	6:34 am
		31. Taurus	8:50 pm		

Summer time to be considered where applicable.

1989 MOON TABLES—GREENWICH TIME

JULY		AUGUST		SEPTEMBER	
Day Moon Enters		**Day Moon Enters**		**Day Moon Enters**	
1. Gemini		1. Leo		1. Virgo	
2. Cancer	9:34 am	2. Leo		2. Libra	1:23 am
3. Cancer		3. Virgo	7:22 am	3. Libra	
4. Leo	2:55 pm	4. Virgo		4. Scorpio	1:50 pm
5. Leo		5. Libra	6:00 pm	5. Scorpio	
6. Virgo	10:49 pm	6. Libra		6. Scorpio	
7. Virgo		7. Libra		7. Sagitt.	2:44 am
8. Virgo		8. Scorpio	6:50 am	8. Sagitt.	
9. Libra	10:00 am	9. Scorpio		9. Capric.	1:29 pm
10. Libra		10. Sagitt.	5:50 pm	10. Capric.	
11. Scorpio	10:53 pm	11. Sagitt.		11. Aquar.	8:09 pm
12. Scorpio		12. Sagitt.		12. Aquar.	
13. Scorpio		13. Capric.	4:26 am	13. Pisces	11:01 pm
14. Sagitt.	10:28 am	14. Capric.		14. Pisces	
15. Sagitt.		15. Aquar.	10:05 am	15. Aries	11:43 pm
16. Capric.	7:07 pm	16. Aquar.		16. Aries	
17. Capric.		17. Pisces	0:40 pm	17. Taurus	11:22 pm
18. Capric.		18. Pisces		18. Taurus	
19. Aquar.	0:35 am	19. Aries	1:50 pm	19. Taurus	
20. Aquar.		20. Aries		20. Gemini	0:35 am
21. Pisces	4:11 am	21. Taurus	3:00 pm	21. Gemini	
22. Pisces		22. Taurus		22. Cancer	4:07 am
23. Aries	6:30 am	23. Gemini	5:46 pm	23. Cancer	
24. Aries		24. Gemini		24. Leo	10:53 am
25. Taurus	9:07 am	25. Cancer	10:34 pm	25. Leo	
26. Taurus		26. Cancer		26. Virgo	8:32 pm
27. Gemini	0:21 pm	27. Cancer		27. Virgo	
28. Gemini		28. Leo	5:33 am	28. Virgo	
29. Cancer	5:08 pm	29. Leo		29. Libra	8:03 am
30. Cancer		30. Virgo	2:31 pm	30. Libra	
31. Leo	11:04 pm	31. Virgo			

Summer time to be considered where applicable.

1989 MOON TABLES—GREENWICH TIME

OCTOBER		NOVEMBER		DECEMBER	
Day Moon Enters		**Day Moon Enters**		**Day Moon Enters**	
1. Scorpio	8:17 pm	1. Sagitt.		1. Capric.	
2. Scorpio		2. Sagitt.		2. Aquar.	5:47 pm
3. Scorpio		3. Capric.	2:53 am	3. Aquar.	
4. Sagitt.	9:11 am	4. Capric.		4. Aquar.	
5. Sagitt.		5. Aquar.	0:11 pm	5. Pisces	0:33 am
6. Capric.	8:37 pm	6. Aquar.		6. Pisces	
7. Capric.		7. Pisces	6:02 pm	7. Aries	4:52 am
8. Capric.		8. Pisces		8. Aries	
9. Aquar.	5:05 am	9. Aries	8:50 pm	9. Taurus	6:38 am
10. Aquar.		10. Aries		10. Taurus	
11. Pisces	9:25 am	11. Taurus	8:56 pm	11. Gemini	7:26 am
12. Pisces		12. Taurus		12. Gemini	
13. Aries	10:32 am	13. Gemini	8:43 pm	13. Cancer	8:13 am
14. Aries		14. Gemini		14. Cancer	
15. Taurus	10:05 am	15. Cancer	9:33 pm	15. Leo	11:10 am
16. Taurus		16. Cancer		16. Leo	
17. Gemini	9:46 am	17. Cancer		17. Virgo	5:27 pm
18. Gemini		18. Leo	1:20 am	18. Virgo	
19. Cancer	11:31 am	19. Leo		19. Virgo	
20. Cancer		20. Virgo	8:56 am	20. Libra	3:52 am
21. Leo	5:01 pm	21. Virgo		21. Libra	
22. Leo		22. Libra	8:24 pm	22. Scorpio	4:27 pm
23. Leo		23. Libra		23. Scorpio	
24. Virgo	2:14 am	24. Libra		24. Scorpio	
25. Virgo		25. Scorpio	9:11 am	25. Sagitt.	5:01 am
26. Libra	2:01 pm	26. Scorpio		26. Sagitt.	
27. Libra		27. Sagitt.	9:31 pm	27. Capric.	3:18 pm
28. Libra		28. Sagitt.		28. Capric.	
29. Scorpio	2:50 am	29. Sagitt.		29. Aquar.	11:42 pm
30. Scorpio		30. Capric.	8:31 am	30. Aquar.	
31. Sagitt.	3:11 pm			31. Aquar.	

Summer time to be considered where applicable.

1989 PHASES OF THE MOON—GREENWICH TIME

New Moon	First Quarter	Full Moon	Last Quarter
Jan. 7	Jan. 14	Jan. 21	Jan. 30
Feb. 6	Feb. 12	Feb. 20	Feb. 28
Mar. 7	Mar. 14	Mar. 22	Mar. 30
Apr. 6	Apr. 12	Apr. 21	Apr. 28
May 5	May 12	May 20	May 28
June 3	June 11	June 19	June 26
July 3	July 11	July 18	July 25
Aug. 1	Aug. 9	Aug. 17	Aug. 23
Aug. 31	Sep. 8	Sep. 15	Sep. 22
Sep. 29	Oct. 8	Oct. 14	Oct. 21
Oct. 29	Nov. 6	Nov. 13	Nov. 20
Nov. 28	Dec. 6	Dec. 12	Dec. 19
Dec. 28	(1990)	(1990)	(1990)

Summer time to be considered where applicable.

1989 PLANTING GUIDE

	Aboveground Crops	Root Crops	Pruning	Weeds Pests
January	11-15-16-19-20	1-2-3-27-28-29-30	2-3-29-30	4-5-22-23-24-25
February	7-8-11-12-16-17	3-4-23-24-25-26-27	26-27	1-2-5-21-22-28
March	11-15-16	2-3-23-24-25-26-30-31	25-26	1-5-27-28
April	7-8-11-12-19-20	3-4-21-22-26-27	3-4-21-22	1-2-5-24-25-28-29
May	9-16-17-18-19	1-23-24-28	1-28	3-21-22-26-30
June	5-6-12-13-14-15-16	1-20-24-25-28-29	24-25	22-26-27-30
July	3-9-10-11-12-13-17	2-21-22-25-26-30-31	2-21-22-30-31	1-19-20-23-24-28
August	6-7-8-9-13-14	18-22-26-27	18-26-27	20-24-25-28-29-30
September	2-3-4-5-6-10-14-30	18-19-22-23	22-23	16-17-20-21-25-26-27-28
October	1-2-3-7-8-11-12-30	16-20-27-28	20	17-18-22-23-24-25
November	3-4-8-12-30	16-17-23-24-25-26	16-17-25-26	14-18-19-20-21
December	1-5-6-9-10-28-29	13-14-20-21-22-23-24	13-14-23-24	16-17-18-19-25-26

1989 FISHING GUIDE

	Good	Best
January	14-18-21-22-23-24	7-19-20-30
February	6-12-18-19-20-21-22-28	17-23
March	14-19-20-21	7-22-23-24-25-30
April	6-18-23-24-28	12-19-20-21-22
May	12-20-21-22	5-17-18-19-23-28
June	3-11-17-18-19-21-22-26	16-20
July	15-16-19-20	3-11-17-18-21-25
August	1-15-16-17-19-20-23-31	9-14-18
September	8-12-13-16-17	14-15-18-22-29
October	13-14-15-17-21	8-11-12-16-29
November	6-10-11-13-14-15-20-28	12-16
December	11-12-15-19	6-9-10-13-14-28

MOON'S INFLUENCE OVER DAILY AFFAIRS

The Moon makes a complete transit of the Zodiac every 27 days 7 hours and 43 minutes. In making this transit the Moon forms different aspects with the planets and consequently has favorable or unfavorable bearings on affairs and events for persons according to the sign of the Zodiac under which they were born.

Whereas the Sun exclusively represents fire, the Moon rules water. The action of the Moon may be described as fluctuating, variable, absorbent and receptive. It is well known that the attraction to the Moon in combination with the movement of the Earth is responsible for the tides. The Moon has a similar effect on men. A clever navigator will make use of the tides to bring his ship to the intended destination. You also can reach your "destination" better by making use of your tides.

When the Moon is in conjunction with the Sun it is called a New Moon; when the Moon and Sun are in opposition it is called a Full Moon. From New Moon to Full Moon, first and second quarter—which takes about two weeks—the Moon is increasing or waxing. From Full Moon to New Moon, third and fourth quarter, the Moon is said to be decreasing or waning. The Moon Table indicates the New Moon and Full Moon and the quarters.

ACTIVITY	MOON IN
Business	
buying and selling	Sagittarius, Aries, Gemini, Virgo
new, requiring public support	1st and 2nd quarter
meant to be kept quiet	3rd and 4th quarter
Investigation	3rd and 4th quarter
Signing documents	1st & 2nd quarter, Cancer, Scorpio, Pisces
Advertising	2nd quarter, Sagittarius
Journeys and trips	1st & 2nd quarter, Gemini, Virgo
Renting offices, etc.	Taurus, Leo, Scorpio, Aquarius
Painting of house/apartment	3rd & 4th quarter, Taurus, Scorpio, Aquarius
Decorating	Gemini, Libra, Aquarius
Buying clothes and accessories	Taurus, Virgo
Beauty salon or barber shop visit	1st & 2nd quarter, Taurus, Leo, Libra, Scorpio, Aquarius
Weddings	1st & 2nd quarter

MOON'S INFLUENCE OVER YOUR HEALTH

ARIES	Head, brain, face, upper jaw
TAURUS	Throat, neck, lower jaw
GEMINI	Hands, arms, lungs, shoulders, nervous system
CANCER	Esophagus, stomach, breasts, womb, liver
LEO	Heart, spine
VIRGO	Intestines, liver
LIBRA	Kidneys, lower back
SCORPIO	Sex and eliminative organs
SAGITTARIUS	Hips, thighs, liver
CAPRICORN	Skin, bones, teeth, knees
AQUARIUS	Circulatory system, lower legs
PISCES	Feet, tone of being

Try to avoid work being done on that part of the body when the Moon is in the sign governing that part.

MOON'S INFLUENCE OVER PLANTS

Centuries ago it was established that seeds planted when the Moon is in certain signs and phases called "fruitful" will produce more than seeds planted when the Moon is in a Barren sign.

FRUITFUL SIGNS	BARREN SIGNS	DRY SIGNS
Taurus	Aries	Aries
Cancer	Gemini	Gemini
Libra	Leo	Sagittarius
Scorpio	Virgo	Aquarius
Capricorn	Sagittarius	
Pisces	Aquarius	

ACTIVITY	MOON IN
Mow lawn, trim plans	Fruitful sign, 1st & 2nd quarter
Plant flowers	Fruitful sign, 2nd quarter; best in Cancer and Libra
Prune	Fruitful sign, 3rd & 4th quarter
Destroy pests; spray	Barren sign, 4th quarter
Harvest potatoes, root crops	Dry sign, 3rd & 4th quarter; Taurus, Leo, and Aquarius

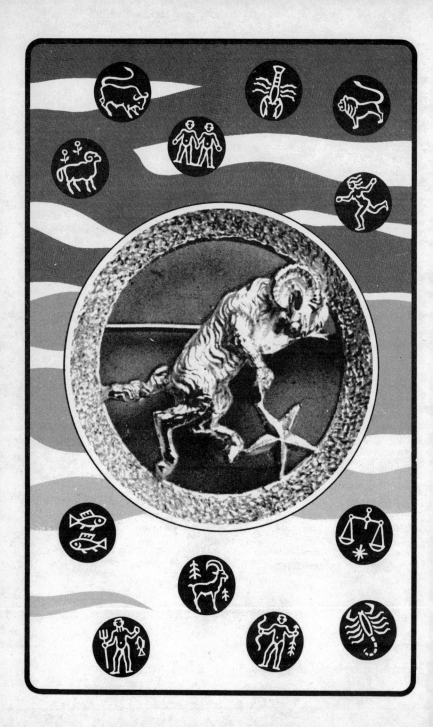

THE SIGNS: DOMINANT CHARACTERISTICS

March 21–April 20

The Positive Side of Aries

The Arien has many positive points to his character. People born under this first sign of the Zodiac are often quite strong and enthusiastic. On the whole, they are forward-looking people who are not easily discouraged by temporary setbacks. They know what they want out of life and they go out after it. Their personalities are strong. Others are usually quite impressed by the Arien's way of doing things. Quite often they are sources of inspiration for others traveling the same route. Aries men and women have a special zest for life that is often contagious; for others, they are often the example of how life should be lived.

The Aries person usually has a quick and active mind. He is imaginative and inventive. He enjoys keeping busy and active. He generally gets along well with all kinds of people. He is interested in mankind, as a whole. He likes to be challenged. Some would say he thrives on opposition, for it is when he is set against that he often does his best. Getting over or around obstacles is a challenge he generally enjoys. All in all, the Arien is quite positive and young-thinking. He likes to keep abreast of new things that are happening in the world. Ariens are often fond of speed. They like things to be done quickly and this sometimes aggravates their slower colleagues and associates.

The Aries man or woman always seems to remain young. Their whole approach to life is youthful and optimistic. They never say die, no matter what the odds. They may have an occasional setback, but it is not long before they are back on their feet again.

The Negative Side of Aries

Everybody has his less positive qualities—and Aries is no exception. Sometimes the Aries man or woman is not very tactful in communicating with others; in his hurry to get things done he is apt to

be a little callous or inconsiderate. Sensitive people are likely to find him somewhat sharp-tongued in some situations. Often in his eagerness to achieve his aims, he misses the mark altogether. At times the Arien is too impulsive. He can occasionally be stubborn and refuse to listen to reason. If things do not move quickly enough to suit the Aries man or woman, he or she is apt to become rather nervous or irritable. The uncultivated Arien is not unfamiliar with moments of doubt and fear. He is capable of being destructive if he does not get his way. He can overcome some of his emotional problems by steadily trying to express himself as he really is, but this requires effort.

April 21–May 20

The Positive Side of Taurus

The Taurus person is known for his ability to concentrate and for his tenacity. These are perhaps his strongest qualities. The Taurus man or woman generally has very little trouble in getting along with others; it's his nature to be helpful toward people in need. He can always be depended on by his friends, especially those in trouble.

The Taurean generally achieves what he wants through his ability to persevere. He never leaves anything unfinished but works on something until it has been completed. People can usually take him at his word; he is honest and forthright in most of his dealings. The Taurus person has a good chance to make a success of his life because of his many positive qualities. The Taurean who aims high seldom falls short of his mark. He learns well by experience. He is thorough and does not believe in short-cuts of any kind. The Taurean's thoroughness pays off in the end, for through his deliberateness he learns how to rely on himself and what he has learned. The Taurus person tries to get along with others, as a rule. He is not overly critical and likes people to be themselves. He is a tolerant person and enjoys peace and harmony—especially in his home life.

The Taurean is usually cautious in all that he does. He is not a person who believes in taking unnecessary risks. Before adopting any one line of action, he will weigh all of the pros and cons. The

Taurus person is steadfast. Once his mind is made up it seldom changes. The person born under this sign usually is a good family person—reliable and loving.

The Negative Side of Taurus

Sometimes the Taurus man or woman is a bit too stubborn. He won't listen to other points of view if his mind is set on something. To others, this can be quite annoying. The Taurean also does not like to be told what to do. He becomes rather angry if others think him not too bright. He does not like to be told he is wrong, even when he is. He dislikes being contradicted.

Some people who are born under this sign are very suspicious of others—even of those persons close to them. They find it difficult to trust people fully. They are often afraid of being deceived or taken advantage of. The Taurean often finds it difficult to forget or forgive. His love of material things sometimes makes him rather avaricious and petty.

May 21–June 20

The Positive Side of Gemini

The person born under this sign of the Heavenly Twins is usually quite bright and quick-witted. Some of them are capable of doing many different things. The Gemini person very often has many different interests. He keeps an open mind and is always anxious to learn new things.

The Geminian is often an analytical person. He is a person who enjoys making use of his intellect. He is governed more by his mind than by his emotions. He is a person who is not confined to one view; he can often understand both sides to a problem or question. He knows how to reason; how to make rapid decisions if need be.

He is an adaptable person and can make himself at home almost anywhere. There are all kinds of situations he can adapt to. He is a person who seldom doubts himself; he is sure of his talents and his

ability to think and reason. The Geminian is generally most satisfied when he is in a situation where he can make use of his intellect. Never short of imagination, he often has strong talents for invention. He is rather a modern person when it comes to life; the Geminian almost always moves along with the times—perhaps that is why he remains so youthful throughout most of his life.

Literature and art appeal to the person born under this sign. Creativity in almost any form will interest and intrigue the Gemini man or woman.

The Geminian is often quite charming. A good talker, he often is the center of attraction at any gathering. People find it easy to like a person born under this sign because he can appear easygoing and usually has a good sense of humor.

The Negative Side of Gemini

Sometimes the Gemini person tries to do too many things at one time—and as a result, winds up finishing nothing. Some Geminians are easily distracted and find it rather difficult to concentrate on one thing for too long a time. Sometimes they give in to trifling fancies and find it rather boring to become too serious about any one thing. Some of them are never dependable, no matter what they promise.

Although the Gemini man or woman often appears to be well-versed on many subjects, this is sometimes just a veneer. His knowledge may be only superficial, but because he speaks so well he gives people the impression of erudition. Some Geminians are sharp-tongued and inconsiderate; they think only of themselves and their own pleasure.

June 21–July 20

The Positive Side of Cancer

The Cancerians's most positive point is his understanding nature. On the whole, he is a loving and sympathetic person. He would never go out of his way to hurt anyone. The Cancer man or woman

is often very kind and tender; they give what they can to others. They hate to see others suffering and will do what they can to help someone in less fortunate circumstances than themselves. They are often very concerned about the world. Their interest in people generally goes beyond that of just their own families and close friends; they have a deep sense of brotherhood and respect humanitarian values. The Cancerian means what he says, as a rule; he is honest about his feelings.

The Cancer man or woman is a person who knows the art of patience. When something seems difficult, he is willing to wait until the situation becomes manageable again. He is a person who knows how to bide his time. The Cancerian knows how to concentrate on one thing at a time. When he has made his mind up he generally sticks with what he does, seeing it through to the end.

The Cancerian is a person who loves his home. He enjoys being surrounded by familiar things and the people he loves. Of all the signs, Cancer is the most maternal. Even the men born under this sign often have a motherly or protective quality about them. They like to take care of people in their family—to see that they are well loved and well provided for. They are usually loyal and faithful. Family ties mean a lot to the Cancer man or woman. Parents and in-laws are respected and loved. The Cancerian has a strong sense of tradition. He is very sensitive to the moods of others.

The Negative Side of Cancer

Sometimes the Cancerian finds it rather hard to face life. It becomes too much for him. He can be a little timid and retiring, when things don't go too well. When unfortunate things happen, he is apt to just shrug and say, "Whatever will be will be." He can be fatalistic to a fault. The uncultivated Cancerian is a bit lazy. He doesn't have very much ambition. Anything that seems a bit difficult he'll gladly leave to others. He may be lacking in initiative. Too sensitive, when he feels he's been injured, he'll crawl back into his shell and nurse his imaginary wounds. The Cancer woman often is given to crying when the smallest thing goes wrong.

Some Cancerians find it difficult to enjoy themselves in environments outside their homes. They make heavy demands on others, and need to be constantly reassured that they are loved.

July 21–August 21

The Positive Side of Leo

Often Leos make good leaders. They seem to be good organizers and administrators. Usually they are quite popular with others. Whatever group it is that he belongs to, the Leo man is almost sure to be or become the leader.

The Leo person is generous most of the time. It is his best characteristic. He or she likes to give gifts and presents. In making others happy, the Leo person becomes happy himself. He likes to splurge when spending money on others. In some instances it may seem that the Leo's generosity knows no boundaries. A hospitable person, the Leo man or woman is very fond of welcoming people to his house and entertaining them. He is never short of company.

The Leo person has plenty of energy and drive. He enjoys working toward some specific goal. When he applies himself correctly, he gets what he wants most often. The Leo person is almost never unsure of himself. He has plenty of confidence and aplomb. He is a person who is direct in almost everything he does. He has a quick mind and can make a decision in a very short time.

He usually sets a good example for others because of his ambitious manner and positive ways. He knows how to stick to something once he's started. Although the Leo person may be good at making a joke, he is not superficial or glib. He is a loving person, kind and thoughtful.

There is generally nothing small or petty about the Leo man or woman. He does what he can for those who are deserving. He is a person others can rely upon at all times. He means what he says. An honest person, generally speaking, he is a friend that others value.

The Negative Side of Leo

Leo, however, does have his faults. At times, he can be just a bit too arrogant. He thinks that no one deserves a leadership position except him. Only he is capable of doing things well. His opinion of himself is often much too high. Because of his conceit, he is sometimes rather unpopular with a good many people. Some Leos are too materialistic; they can only think in terms of money and profit.

Some Leos enjoy lording it over others—at home or at their place of business. What is more, they feel they have the right to. Egocentric to an impossible degree, this sort of Leo cares little about how others think or feel. He can be rude and cutting.

August 22–September 22

The Positive Side of Virgo

The person born under the sign of Virgo is generally a busy person. He knows how to arrange and organize things. He is a good planner. Above all, he is practical and is not afraid of hard work.

The person born under this sign, Virgo, knows how to attain what he desires. He sticks with something until it is finished. He never shirks his duties, and can always be depended upon. The Virgo person can be thoroughly trusted at all times.

The man or woman born under this sign tries to do everything to perfection. He doesn't believe in doing anything half-way. He always aims for the top. He is the sort of a person who is constantly striving to better himself—not because he wants more money or glory, but because it gives him a feeling of accomplishment.

The Virgo man or woman is a very observant person. He is sensitive to how others feel, and can see things below the surface of a situation. He usually puts this talent to constructive use.

It is not difficult for the Virgoan to be open and earnest. He believes in putting his cards on the table. He is never secretive or under-handed. He's as good as his word. The Virgo person is generally plain-spoken and down-to-earth. He has no trouble in expressing himself.

The Virgo person likes to keep up to date on new developments in his particular field. Well-informed, generally, he sometimes has a keen interest in the arts or literature. What he knows, he knows well. His ability to use his critical faculties is well-developed and sometimes startles others because of its accuracy.

The Virgoan adheres to a moderate way of life; he avoids excesses. He is a responsible person and enjoys being of service.

The Negative Side of Virgo

Sometimes a Virgo person is too critical. He thinks that only he can do something the way it should be done. Whatever anyone else does is inferior. He can be rather annoying in the way he quibbles over insignificant details. In telling others how things should be done, he can be rather tactless and mean.

Some Virgos seem rather emotionless and cool. They feel emo-

tional involvement is beneath them. They are sometimes too tidy, too neat. With money they can be rather miserly. Some try to force their opinions and ideas on others.

September 23–October 22

The Positive Side of Libra

Librans love harmony. It is one of their most outstanding character traits. They are interested in achieving balance; they admire beauty and grace in things as well as in people. Generally speaking, they are kind and considerate people. Librans are usually very sympathetic. They go out of their way not to hurt another person's feelings. They are outgoing and do what they can to help those in need.

People born under the sign of Libra almost always make good friends. They are loyal and amiable. They enjoy the company of others. Many of them are rather moderate in their views; they believe in keeping an open mind, however, and weighing both sides of an issue fairly before making a decision.

Alert and often intelligent, the Libran, always fair-minded, tries to put himself in the position of the other person. They are against injustice; quite often they take up for the underdog. In most of their social dealings, they try to be tactful and kind. They dislike discord and bickering, and most Libras strive for peace and harmony in all their relationships.

The Libra man or woman has a keen sense of beauty. They appreciate handsome furnishings and clothes. Many of them are artistically inclined. Their taste is usually impeccable. They know how to use color. Their homes are almost always attractively arranged and inviting. They enjoy entertaining people and see to it that their guests always feel at home and welcome.

The Libran gets along with almost everyone. He is well-liked and socially much in demand.

The Negative Side of Libra

Some people born under this sign tend to be rather insincere. So eager are they to achieve harmony in all relationships that they will even go so far as to lie. Many of them are escapists. They find facing

the truth an ordeal and prefer living in a world of make-believe.

In a serious argument, some Librans give in rather easily even when they know they are right. Arguing, even about something they believe in, is too unsettling for some of them.

Librans sometimes care too much for material things. They enjoy possessions and luxuries. Some are vain and tend to be jealous.

October 23–November 22

The Positive Side of Scorpio

The Scorpio man or woman generally knows what he or she wants out of life. He is a determined person. He sees something through to the end. The Scorpion is quite sincere, and seldom says anything he doesn't mean. When he sets a goal for himself he tries to go about achieving it in a very direct way.

The Scorpion is brave and courageous. They are not afraid of hard work. Obstacles do not frighten them. They forge ahead until they achieve what they set out for. The Scorpio man or woman has a strong will.

Although the Scorpion may seem rather fixed and determined, inside he is often quite tender and loving. He can care very much for others. He believes in sincerity in all relationships. His feelings about someone tend to last; they are profound and not superficial.

The Scorpio person is someone who adheres to his principles no matter what happens. He will not be deterred from a path he believes to be right.

Because of his many positive strengths, the Scorpion can often achieve happiness for himself and for those that he loves.

He is a constructive person by nature. He often has a deep understanding of people and of life, in general. He is perceptive and unafraid. Obstacles often seem to spur him on. He is a positive person who enjoys winning. He has many strengths and resources; challenge of any sort often brings out the best in him.

The Negative Side of Scorpio

The Scorpio person is sometimes hypersensitive. Often he imagines injury when there is none. He feels that others do not bother to

recognize him for his true worth. Sometimes he is given to excessive boasting in order to compensate for what he feels is neglect

The Scorpio person can be rather proud and arrogant. They can be rather sly when they put their minds to it and they enjoy outwitting persons or institutions noted for their cleverness.

Their tactics for getting what they want are sometimes devious and ruthless. They don't care too much about what others may think. If they feel others have done them an injustice, they will do their best to seek revenge. The Scorpion often has a sudden, violent temper; and this person's interest in sex is sometimes quite unbalanced or excessive.

November 23–December 20

The Positive Side of Sagittarius

People born under this sign are often honest and forthright. Their approach to life is earnest and open. The Sagittarian is often quite adult in his way of seeing things. They are broadminded and tolerant people. When dealing with others the person born under the sign of Sagittarius is almost always open and forthright. He doesn't believe in deceit or pretension. His standards are high. People who associate with the Sagittarian, generally admire and respect him.

The Sagittarian trusts others easily and expects them to trust him. He is never suspicious or envious and almost always thinks well of others. People always enjoy his company because he is so friendly and easy-going. The Sagittarius man or woman is often good-humored. He can always be depended upon by his friends, family, and co-workers.

The person born under this sign of the Zodiac likes a good joke every now and then; he is keen on fun and this makes him very popular with others.

A lively person, he enjoys sports and outdoor life. The Sagittarian is fond of animals. Intelligent and interesting, he can begin an animated conversation with ease. He likes exchanging ideas and discussing various views.

He is not selfish or proud. If someone proposes an idea or plan that is better than his, he will immediately adopt it. Imaginative yet practical, he knows how to put ideas into practice.

He enjoys sport and game, and it doesn't matter if he wins or loses. He is a forgiving person, and never sulks over something that has not worked out in his favor.

He is seldom critical, and is almost always generous.

The Negative Side of Sagittarius

Some Sagittarians are restless. They take foolish risks and seldom learn from the mistakes they make. They don't have heads for money and are often mismanaging their finances. Some of them devote much of their time to gambling.

Some are too outspoken and tactless, always putting their feet in their mouths. They hurt others carelessly by being honest at the wrong time. Sometimes they make promises which they don't keep. They don't stick close enough to their plans and go from one failure to another. They are undisciplined and waste a lot of energy.

December 21–January 19

The Positive Side of Capricorn

The person born under the sign of Capricorn is usually very stable and patient. He sticks to whatever tasks he has and sees them through. He can always be relied upon and he is not averse to work.

An honest person, the Capricornian is generally serious about whatever he does. He does not take his duties lightly. He is a practical person and believes in keeping his feet on the ground.

Quite often the person born under this sign is ambitious and knows how to get what he wants out of life. He forges ahead and never gives up his goal. When he is determined about something, he almost always wins. He is a good worker—a hard worker. Although things may not come easy to him, he will not complain, but continue working until his chores are finished.

He is usually good at business matters and knows the value of money. He is not a spendthrift and knows how to put something away for a rainy day; he dislikes waste and unnecessary loss.

The Capricornian knows how to make use of his self-control. He

can apply himself to almost anything once he puts his mind to it. His ability to concentrate sometimes astounds others. He is diligent and does well when involved in detail work.

The Capricorn man or woman is charitable, generally speaking, and will do what is possible to help others less fortunate. As a friend, he is loyal and trustworthy. He never shirks his duties or responsibilities. He is self-reliant and never expects too much of the other fellow. He does what he can on his own. If someone does him a good turn, then he will do his best to return the favor.

The Negative Side of Capricorn

Like everyone, the Capricornian, too, has his faults. At times, he can be over-critical of others. He expects others to live up to his own high standards. He thinks highly of himself and tends to look down on others.

His interest in material things may be exaggerated. The Capricorn man or woman thinks too much about getting on in the world and having something to show for it. He may even be a little greedy.

He sometimes thinks he knows what's best for everyone. He is too bossy. He is always trying to organize and correct others. He may be a little narrow in his tninking.

January 20–February 18

The Positive Side of Aquarius

The Aquarius man or woman is usually very honest and forthright. These are his two greatest qualities. His standards for himself are generally very high. He can always be relied upon by others. His word is his bond.

The Aquarian is perhaps the most tolerant of all the Zodiac personalities. He respects other people's beliefs and feels that everyone is entitled to his own approach to life.

He would never do anything to injure another's feelings. He is never unkind or cruel. Always considerate of others, the Aquarian is always willing to help a person in need. He feels a very strong tie between himself and all the other members of mankind.

The person born under this sign is almost always an individualist. He does not believe in teaming up with the masses, but prefers going his own way. His ideas about life and mankind are often quite advanced. There is a saying to the effect that the average Aquarian is fifty years ahead of his time.

He is broadminded. The problems of the world concern him greatly. He is interested in helping others no matter what part of the globe they live in. He is truly a humanitarian sort. He likes to be of service to others.

Giving, considerate, and without prejudice, Aquarians have no trouble getting along with others.

The Negative Side of Aquarius

The Aquarian may be too much of a dreamer. He makes plans but seldom carries them out. He is rather unrealistic. His imagination has a tendency to run away with him. Because many of his plans are impractical, he is always in some sort of a dither.

Others may not approve of him at all times because of his unconventional behavior. He may be a bit eccentric. Sometimes he is so busy with his own thoughts, that he loses touch with the realities of existence.

Some Aquarians feel they are more clever and intelligent than others. They seldom admit to their own faults, even when they are quite apparent. Some become rather fanatic in their views. Their criticism of others is sometimes destructive and negative.

February 19–March 20

The Positive Side of Pisces

The Piscean can often understand the problems of others quite easily. He has a sympathetic nature. Kindly, he is often dedicated in the way he goes about helping others. The sick and the troubled often turn to him for advice and assistance.

He is very broadminded and does not criticize others for their faults. He knows how to accept people for what they are. On the whole, he is a trustworthy and earnest person. He is loyal to his

friends and will do what he can to help them in time of need. Generous and good-natured, he is a lover of peace; he is often willing to help others solve their differences. People who have taken a wrong turn in life often interest him and he will do what he can to persuade · them to rehabilitate themselves.

He has a strong intuitive sense and most of the time he knows how to make it work for him; the Piscean is unusually perceptive and often knows what is bothering someone before that person, himself, is aware of it. The Pisces man or woman is an idealistic person, basically, and is interested in making the world a better place in which to live. The Piscean believes that everyone should help each other. He is willing to do more than his share in order to achieve cooperation with others.

The person born under this sign often is talented in music or art. He is a receptive person; he is able to take the ups and downs of life with philosophic calm.

The Negative Side of Pisces

Some Pisceans are often depressed; their outlook on life is rather glum. They may feel that they have been given a bad deal in life and that others are always taking unfair advantage of them. The Piscean sometimes feel that the world is a cold and cruel place. He is easily discouraged. He may even withdraw from the harshness of reality into a secret shell of his own where he dreams and idles away a good deal of his time.

The Piscean can be rather lazy. He lets things happen without giving the least bit of resistance. He drifts along, whether on the high road or on the low. He is rather short on willpower.

Some Pisces people seek escape through drugs or alcohol. When temptation comes along they find it hard to resist. In matters of sex, they can be rather permissive.

THE SIGNS AND
THEIR KEY WORDS

		POSITIVE	NEGATIVE
ARIES	self	courage, initiative, pioneer instinct	brash rudeness, selfish impetuosity
TAURUS	money	endurance, loyalty, wealth	obstinacy, gluttony
GEMINI	mind	versatility	capriciousness, unreliability
CANCER	family	sympathy, homing instinct	clannishness, childishness
LEO	children	love, authority, integrity	egotism, force
VIRGO	work	purity, industry, analysis	fault-finding, cynicism
LIBRA	marriage	harmony, justice	vacillation, superficiality
SCORPIO	sex	survival, regeneration	vengeance, discord
SAGITTARIUS	travel	optimism, higher learning	lawlessness
CAPRICORN	career	depth	narrowness, gloom
AQUARIUS	friends	human fellowship, genius	perverse unpredictability
PISCES	confine-ment	spiritual love, universality	diffusion, escapism

THE ELEMENTS AND QUALITIES OF THE SIGNS

ELEMENT	SIGN	QUALITY	SIGN
FIRE...................	ARIES LEO SAGITTARIUS	CARDINAL.........	ARIES LIBRA CANCER CAPRICORN
EARTH...............	TAURUS VIRGO CAPRICORN	FIXED................	TAURUS LEO SCORPIO AQUARIUS
AIR.....................	GEMINI LIBRA AQUARIUS		
WATER..............	CANCER SCORPIO PISCES	MUTABLE.........	GEMINI VIRGO SAGITTARIUS PISCES

Every sign has both an element and a quality associated with it. The element indicates the basic makeup of the sign, and the quality describes the kind of activity associated with each.

Signs can be grouped together according to their *element* and *quality*. Signs of the same element share many basic traits in common. They tend to form stable configurations and ultimately harmonious relationships. Signs of the same quality are often less harmonious, but they share many dynamic potentials for growth as well as profound fulfillment.

THE FIRE SIGNS

SAGITTARIUS

ARIES

LEO

This is the fire group. On the whole these are emotional, volatile types, quick to anger, quick to forgive. They are adventurous, powerful people and act as a source of inspiration for everyone. They spark into action with immediate exuberant impulses. They are intelligent, self-involved, creative and idealistic. They all share a certain vibrancy and glow that outwardly reflects an inner flame and passion for living.

THE EARTH SIGNS

CAPRICORN

TAURUS   VIRGO

This is the earth group. They are in constant touch with the material world and tend to be conservative. Although they are all capable of spartan self-discipline, they are earthy, sensual people who are stimulated by the tangible, elegant and luxurious. The thread of their lives is always practical, but they do fantasize and are often attracted to dark, mysterious, emotional people. They are like great cliffs overhanging the sea, forever married to the ocean but always resisting erosion from the dark, emotional forces that thunder at their feet.

THE AIR SIGNS

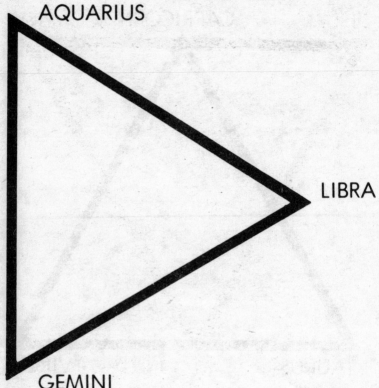

AQUARIUS

LIBRA

GEMINI

This is the air group. They are light, mental creatures desirous of contact, communication and relationship. They are involved with people and the forming of ties on many levels. Original thinkers, they are the bearers of human news. Their language is their sense of word, color, style and beauty. They provide an atmosphere suitable and pleasant for living. They add change and versatility to the scene, and it is through them that we can explore new territory of human intelligence and experience.

THE WATER SIGNS

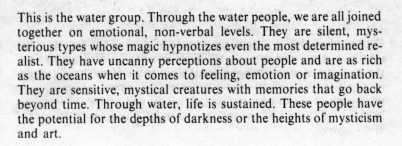

This is the water group. Through the water people, we are all joined together on emotional, non-verbal levels. They are silent, mysterious types whose magic hypnotizes even the most determined realist. They have uncanny perceptions about people and are as rich as the oceans when it comes to feeling, emotion or imagination. They are sensitive, mystical creatures with memories that go back beyond time. Through water, life is sustained. These people have the potential for the depths of darkness or the heights of mysticism and art.

THE CARDINAL SIGNS

CAPRICORN

ARIES LIBRA

CANCER

Put together, this is a clear-cut picture of dynamism, activity, tremendous stress and remarkable achievement. These people know the meaning of great change since their lives are often characterized by significant crises and major successes. This combination is like a simultaneous storm of summer, fall, winter and spring. The danger is chaotic diffusion of energy; the potential is irrepressible growth and victory.

THE FIXED SIGNS

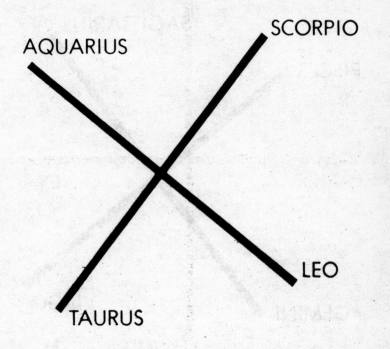

Fixed signs are always establishing themselves in a given place or area of experience. Like explorers who arrive and plant a flag, these people claim a position from which they do not enjoy being deposed. They are staunch, stalwart, upright, trusty, honorable people, although their obstinacy is well-known. Their contribution is fixity, and they are the angels who support our visible world.

THE MUTABLE SIGNS

SAGITTARIUS

PISCES

GEMINI

VIRGO

Mutable people are versatile, sensitive, intelligent, nervous and deeply curious about life. They are the translators of all energy. They often carry out or complete tasks initiated by others. Combinations of these signs have highly developed minds; they are imaginative and jumpy and think and talk a lot. At worst their lives are a Tower of Babel. At best they are adaptable and ready creatures who can assimilate one kind of experience and enjoy it while anticipating coming changes.

HOW TO APPROXIMATE YOUR RISING SIGN

Apart from the month and day of birth, the exact *time* of birth is another vital factor in the determination of an accurate horoscope. Not only do the planets move with great speed, but one must know how far the Earth has turned during the day. That way you can determine exactly where the planets are located with respect to the precise birthplace of an individual. This makes *your* horoscope *your* horoscope. In addition to these factors, another grid is laid upon that of the Zodiac and the planets: the houses. After all three have been considered, specific planetary relationships can be measured and analyzed in accordance with certain ordered procedures. It is the skillful translation of all this complex astrological language that a serious astrologer strives for in his attempt at coherent astrological synthesis. Keep this in mind.

The horoscope sets up a kind of framework around which the life of an individual grows like wild ivy, this way and that, weaving its way around the trellis of the natal positions of the planets. The year of birth tells us the positions of the distant, slow-moving planets like Jupiter, Saturn, Uranus and Pluto. The month of birth indicates the Sun sign, or birth sign as it is commonly called, as well as indicating the positions of the rapidly moving planets like Venus, Mercury and Mars. The day of birth locates the position of our Moon, and the moment of birth determines the houses through what is called the Ascendant, or Rising Sign.

As the Earth rotates on its axis once every 24 hours, each one of the twelve signs of the Zodiac appears to be "rising" on the horizon, with a new one appearing about every two hours. Actually it is the turning of the Earth that exposes each sign to view, but you will remember that in much of our astrological work we are discussing "apparent" motion. This *Rising Sign* marks the Ascendant and it colors the whole orientation of a horoscope. It indicates the sign governing the first house of the chart, and will thus determine which signs will govern all the other houses. The idea is a bit complicated at first, and we needn't dwell on complications in this introduction, but if you can imagine two color wheels with twelve divisions superimposed upon each other, one moving slowly and the other remaining still, you will have some idea of how the signs keep shifting the "color" of the houses as the Rising Sign continues to change every two hours.

The important point is that the birth chart, or horoscope, actually does define specific factors of a person's makeup. It contains a picture of being, much the way the nucleus of a tiny cell contains the potential for an entire elephant, or a packet of seeds contains a rosebush. If there were no order or continuity to the world, we could plant roses and get elephants. This same order that gives continuous flow to our lives often annoys people if it threatens to determine too much of their lives. We must grow from what we were planted, and there's no reason why we can't do that magnificently. It's all there in the horoscope. Where there is limitation, there is breakthrough; where there is crisis, there is transformation. Accurate analysis of a horoscope can help you find these points of breakthrough and transformation, and it requires knowledge of subtleties and distinctions that demand skillful judgment in order to solve even the simplest kind of personal question.

It is still quite possible, however, to draw some conclusions based upon the sign occupied by the Sun alone. In fact, if you're just being introduced to this vast subject, you're better off keeping it simple. Otherwise it seems like an impossible jumble, much like trying to read a novel in a foreign language without knowing the basic vocabulary. As with anything else, you can progress in your appreciation and understanding of astrology in direct proportion to your interest. To become really good at it requires study, experience, patience and above all—and maybe simplest of all—a fundamental understanding of what is actually going on right up there in the sky over your head. It is a vital living process you can observe, contemplate and ultimately understand. You can start by observing sunrise, or sunset, or even the full Moon.

In fact you can do a simple experiment after reading this introduction. You can erect a rough chart by following the simple procedure below:

1. Draw a circle with twelve equal segments.

2. Starting at what would be the nine o'clock position on a clock, number the segments, or houses, from 1 to 12 in a *counterclockwise direction*.

3. Label house number 1 in the following way: 4 A.M.-6 A.M.

4. In a counterclockwise direction, label the rest of the houses: 2 A.M.-4 A.M., MIDNIGHT-2 A.M., 10 P.M-MIDNIGHT, 8 P.M.-10 P.M., 6 P.M.-8 P.M., 4 P.M.-6 P.M., 2 P.M.-4 P.M., NOON-2 P.M., 10 A.M.-NOON, 8 A.M.-10 A.M., and 6 A.M.-8 A.M.

5. Now find out what time you were born and place the sun in the appropriate house.

6. Label the edge of that house with your Sun sign. You now have a description of your basic character and your fundamental drives. You can also see in what areas of life on Earth you will be most likely to focus your constant energy and center your activity.

7. If you are really feeling ambitious, label the rest of the houses with the signs, starting with your Sun sign, in order, still in a *counterclockwise direction*. When you get to Pisces, start over with Aries and keep going until you reach the house behind the Sun.

8. Look to house number 1. The sign that you have now labeled and attached to house number 1 is your Rising sign. It will color your self-image, outlook, physical constitution, early life and whole orientation to life. Of course this is a mere approximation, since there are many complicated calculations that must be made with respect to adjustments for birth time, but if you read descriptions of the sign preceding and the sign following the one you have calculated in the above manner, you may be able to identify yourself better. In any case, when you get through labeling all the houses, your drawing should look something like this:

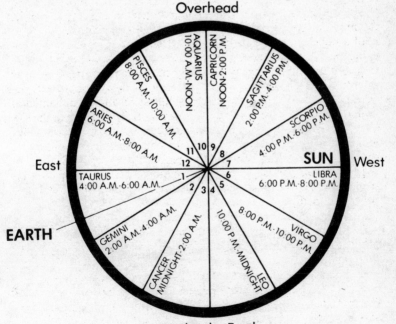

Overhead

East

West

EARTH

Under the Earth

Basic chart illustrating the position of the Sun in Scorpio, with the Ascendant Taurus as the Rising Sign.

This individual was born at 5:15 P.M. on October 31 in New York City. The Sun is in Scorpio and is found in the 7th house. The Rising sign, or the sign governing house number 1, is Taurus, so this person is a blend of Scorpio and Taurus.

Any further calculation would necessitate that you look in an ephemeris, or table of planetary motion, for the positions of the rest of the planets for your particular birth year. But we will take the time to define briefly all the known planets of our Solar System and the Sun to acquaint you with some more of the astrological vocabulary that you will be meeting again and again. (See page 21 for a full explanation of the Moon in all the Signs.)

THE PLANETS AND SIGNS THEY RULE

The signs of the Zodiac are linked to the planets in the following way. Each sign is governed or ruled by one or more planets. No matter where the planets are located in the sky at any given moment, they still rule their respective signs, and when they travel through the signs they rule, they have special dignity and their effects are stronger.

Following is a list of the planets and the signs they rule. After looking at the list, go back over the definitions of the planets and see if you can determine how the planet ruling *your* Sun sign has affected your life.

SIGNS	RULING PLANETS
Aries	Mars, Pluto
Taurus	Venus
Gemini	Mercury
Cancer	Moon
Leo	Sun
Virgo	Mercury
Libra	Venus
Scorpio	Mars, Pluto
Sagittarius	Jupiter
Capricorn	Saturn
Aquarius	Saturn, Uranus
Pisces	Jupiter, Neptune

THE PLANETS
OF THE
SOLAR SYSTEM

Here are the planets of the Solar System. They all travel around the Sun at different speeds and different distances. Taken with the Sun, they all distribute individual intelligence and ability throughout the entire chart.

The planets modify the influence of the Sun in a chart according to their own particular natures, strengths and positions. Their positions must be calculated for each year and day, and their function and expression in a horoscope will change as they move from one area of the Zodiac to another.

Following, you will find brief statements of their pure meanings.

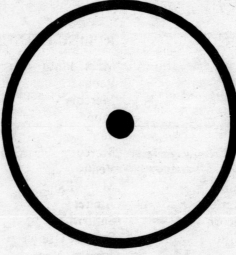

THE SUN

SUN

This is the center of existence. Around this flaming sphere all the planets revolve in endless orbits. Our star is constantly sending out its beams of light and energy without which no life on Earth would be possible. In astrology it symbolizes everything we are trying to become, the center around which all of our activity in life will always revolve. It is the symbol of our basic nature and describes the natural and constant thread that runs through everything that we do from birth to death on this planet.

To early astrologers, the sun seemed to be another planet because it crossed the heavens every day, just like the rest of the bodies in the sky.

It is the only star near enough to be seen well—it is, in fact, a dwarf star. Approximately 860,000 miles in diameter, it is about ten times as wide as the giant planet Jupiter. The next nearest star is nearly 300,000 times as far away, and if the Sun were located as far away as most of the bright stars, it would be too faint to be seen without a telescope.

Everything in the horoscope ultimately revolves around this singular body. Although other forces may be prominent in the charts of some individuals, still the Sun is the total nucleus of being and symbolizes the complete potential of every human being alive. It is vitality and the life force. Your whole essence comes from the position of the Sun.

You are always trying to express the Sun according to its position by house and sign. Possibility for all development is found in the Sun, and it marks the fundamental character of your personal radiations all around you.

It is the symbol of strength, vigor, wisdom, dignity, ardor and generosity, and the ability for a person to function as a mature individual. It is also a creative force in society. It is consciousness of the gift of life.

The underdeveloped solar nature is arrogant, pushy, undependable and proud, and is constantly using force.

MERCURY

Mercury is the planet closest to the Sun. It races around our star, gathering information and translating it to the rest of the system. Mercury represents your capacity to understand the desires of your own will and to translate those desires into action.

In other words it is the planet of Mind and the power of communication. Through Mercury we develop an ability to think, write, speak and observe—to become aware of the world around us. It colors our attitudes and vision of the world, as well as our capacity to communicate our inner responses to the outside world. Some people who have serious disabilities in their power of verbal communication have often wrongly been described as people lacking intelligence.

Although this planet (and its position in the horoscope) indicates your power to communicate your thoughts and perceptions to the world, intelligence is something deeper. Intelligence is distributed throughout all the planets. It is the relationship of the planets to each other that truly describes what we call intelligence. Mercury rules speaking, language, mathematics, draft and design, students, messengers, young people, offices, teachers and any pursuits where the mind of man has wings.

VENUS

Venus is beauty. It symbolizes the harmony and radiance of a rare and elusive quality: beauty itself. It is refinement and delicacy, softness and charm. In astrology it indicates grace, balance and the aesthetic sense. Where Venus is we see beauty, a gentle drawing in of energy and the need for satisfaction and completion. It is a special touch that finishes off rough edges. It is sensitivity, and affection, and it is always the place for that other elusive phenomenon: love. Venus describes our sense of what is beautiful and loving. Poorly developed, it is vulgar, tasteless and self-indulgent. But its ideal is the flame of spiritual love—Aphrodite, goddess of love, and the sweetness and power of personal beauty.

MARS

This is raw, crude energy. The planet next to Earth but outward from the Sun is a fiery red sphere that charges through the horoscope with force and fury. It represents the way you reach out for new adventure and new experience. It is energy and drive, initiative, courage and daring. The power to start something and see it through. It can be thoughtless, cruel and wild, angry and hostile, causing cuts, burns, scalds and wounds. It can stab its way through a chart, or it can be the symbol of healthy spirited adventure, well-channeled constructive power to begin and keep up the drive. If you have trouble starting things, if you lack the get-up-and-go to start the ball rolling, if you lack aggressiveness and self-confidence, chances are there's another planet influencing your Mars. Mars rules soldiers, butchers, surgeons, salesmen—any field that requires daring, bold skill, operational technique or self-promotion.

JUPITER

This is the largest planet of the Solar System. Scientists have recently learned that Jupiter reflects more light than it receives from the Sun. In a sense it is like a star itself. In astrology it rules good luck and good cheer, health, wealth, optimism, happiness, success and joy. It is the symbol of opportunity and always opens the way for new possibilities in your life. It rules exuberance, enthusiasm, wisdom, knowledge, generosity and all forms of expansion in general. It rules actors, statesmen, clerics, professional people, religion, publishing and the distribution of many people over large areas.

Sometimes Jupiter makes you think you deserve everything, and you become sloppy, wasteful, careless and rude, prodigal and lawless, in the illusion that nothing can ever go wrong. Then there is the danger of over-confidence, exaggeration, undependability and over-indulgence.

Jupiter is the minimization of limitation and the emphasis on spirituality and potential. It is the thirst for knowledge and higher learning.

SATURN

Saturn circles our system in dark splendor with its mysterious rings, forcing us to be awakened to whatever we have neglected in the past. It will present real puzzles and problems to be solved, causing delays, obstacles and hindrances. By doing so, Saturn stirs our own sensitivity to those areas where we are laziest.

Here we must patiently develop *method,* and only through painstaking effort can our ends be achieved. It brings order to a horoscope and imposes reason just where we are feeling least reasonable. By creating limitations and boundary, Saturn shows the consequences of being human and demands that we accept the changing cycles inevitable in human life. Saturn rules time, old age and sobriety. It can bring depression, gloom, jealousy and greed, or serious acceptance of responsibilities out of which success will develop. With Saturn there is nothing to do but face facts. It rules laborers, stones, granite, rocks and crystals of all kinds.

The Outer Planets

The following three are the outer planets. They liberate human beings from cultural conditioning, and in that sense are the law breakers. In early times it was thought that Saturn was the last planet of the system—the outer limit beyond which we could never go. The discovery of the next three planets ushered in new phases of human history, revolution and technology.

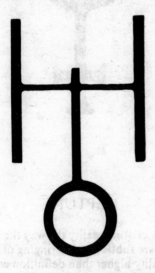

URANUS

Uranus rules unexpected change, upheaval, revolution. It is the symbol of total independence and asserts the freedom of an individual from all restriction and restraint. It is a breakthrough planet and indicates talent, originality and genius in a horoscope. It usually causes last-minute reversals and changes of plan, unwanted separations, accidents, catastrophes and eccentric behavior. It can add irrational rebelliousness and perverse bohemianism to a personality or a streak of unaffected brilliance in science and art. It rules technology, aviation and all forms of electrical and electronic advancement. It governs great leaps forward and topsy-turvy situations, and *always* turns things around at the last minute. Its effects are difficult to ever really predict, since it rules sudden last-minute decisions and events that come like lightning out of the blue.

NEPTUNE

Neptune dissolves existing reality the way the sea erodes the cliffs beside it. Its effects are subtle like the ringing of a buoy's bell in the fog. It suggests a reality higher than definition can usually describe. It awakens a sense of higher responsibility often causing guilt, worry, anxieties or delusions. Neptune is associated with all forms of escape and can make things seem a certain way so convincingly that you are absolutely sure of something that eventually turns out to be quite different.

It is the planet of illusion and therefore governs the invisible realms that lie beyond our ordinary minds, beyond our simple factual ability to prove what is "real." Treachery, deceit, disillusionment and disappointment are linked to Neptune. It describes a vague reality that promises eternity and the divine, yet in a manner so complex that we cannot really fathom it at all. At its worst Neptune is a cheap intoxicant; at its best it is the poetry, music and inspiration of the higher planes of spiritual love. It has dominion over movies, photographs and much of the arts.

PLUTO

Pluto lies at the outpost of our system and therefore rules finality in a horoscope—the final closing of chapters in your life, the passing of major milestones and points of development from which there is no return. It is a final wipeout, a closeout, an evacuation. It is a distant, subtle but powerful catalyst in all transformations that occur. It creates, destroys, then recreates. Sometimes Pluto starts its influence with a minor event or insignificant incident that might even go unnoticed. Slowly but surely, little by little, everything changes, until at last there has been a total transformation in the area of your life where Pluto has been operating. It rules mass thinking and the trends that society first rejects, then adopts and finally outgrows.

Pluto rules the dead and the underworld—all the powerful forces of creation and destruction that go on all the time beneath, around and above us. It can bring a lust for power with strong obsessions.

It is the planet that rules the metamorphoses of the caterpillar into a butterfly, for it symbolizes the capacity to change totally and forever a person's life style, way of thought and behavior.

FAMOUS PERSONALITIES

ARIES: Hans Christian Andersen, Pearl Bailey, Marlon Brando, Wernher Von Braun, Charlie Chaplin, Joan Crawford, Da Vinci, Bette Davis, Doris Day, W. C. Fields, Alec Guinness, Adolf Hitler, Billie Holiday, Thomas Jefferson, Nikita Khrushchev, Elton John, Arturo Toscanini, J. P. Morgan, Paul Robeson, Gloria Steinem, Lowell Thomas, Vincent van Gogh, Tennessee Williams

TAURUS: Fred Astaire, Charlote Brontë, Carol Burnett, Irving Berlin, Bing Crosby, Salvador Dali, Tchaikovsky, Queen Elizabeth II, Duke Ellington, Ella Fitzgerald, Henry Fonda, Sigmund Freud, Orson Welles, Joe Louis, Lenin, Karl Marx, Golda Meir, Eva Peron, Bertrand Russell, Shakespeare, Kate Smith, Benjamin Spock, Barbra Streisand, Shirley Temple, Harry Truman

GEMINI: Mikhail Baryshnikov, Boy George, Igor Stravinsky, Carlos Chavez, Walt Whitman, Bob Dylan, Ralph Waldo Emerson, Judy Garland, Paul Gauguin, Allen Ginsberg, Benny Goodman, Bob Hope, Burl Ives, John F. Kennedy, Peggy Lee, Marilyn Monroe, Joe Namath, Cole Porter, Laurence Olivier, Harriet Beecher Stowe, Queen Victoria, John Wayne, Frank Lloyd Wright

CANCER: "Dear Abby," David Brinkley, Yul Brynner, Pearl Buck, Marc Chagall, Jack Dempsey, Mildred (Babe) Zaharias, Mary Baker Eddy, Henry VIII, John Glenn, Ernest Hemingway, Lena Horne, Oscar Hammerstein, Helen Keller, Ann Landers, George Orwell, Nancy Reagan, Rembrandt, Richard Rodgers, Ginger Rogers, Rubens, Jean-Paul Sartre, O. J. Simpson

LEO: Neil Armstrong, Russell Baker, James Baldwin, Emily Brontë, Wilt Chamberlain, Julia Child, Cecil B. De Mille, Ogden Nash, Amelia Earhart, Edna Ferber, Arthur Goldberg, Dag Hammarskjöld, Alfred Hitchcock, Mick Jagger, George Meany, George Bernard Shaw, Napoleon, Jacqueline Onassis, Henry Ford, Francis Scott Key, Andy Warhol, Mae West, Orville Wright

VIRGO: Ingrid Bergman, Warren Burger, Maurice Chevalier, Agatha Christie, Sean Connery, Lafayette, Peter Falk, Greta Garbo, Althea Gibson, Arthur Godfrey, Goethe, Buddy Hackett, Michael Jackson, Lyndon Johnson, D. H. Lawrence, Sophia Loren, Grandma Moses, Arnold Palmer, Queen Elizabeth I, Walter Reuther, Peter Sellers, Lily Tomlin, George Wallace

LIBRA: Brigitte Bardot, Art Buchwald, Truman Capote, Dwight D. Eisenhower, William Faulkner, F. Scott Fitzgerald, Gandhi, George Gershwin, Micky Mantle, Helen Hayes, Vladimir Horowitz, Doris Lessing, Martina Navratalova, Eugene O'Neill, Luciano Pavarotti, Emily Post, Eleanor Roosevelt, Bruce Springsteen, Margaret Thatcher, Gore Vidal, Barbara Walters, Oscar Wilde

SCORPIO: Vivien Leigh, Richard Burton, Art Carney, Johnny Carson, Billy Graham, Grace Kelly, Walter Cronkite, Marie Curie, Charles de Gaulle, Linda Evans, Indira Gandhi, Theodore Roosevelt, Rock Hudson, Katherine Hepburn, Robert F. Kennedy, Billie Jean King, Martin Luther, Georgia O'Keeffe, Pablo Picasso, Jonas Salk, Alan Shepard, Robert Louis Stevenson

SAGITTARIUS: Jane Austen, Louisa May Alcott, Woody Allen, Beethoven, Willy Brandt, Mary Martin, William F. Buckley, Maria Callas, Winston Churchill, Noel Coward, Emily Dickinson, Walt Disney, Benjamin Disraeli, James Doolittle, Kirk Douglas, Chet Huntley, Jane Fonda, Chris Evert Lloyd, Margaret Mead, Charles Schulz, John Milton, Frank Sinatra, Steven Spielberg

CAPRICORN: Muhammad Ali, Isaac Asimov, Pablo Casals, Dizzy Dean, Marlene Dietrich, James Farmer, Ava Gardner, Barry Goldwater, Cary Grant, J. Edgar Hoover, Howard Hughes, Joan of Arc, Gypsy Rose Lee, Martin Luther King, Jr., Rudyard Kipling, Mao Tse-tung, Richard Nixon, Gamal Nasser, Louis Pasteur, Albert Schweitzer, Stalin, Benjamin Franklin, Elvis Presley

AQUARIUS: Marian Anderson, Susan B. Anthony, Jack Benny, Charles Darwin, Charles Dickens, Thomas Edison, John Barrymore, Clark Gable, Jascha Heifetz, Abraham Lincoln, John McEnroe, Yehudi Menuhin, Mozart, Jack Nicklaus, Ronald Reagan, Jackie Robinson, Norman Rockwell, Franklin D. Roosevelt, Gertrude Stein, Charles Lindbergh, Margaret Truman

PISCES: Edward Albee, Harry Belafonte, Alexander Graham Bell, Frank Borman, Chopin, Adelle Davis, Albert Einstein, Jackie Gleason, Winslow Homer, Edward M. Kennedy, Victor Hugo, Mike Mansfield, Michelangelo, Edna St. Vincent Millay, Liza Minelli, John Steinbeck, Linus Pauling, Ravel, Diana Ross, William Shirer, Elizabeth Taylor, George Washington

ARIES

CHARACTER ANALYSIS

People born under the astrological sign of Aries are often strong-willed and energetic. Ariens are seldom afraid of taking a risk, provided that it is well-calculated. They are people who dare; they are sometimes impulsive but almost never irrational. The Aries man or woman likes to keep busy. They are not a people who like to while away the time in an aimless fashion. Ariens are known for their drive and their boldness. They generally know how to make proper use of their energies; they are positive and productive people who seldom doubt themselves. They know what they want out of life and they go after it. They generally have a pioneering sort of spirit and are always anxious to begin something new. They know how to make use of opportunity when it appears. Many Ariens have no trouble in achieving success.

The strong and positive sort of Arien knows how to channel his energies properly so that he will get the most out of what life has to offer. He is a sensible, practical person, who does not only think about himself but does what he can to help those in less fortunate positions than himself. If a plan goes awry, he does not hesitate to see what he can do to fix it. The Arien is usually quick to initiate a change if it seems necessary to do so. He is an activist, generally, and does not believe in sitting about, waiting for good things to tumble into his lap. If good fortune does not appear, the positive Arien will go out and look for it; his search does not end until he has it. Obstacles do not frighten the Aries man or woman. In fact, contrary situations or people seem to spur him on. The Arien often thrives on adversity. He knows how to turn a disadvantage to an advantage in short order. Not easily discouraged, he will forge ahead on a plan or idea until it is exactly the way he wants it. The

Arien knows how to shift for himself. He won't wait for others to lend a helping hand, but starts himself, without assistance. Some find the Aries person a little too ruthless in his manner for getting what he wants. Patience is a virtue some Ariens lack; they are people who are usually interested in fast results. They want to see the fruits of their investments as quickly as possible.

The average Arien is a person who has many ideas; he is never at a loss for a new approach to an old or familiar situation. He is ever adaptable and knows how to make a profit out of a loss. In emergency situations, the Arien is always quick to act. When an accident occurs, he often knows the proper remedy. Decision-making does not frighten the strong Aries man or woman. They have the ability to think clearly and to direct their interests and energies toward their ultimate goal. Aries people are easily attracted to anything that is new and interesting. They have naturally inquiring minds.

Although Ariens are often alert and quick to act, they are sometimes easily distracted by side issues. Almost everything interests them and this can have its disadvantages, especially when a one-track mind is needed in order to solve a problem. Ariens can sometimes make a mess of things in their eagerness to get things done as soon as possible.

The weak or poorly directed Arien sometimes has a problem trying to put all of his eggs in one basket. He is easily distracted and often argumentative. He sometimes finds it difficult to see the forest for the trees. In trying to get many things accomplished at one time, he achieves nothing. In spite of his short-comings, he is apt to be quite caught up with what he fancies to be his virtues. He will underestimate the intelligence and abilities of others, especially if they seem to threaten his position in one way or another. The confused Arien is always ready for a quarrel. He will often refuse to see the other person's point of view and dismiss their opinions as so much poppy-cock. The Aries man or woman who does not know how to concentrate his or her energies effectively, easily jumps from one mistake to another, leaving things in an incomplete and jumbled state. The weak Arien will seldom admit his faults, although he will eagerly point out those of others . . . or what he imagines to be those of others.

The misdirected Arien more often than not misses his mark. He is too anxious to succeed. He wants success fast and is in too much of a hurry to prepare himself adequately. The weak Aries man or woman can be as stubborn as a mule. When intent on some illusory goal they will seldom take the time to listen to others. Not afraid of taking a risk, the ill-prepared Arien often finds himself leaping from one unsuccessful plan to the other. His optimism often makes a fool of him. He is the type of person who leaps before looking. Although he is easy to anger, his temper quickly cools off. When hurt, he can rant and rave for an hour but once he has defended himself, he will drop the matter altogether and move on to something else. The Arien seldom carries a grudge. In love, too, the Aries man or woman who has not learned how to curb impulsiveness, often finds him- or her- self in a pot of hot water. Love at first sight is not uncommon to this sort of Aries person; he is romantic for as long as the impulse carries him. He is not averse to fly-by-night romances, and is liable to throw caution to the winds when in love.

Because the Aries person has an enterprising nature, he never finds it difficult to keep busy. He is an extremely independent person —sometimes to a fault. Others sometimes find him rather haughty and arrogant. This weak sort of Aries finds it difficult to be objective in anything. He resents criticism even when it is due, yet he will not find it difficult to criticize others. He is the kind of person who takes any dare as an opportunity to prove his worth. Others are often annoyed by the manner in which he presses an issue. He is capable of becoming quite aggressive when the situation calls for tact and understanding. If the weak Arien made an attempt to see or understand both sides of one story, he could improve his own insight into problems. He should do what he can to develop a balanced sense of judgment. It is important for this sort of Aries person to prepare himself adequately before taking on a new project. He should avoid overdoing as that only ends in total exhaustion and very little actual progress is made.

Health

People born under the sign of Aries are generally quite healthy. Their physical condition tends to be good. Still, it is necessary that they take steps not to abuse their health by overdoing. The Arien is sometimes accident-prone because he is careless in his actions, particularly when intent on achieving a particular goal. The head and the face are areas of the body that are often injured. It is important that Ariens learn to relax. The Aries man or woman usually does fairly well in sports. Their bodies are generally well-developed and lithe. The Arien's constitution is almost always good. He is capable of great physical strength for short periods of time. This, or course, has its disadvantages as well as advantages. The Arien can achieve more if he learns how to apply his spurts of strength correctly. Sports where staying power is important are not likely to be ones in which he can excel. The sign of Aries governs the head; nerves, head, and stomach are apt to be the weak points under this sign.

Headaches and fevers are not uncommon complaints. As was mentioned before, it is essential that the person born under this first sign of the Zodiac learn how to relax. It is often the case that they wear out easily because they are impulsive and headstrong; they do not know how to channel their energies in a consistent manner. This can sometimes lead to a breakdown. The Arien is so intent on achieving his goal that he allows himself to overwork. Self-control must also be learned. Sometimes the Arien is too free in expressing himself—this can lead to emotional bankruptcy. He is a person who is quick to anger; he worries. Controlling negative emotions is vitally important as bad moods can often affect his health. People born under this sign should always get their proper rest. Adequate sleep can help an exhausted Arien to regain his strength. A sensible, well-balanced diet is also important. Overeating or immoderate drinking habits can, to some extent, incorrectly influence the general disposition of the Aries man or woman. The Arien does not like to be ill. Sickness makes him restless and impatient. He does not like to spend too much time recuperating from an illness. Because of his drive and enthusiasm, the Arien often recovers more quickly than others. An illness may strike him hard, but he is soon on his feet again. The person born under this sign is almost lively and enterprising. Ariens generally lead long and active lives; to some, they never seem to grow old. The Aries person who learns how to conserve his energies as well as to correctly channel them, can add years to his life-span. Good health habits should be continually observed.

Occupation

The Arien is an active, industrious person. He should find a career in which he can best put his talents to use. Although an Arien is apt to have many interests, he should try to find out which interest is the most suited to his actual means and abilities. He is a person who is sincerely interested in getting on in the world and making a success of himself.

The sign of Aries governs the head and the intellect. The person born during the period, March 21 to April 20, is usually quite ambitious and enterprising. He is not a person who can sit still when there is something to do. Some Ariens have an artistic bent and do well in creative work. Others have some trouble in making up their minds about what kind of work they should do because they are interested in so many things and can handle them all reasonably well. Generally speaking, whatever profession the Arien chooses to enter, he makes a good job of it. The Aries man or woman is never lacking in personality and charm. Quite often they do well in work that requires them to come in direct contact with the public. Quite often they are clever conversationalists. They know how to deal with people—how to amuse them, how to convince them. Others often turn to Aries for advice or counsel when in difficulty. The Aries person can usually handle a position that requires authoratative behavior without any problem at all. They make good leaders and advisors. Ariens are inventive and forward-looking. They have plenty of energy and drive; many have a talent for successfully realizing their plans and dreams.

Aries is a person of action. Quite often he does well in the military or in organized sports. Some Ariens make excellent doctors and nurses. Other do remarkably well as dentists and draftsmen. They are a resourceful people—men and women who often know what they want to achieve in life.

The person born under the sign of Aries is more often than not an individualist. He prefers giving orders to taking them. He is not a "group" sort of person. He enjoys working by himself more than working in a team. A modern person, he usually sees to it that he keeps abreast of the new developments in his field.

One fault often found in the underdeveloped Arien, is that he will undertake a project with much enthusiasm, then as his interest flags he will readily give it up for something new. In such cases, he will often pass the unfinished chore or project on to someone else. Some Ariens make a habit of starting things, then turning them over to others. The sort of Arien who falls into this habit often does it unknowingly. New plans and ideas attract people of this sign quickly. They are always off for new fields to conquer. The strong Arien, however, seldom has difficulties of this sort; he knows how to stick with one job until it is done. He will do his utmost to direct his efforts and energies toward one goal. This sort of Ram makes a success of his life without much effort.

The Aries man or woman is seldom a person who is only interested in work and material gain. He or she knows how to go about having a good time. Some are quite happy when they are able to combine business with pleasure. Ariens usually are not hard materialists, but they know well what money can do. They busy themselves earning money, but they sometimes spend it as soon as it comes into their pockets. The Aries man or woman is generally honest when it comes to money matters. If he or she directs him- or her- self to one goal, there is a good chance that it will be attained without too much effort. The Arien has a driving and courageous personality. In work, this often stands him in good stead.

People born under the sign of Aries generally like to be surrounded by fashionable furnishings and the like. Luxury makes them feel comfortable and successful and often has an important influence in making them positive and enterprising. Shabby or old surroundings are apt to depress the Aries person. He is modern and forward-looking; he must live in an environment that is suited to his general disposition.

Some Ariens tend to be rather careless with their money. Saving is something of a problem for them. They would rather spend what they earn instead of putting something aside for a rainy day. They know how to live for the moment. The weak Arien often invests unwisely or mismanages his joint finances without regard for his partner or mate. The wise Arien avoids impulsive spending and thinks of the future. He sees to it that he learns how to budget his expenses in an effective manner.

Home and Family

The Aries man or woman is a home-loving person by nature. Home means a lot to the Ram. Here he can relax at the end of a hard day and enjoy the comfort of his surroundings. Aries woman are generally excellent home-makers. They have a way with furnishings and color arrangement. They know how to make a home radiate harmony and comfort. Invariably, they have good taste. They can beautify a room or a home without much difficulty. The Aries home usually gives one the feeling of freedom and roominess. A guest is not apt to feel himself confined or uncomfortable.

The Arien enjoys entertaining his friends and family. Nothing pleases him more than people dropping in. He knows how to make the best of a social situation even if it occurs on the spur of the moment. They know how to please visitors and enjoy company. Friends generally respect them and their homes.

In family matters, the Aries man or woman is very emotional— in the good sense of the word. Affection and love between members of his or her immediate family are essential for getting along. The Arien is keenly interested in keeping his home peaceful and harmonious. If possible, the Aries husband or wife tries to exert a strong influence in household matters. The Arien feels that his guidance is important to others.

The person born under this sign of the Zodiac is usually quite fond of children. They understand children and children usually feel close to them. The Arien himself usually has something youthful about his nature. Children have no difficulty in getting along with them and generally enjoy having them join them in some of their activities. Ariens know the value of a good joke and children love them for this. A sense of humor that is rich and well-balanced makes them a favorite with children. Aries people seldom forget the joys of their own youth and enjoy living somewhat vicariously through the adventures and games of their own children.

Although the Aries man or woman is not much of a disciplinarian, they do become rather disappointed if their children do not live up to their expectations in later life. Aries generally thinks he knows what is best for his children and can become rather overbearing if his children are not inclined to agree. The Arien is a person who enjoys being popular and respected and he can be a proud parent.

Social Relationships

The Aries person usually has no trouble in making new friends. He is generally outgoing and generous. He enjoys having many friends. People are easily attracted to the Arien because of his bright and pleasant personality. He knows how to make people feel at ease and encourages them in their self-expression. People often turn to an Arien when they are in trouble. The Aries man or woman knows how to counsel a friend in trouble; he or she is sometimes willing to share the burden or responsibilities of a good friend.

On the other hand, Aries people often make a habit of jumping from one friend to another. As long as a person remains new, interesting, and somewhat mysterious, he remains a friend. As soon as an Arien becomes aware of this friend's limitations, he is apt to try to find someone new to replace him. This is the pattern an uncultivated Arien follows in work. As long as the project is new, it absorbs his interest. As soon as it becomes old hat, he turns it over to someone else and starts something new.

Ariens make friends quickly. If they are really impressed, they will place the new friend on a very high pedestal. Some Ariens become very possessive of their friends and if someone else shows an interest in them, they become rather jealous and resentful. If a friend becomes tiresome or dull, the tactless Arien will not hesitate to handle him in an inconsiderate manner.

Although Ariens generally have a talent for making friends quickly, they also are apt to lose them rather fast if they are not careful. Some Ariens tend to neglect their friends and acquaintances as soon as something new catches their fancies. The weak Arien is sometimes a bit of a gossip and finds it hard not to supply others with the secrets of their friends. This sort of Aries person generally takes people for what they appear to be and not for what they actually are.

LOVE AND MARRIAGE

Romance and the Aries Woman

The Aries woman is more often than not charming. The opposite sex generally find her attractive, even glamorous. She is a woman who is very interested in love and romance. The female Arien has plenty of affection to give to the right man—when she meets him. Women born under this sign are usually very active and vigorous; their intelligence and strong character are also qualities which make them attractive to men. The Aries woman has no trouble in communicating with a man on an intellectual plane; she can easily hold her own in any conversation. She should, however, try to curb her eagerness to talk; quite often she winds up dominating the conversation. The Arien who has cultivated the talent of being a good listener generally does not have any trouble in attracting the sort of man who might propose to her.

The Aries woman is not the sort to sit back and wait for the right man to come along. If she sees someone who interests her, she will more than likely take the lead. She can usually do this in such a charming fashion, that the object of her affection hardly notices that he is being coaxed into a romance.

The Aries woman has no trouble in being true to the man she loves. She is true to herself and believes in remaining faithful to the man she has chosen. She usually makes a thoughtful and considerate companion. When her man is in need of advice she is often able to give him wise counsel. Aries women are generally able to voice an intelligent opinion on just about any subject. Their range of knowledge—just as their range of interests—is quite broad. They are imaginative and know how to keep a relationship alive and interesting.

The woman born under the sign of the Ram makes an excellent wife. It is seldom that she will bother her mate or partner with matters that she can easily handle herself. She has a way of transforming almost any house or apartment into a very comfortable home. With household budgeting, she often turns out to be a mastermind. All in all, the Aries woman is very considerate and dependable; she has all the qualities it takes to make an excellent wife or partner. She knows how to bring up children correctly. She is fond of children and affectionate. She is often the kind of mother who enjoys a large family.

Romance and the Aries Man

The Aires man is often quite romantic and charming when courting the opposite sex. He knows how to win the heart of the woman he loves. The Arien in love is as persuasive and energetic as he is in anything else that interests him. He makes an attentive and considerate lover. A direct and positive person, he has no trouble in attracting women. They are often taken by his charming and dashing manner. The opposite sex feels very safe and confident when with an Aries man—for he knows how to make a woman feel wanted and appreciated. However, the Aries man is sometimes so sure of himself that he frightens the more sensitive woman away.

Although the man born under the sign of the Ram, is usually quite faithful when married, he does not mind "playing the field" as long as he remains single. He can be quite a flirt; sometimes the Aries man goes from one romance to the other until he finds the right girl. Making conquests on the battlefield of love is apt to give his ego quite a boost. The Aries man never has very much trouble with rivals. When he is intent on love he knows how to do away with all opposition—and in short order. The Arien is a man who is very much in need of love and affection; he is quite open about this and goes about attaining it in a very open way.

He may be quite adventurous in love while he is single, but once he settles down, he becomes a very reliable and responsible mate. The Aries man is really a family-type man. He enjoys the company of his immediate family; he appreciates the comforts of home. A well-furnished and inviting home is important to a man born under this sign. Some of the furnishings may be a little on the luxurious side; the Arien feels often inspired to do better if he is surrounded by a show of material comfort. Success-oriented, he likes his home to radiate success.

The Aries man often likes to putter around the house, making minor repairs and installing new household utensils. He is a man who does not mind being tied down as long as he does not really feel it. He will be the head of the house; he does not like the woman to wear the pants in the family. He wants to be the one who keeps things in order. He remains romantic, even after marriage. He is tremendously fond of children and is quite apt to spoil them a bit. He makes an affectionate father. Children make him happy when they make him feel proud of them.

Man—Woman

ARIES MAN
ARIES WOMAN

The Aries man will be contented with the Aries woman so long as she reflects his qualities and interests without trying to outshine him. Although he may be progressive and modern in many things, when it comes to pants-wearing, he's downright conventional: it's strictly male attire. The best position an Aries woman can take in the relationship is a supporting one. He's the boss and that's that. Once that is settled and thoroughly accepted by his Aries spouse, then it's clear sailing.

The Aries man, with his seemingly endless drive and energy, likes to relax in the comfort of his home at the end of an action-packed day, and the Aries wife who is a good homemaker can be sure of his undying affection. He's a lover of slippers and pipe and a comfortable armchair. The Aries wife who sees to it that everything in the house is where her man expects to find it—including herself—will have no difficulty keeping the relationship ship-shape.

When it comes to love, the Aries man is serious and constant, and the object of his affection should be likewise. He is generally not interested in a clinging-vine kind of wife; he justs wants someone who is there when he needs her; someone who listens and understands what he says; someone who can give advice if he should ever have to ask for it—which is not likely to be often. Although he can appreciate a woman who can intelligently discuss things that matter to him, he is not interested in a ranting chatterbox who, through her fondness for earbending, is liable to let the apple pie burn up in the oven.

The Aries man wants a woman who is a good companion and a good sport; someone who will look good on his arm without hanging on it too heavily. He is looking for a woman who has both feet on the ground and yet is mysterious and enticing . . . a kind of domestic Helen of Troy whose face or fine dinner can launch a thousand business deals if need be. The cultivated Aries woman should have no difficulty in filling such a role.

The Aries man and woman have similar tastes when it comes to family style: they both like large ones. The Aries woman is crazy about kids and the more she has, the more she feels like a wife. Children love and admire the affectionate Aries mother. She knows how to play with them and how to understand them. She's very anxious that they do well in life and reflect their good homelife and upbringing. However, both Aries parents should try not to smother their offspring with too much love. They should be urged to make their own decisions—especially as they grow older—and not rely unnecessarily on the advice of their partents.

ARIES MAN
TAURUS WOMAN

The woman born under Taurus may lack the sparkle or dazzle you often like your women to have. In many respects, she's very basic—never flighty—and puts great store in keeping her feet flat on the ground. She may fail to appreciate your willingness to jump here, then there, especially if she's under the impression that there's no profit in it. On the other hand, if you do manage to hit it off with a Taurus woman you won't be disappointed at all in the romance area. The Taurus woman is all woman and proud of it, too. She can be very devoted and loving once she decides that her relationship with you is no fly-by-night romance. She's pretty rugged, too, or can be, when the situation calls for a stiff upper lip. It's almost certain that if the going ever gets too rough she won't go running home to mother. She'll stick by you, talk it out, fight it out, or whatever. When bent on a particular point of view, she can be as hard as nails —without having it adversely affect her femininity. She'll stick by you through thick and thin. She can adjust to hard times just as graciously as she can to good times. You may lose your patience with her, though, if when trying to explain some new project or plan to her, she doesn't seem to want to understand or appreciate your enthusiasm and ambition. With your quick wit and itchy feet, you may find yourself miles ahead of your Taurus woman. At times, you are likely to find this distressing. But if you've developed a talent for patience, you won't mind waiting for her to catch up. Never try grabbing her hand and pulling her along at your normal speed—it is likely not to work. It could lead to flying pots and pans and a fireworks display that would put the Fourth of July to shame. The Taurus woman doesn't anger readily but when prodded often enough, she's capable of letting loose with a cyclone of illwill. If you treat her correctly, you'll have no cause for complaint. The Taurus woman loves doing things for her man. She's a whiz in the kitchen and can whip up feasts fit for a king if she thinks they will be royally appreciated. She may not fully understand you but she'll adore you and be faithful to you if she feels you're worthy of it. She won't see green, either, if you compliment another woman in her presence. When you come home late occasionally and claim that there were a lot of last-minute things to attend to at the office, she won't insinuate that one of those last-minute things was most likely your new, shapely secretary. Her mind doesn't run like that. She's not gullible, but she won't doubt your every word if she feels there is no reason to. The woman born under Taurus will make a wonderful mother for your children. She's a master at keeping children cuddled, well-loved, and warm. You may find, however, that when your offspring reach the adolescent stage you'll have to intervene: Taureans are not very sympathetic to the whims of ever-changing teenagers.

ARIES MAN
GEMINI WOMAN

You may find a romance with a woman born under the sign of the Twins, a many-splendored thing. In her you can find the intellectual companionship you often crave and so seldom find. A Gemini girlfriend can appreciate your aims and desires because she travels pretty much the same route as you do, intellectually . . . that is, at least part of the way. She may share your interests, but she will lack your stick-to-it-iveness. Her feet are much itchier than yours, and as a result, she can be here, there—all over the place, and all at the same time, or so it seems. It may make you dizzy. However, you'll enjoy and appreciate her liveliness and mental agility.

Geminians often have sparkling personalities; you'll be attracted by her warmth and grace. While she's on your arm, you'll probably notice that many male eyes are drawn to her—she may even return a gaze or two, but don't let that worry you. All women born under this sign have nothing against a harmless flirtation; they enjoy this sort of attention and, if they feel they're already spoken for, they'll never let it get out of hand.

Although she may not be as handy in the kitchen as you'd like, you'll never go hungry for a filling and tasty meal. She's in as much a hurry as you and won't feel like she's cheating by breaking out the instant mashed potatoes or the frozen vegetables. She may not be handy at the kitchen range but she can be clever—and with a dash of this and a suggestion of that, she can make an uninteresting TV dinner taste like something out of a Jim Beard cookbook. Then again, maybe you've struck it rich with your Gemini and have one who finds complicated recipes a challenge to her intellect. If so, you'll find every meal a tantalizing and mouth-watering surprise.

When you're exercizing your brain over the Sunday crossword puzzle and find yourself bamboozled over 23 Down and 11 Across, just ask your Gemini friend; she'll give you the right answers without batting an eye. Chances are she probably went through the crossword phase herself years ago and gave them up because she found them too easy.

She loves all kinds of people—just like you do. Still, you're apt to find that you're more particular than she. Often, all that a Gemini requires is that her friends be interesting—and stay interesting. One thing she's not able to abide is a dullard.

Leave the party-organizing to your Gemini sweetheart or mate and you'll never know what a dull moment is. She'll bring the swinger out in you if you give her half a chance.

With kids, woman born under Gemini seem to work wonders. Perhaps this is because they are like children themselves in a way:

restless, adventurous, and easily bored. At any rate, the Gemini mother is loving, gentle, and affectionate with her children.

ARIES MAN
CANCER WOMAN

Romancing a girl born under the sign of the Crab may occasionally give you a case of the jitters. It may leave you with one of those "Oh, brother . . . what did I get into now" feelings. In one hour she can unravel a whole gamut of emotions that will leave you in a tizzy. If you do fall in love with a Cancerian, be prepared for anything. She'll keep you guessing, that's for sure. You may find her a little too uncertain and sensitive for your tastes. You'll most likely have to spend a good deal of your time encouraging her, helping her to erase her foolish fears. Tell her she's a living doll a dozen times a day and you'll be well-loved in return. Be careful of the jokes you make when you are with her—and for heaven's sake don't let any of them revolve around her, her personal interests, or her relatives. Chances are if you do, you'll reduce her to tears. She can't stand being made fun of. It will take bushels of roses and tons of chocolates, not to mention the "I'm sorrys", to get you back in her good graces again.

In matters of money-managing, she may not easily come around to your way of thinking. Ariens are often apt to let money burn a hole in their pockets. Cancerians are just the opposite. You may think your Cancerian sweetheart or mate is a direct descendant of Scrooge. If she has it her way, she'll hang onto that first dollar you ever earned. She's not only that way with money, but with everything from bakery string right on to jelly jars. She's a saver and never discards anything no matter how trivial.

Once she returns your "I love you", you'll find that you have a very loving, self-sacrificing and devoted friend on your hands. Her love for you will never alter unless you want it to. She'll put you high up on a pedestal and will do everything—even if it's against your will—to see that you stay up there.

Cancer women make reputedly the best mothers of all the signs of the Zodiac. She'll consider every minor complaint of her child a major catastrophe. She's not the kind of mother who will do anything to get her children off her hands; with her, kids come first. You'll run a close second. You'll perhaps see her as too devoted and you may have a hard time convincing her that the length of her apron-strings is a little too long. When Junior or Sis is ready for that first date, you may have to lock your Cancer wife in the broom closet to keep her from going along. As an Arien you are apt to understand your children more as individuals than your wife. No matter how many times your Cancer wife insists that no man is good enough for your daughter, you'll know it's all nonsense. If you don't help her to curb her super-maternal tendencies, your Cancer wife may have a good chance of turning into a formidable mother-in-law.

ARIES MAN
LEO WOMAN

If you can manage a girl who likes to kick up her heels every once in a while, the Leo woman's your mate. You'll have to learn how to put away your jealous fears—or at least forget about them—when you take up with a woman born under this sign, because she's often the sort that makes heads turn and sometimes tongues wag. You don't necessarily have to believe any of what you hear; it's most likely just jealous gossip or wishful thinking. She's usually got more than a good share of grace and glamor. She knows it, generally, and knows how to put it to good use. Needless to say, other women in her vicinity turn green with envy and will try anything short of shoving her into the nearest lake in order to put her out of commission, especially if she appears to be cramping their style.

If she has captured your heart and fancy, woo her full-force if your intention is to eventually win her. Shower her with expensive gifts, take her regularly to Ciro's, and promise her the moon—if you're in a position to go that far—and you'll find that Miss Leo's resistance will begin to weaken. It's not that she's so difficult—she'll probably make a lot over you once she's decided you're the man for her—but she does enjoy a lot of attention. What's more, she feels she's entitled to it. Her mild arrogance, though, is becoming. The Leo woman knows how to transform the crime of excessive pride into a very charming misdemeanor. It sweeps most men right off their feet . . . in fact, all men. Those that do not succumb to her leonine charm are few and far between.

If you've got an important business deal to clinch and you have doubts as to whether it will go over well or not, bring your Leo wife along to that business luncheon or cocktail party and it will be a cinch that you'll have that contract in your pocket before the meeting is over. She won't have to say or do anything . . . just be there at your side. The grouchiest oil magnate can be transformed into a gushing, dutiful schoolboy if there's a Leo woman in the room.

If you're a rich Arien, you may have to see to it that your Leo wife doesn't become to heavy-handed with the charge accounts and credit cards. When it comes to spending, Leos tend to overdo. If you're a poor Arien, then you have nothing to fear—for Miss Leo, with her love of luxury, will most likely never give you the time of day, let alone exchange vows.

As a mother, she can be strict and easy-going at the same time. She can pal around with her children and still see to it that they know their places.

ARIES MAN
VIRGO WOMAN

The Virgo woman may be a little too difficult for you to understand at first. Her waters run deep. Even when you think that you do know her, don't take any bets on it: she's capable of keeping things hidden in the deep recesses of her womanly soul—things she'll only reveal when she is sure that you're the one she's been looking for. It may take her sometime to come around to this decision. Virgo women are finnicky about almost everything; everything has to be letter-perfect before they're satisfied. Many of them have the idea that the only people who can do things correctly are other Virgos. Nothing offends a Virgo woman more than sloppy dress, character, or careless display of affection. Make sure your tie's not crooked and your shoes sport a bright shine before you go calling on this lady. Keep your off-color jokes for the locker-room; she'll have none of that. Take her arm when crossing the street. Don't rush the romance. Trying to corner her in the back of a cab may be one way of striking out. Never criticize the way she looks—in fact, the best policy would be to agree with her as much as possible. The Arien, however, with his outspoken, direct, and sensible nature, may find a Virgo relationship too trying. All those Do's and Don't's you'll have to observe if you want to get to first base with a Virgo may be just a little too much to ask of you. After a few dates, you may come to the conclusion that she just isn't worth all that trouble. However, the Virgo woman is mysterious enough, generally, to keep her men running back for more. Chances are you'll be intrigued by her airs and graces.

Love means a lot to you and you may be disappointed at first in Virgo's cool ways. However, underneath that glacial facade lies a hot cauldron of seething excitement. If you're patient and artful in your romantic approach, you'll find that all that caution was well worth the trouble. When Virgos love, they don't stint. It's all or nothing as far as they're concerned. Once they're convinced that they love you, they go all the way right off the bat, tossing all cares to the wind. One thing a Virgo can't stand in love is hypocrisy. They don't give a hoot about what the neighbors might say as long as their hearts tell them "go ahead." They're very concerned with human truths. So much so that if their hearts stumble upon another fancy, they're liable to take up with that new heart-throb and leave you standing in the rain. She's that honest—to her own heart, at any rate. But if you are earnest about your interests in her, she'll know, and will respect and reciprocate your love. Do her wrong once, however, and you can be sure she'll come up with a pair of sharp scissors and cut the soiled ribbon of your relationship.

As a housewife, she'll be neat and orderly. With children, she can be tender and strict at the same time. She can be a devoted and loving wife—it all depends on you.

ARIES MAN
LIBRA WOMAN

That girl born under the sign of Libra is worth more than her weight in gold. She's a woman after your own heart. With her, you'll always come first, make no mistake about that. She'll always be behind you, no matter what you do. And when you ask her for advice about almost anything, you'll most likely get a very balanced and realistic opinion. She's good at thinking things out and never lets her emotions run away with her when clear logic is called for. As a homemaker, she's hard to beat. She is very concerned with harmony and balance; your home will be tastefully furnished and decorated. A Libran cannot stand filth or disarray—it gives her goose bumps. Anything that does not radiate harmony, in fact, runs against her orderly grain.

She's chock-full of charm and womanly ways; she can sweep just about any man off his feet with one winning smile. When it comes to using her brains, she can out-think anyone and sometimes with half the effort. She's diplomatic enough, though, never to let this become glaringly apparent. She may even turn the conversation so that you think that you were the one who did all the brain work. She couldn't care less, really, just as long as you wind up doing what is right. She's got you up there on a pretty high pedestal. You're her man and she's happy if you make all the decisions, big and small—with a little help from her if necessary. In spite of her masculine approach to reason, she remains all woman in her approach to love and affection. You'll literally be showered with hugs and kisses during your romance with a Libra woman. She doesn't believe in holding out. You shouldn't, either, if you want to hang on to her. She's the kind of girl who likes to snuggle up to you in front of the fire on chilly autumn nights. She'll bring you breakfast in bed Sundays then cuddle beside you and tuck a napkin under your chin so you won't get any crumbs on the blankets.

She's very thoughtful about anything that concerns you. If anyone dares suggest that you're not the grandest guy in the world, your Libran is bound to defend you. She'll defend you with her dying breath. When she makes those marriage vows she means every word. As an Arien who also has a tendency to place people you like on a pedestal, you won't be let down by a girl born under the sign of Libra. She'll be everything you believe she is . . . even more. As a mother of your children, she'll be very attentive and loving. However, you won't have to take the backseat when Junior comes along. You'll always come first with her—no matter if it's the kids, the dog, or her maiden aunt from Keokuk. Your children will be well-mannered and respectful. She'll do everything in her power to see that you're treated like a prince.

ARIES MAN
SCORPIO WOMAN

The Scorpio woman can be a whirlwind of passion—perhaps too much passion to suit you. When her temper flies, better lock up the family heirlooms and take cover. When she chooses to be sweet, you're apt to think that butter wouldn't melt in her mouth . . . but of course, it would. She can be as hot as a *tamale* or as cool as a cucumber, but whatever mood she is in, it's no pose. She doesn't believe in putting on airs.

Scorpio women are often quite seductive and sultry—their charm can pierce through the hardest of hearts like a laser ray. She doesn't have to look like Mata Hari (quite often Scorpio women resemble the tomboy next door) but once you've looked into those tantalizing eyes, you're a goner. Life with her won't be all smiles and smooth-sailing; when prompted she can unleash a gale of venom. Generally, she will have the good grace to keep family battles within the walls of your home; when company visits she's apt to give the impression that married life with you is one great big joy-ride. It's just one of her ways of expressing her loyalty to you—at least in front of others. She may fight you tooth and nail in the confines of your living room but at a ball or during an evening out, she'll hang on your arm and have stars in her eyes. She doesn't consider this hypocrisy; she just firmly believes that family quarrels should stay a private matter.

She's pretty good at keeping secrets. She may even keep a few hidden from you if she feels like it. This sort of attitude, of course, goes against the Arien's grain; you believe in being open and straight-from-the-shoulder.

Never cross her up, not even in little things; when it comes to revenge, she's an eye-for-an-eye woman. She's not keen on forgiveness if she feels she's been done wrong. You'd be well-advised not to give her cause to be jealous, either. When she sees green, your life will be made far from rosy. Once she's put you in the dog-house, you can be sure that you're going to stay there an awfully long time.

There's a good possibility that you may find your relationship with a Scorpio too draining. Although she may be full of the old paprika and bursting with dynamite, she still is not the girl you'd exactly like to spend the rest of your natural life with. You'd prefer someone gentler and more direct; someone who won't go throwing pots and pans at the mention of your secretary's name; someone who's flexible and understanding; someone who can take the highs along with the lows and not bellyache; someone who can ride with the punches. If you've got your sights set on a shapely Scorpio, you'd better forget that sweet girl of your dreams. True: a woman born under Scorpio can be heavenly, but she can also be the very devil when she chooses.

ARIES MAN
SAGITTARIUS WOMAN

You most likely won't come across a more good-natured girl than the one born under the sign of Sagittarius. Generally, they're full of bounce and good cheer. Their sunny dispositions seem almost permanent and can be relied upon even on the rainiest of days. No matter what she'll ever say or do, you'll know that she always means well. Women born under this sign are almost never malicious. If ever they seem to be, it is only superficial. Sagittarians are quite often a little short on tact and say literally anything that comes into their pretty little heads, no matter what the occasion. Sometimes the words that tumble out of their mouths seem downright cutting and cruel. They're quite capable of losing their friends—and perhaps even yours—through a careless slip of the lip. On the other hand, you're liable to appreciate their honesty and good intentions. To you, qualities of this sort play an important part in life. With a little patience and practice, you can probably help cure your Sagittarian of her loose tongue; in most cases, it will be worth the effort.

Chances are she'll be the outdoors-type of girlfriend; long hikes, fishing trips, and water skiing will most likely appeal to her. She's a busy person; she could never be called a slouch. She sets great store in being able to move about. She's like you in that respect: she has itchy feet. You won't mind taking her along on camping or hunting trips. She is great company most of the time and generally a lot of fun. Even if your buddies drop by for an evening of poker and beer, she'll manage to fit right in. In fact, they'll probably resent it if she doesn't join in the game. On the whole, she is a very kind and sympathetic woman. If she feels she's made a mistake she'll be the first to call your attention to it. She's not afraid of taking the blame for a foolish deed.

You might lose your patience with her once or twice, but after she's seen how upset you get over her short-sightedness, and her tendency to talk too much, chances are she'll do everything in her power not to do it again. She is not the kind of wife who will pry into your business affairs. But she'll always be there, ready to offer advice if you ask for it. If you come home from a night out with the boys and tell your Sagittarius wife that the red stains on your collar came from cranberry sauce, she'll believe you. She'll seldom be suspicious; your word will almost always be good enough for her.

Although she can be a good housewife, her interests are generally too far-reaching and broad to allow her to confine her activities to just taking care of the house. She's interested in what is going on everywhere.

As a mother, she'll be a wonderful and loving friend to her children. She's apt to spoil them if she is not careful.

ARIES MAN
CAPRICORN WOMAN

If you're not a successful businessman or at least on your way to success, it's quite possible that a Capricorn woman will have no interest in entering your life. She's generally a very security-minded female and will see to it that she only invests her time and interests in sure things. Men who whittle away their time and energy on one unsuccessful scheme or another, seldom attract a Capricorn. Men who are interested in getting somewhere in life and keep their noses close to the grindstone quite often have a Capricorn woman behind them, helping them to get ahead. Although she is a climber herself, she is not what one could call cruel or hard-hearted. Beneath that cool, seemingly calculating exterior there's a warm and desirable woman. She just happens to feel that it's just as easy to fall in love with a rich or ambitious man as it is with a poor or lazy one. She's practical. Although she is keenly interested in rising to the top, she's not aggressive about it. She'll seldom step on someone's feet or nudge competitors away with her elbows. She's quiet about her wishes. She sits, waits, and watches. When an opening or an opportunity does appear, she'll latch on to it, lickety-split. For an on-the-go Arien, an ambitious Capricorn wife or girlfriend can be quite an asset. She can probably give you some very good advice about your business affairs and when you invite the boss and his wife to dinner, she'll charm them both right off the ground. She's generally thorough in whatever she undertakes. She'll see to it that she is second to none in good housekeeping.

Capricorn women make excellent hostesses as well as guests. Generally, they are very well-mannered and gracious, no matter what their background is. They seem to have a built-in sense of what is right and proper. Crude behavior or a careless comment can offend them no end.

If you should marry a woman born under Capricorn you need never worry about her going on a wild shopping spree. Capricorns are very careful about every cent that comes into their hands. They understand the value of money better than most women and have no room in their lives for careless spending. If you turn over your paycheck to her at the end of the week, you can be sure that a good hunk of it will wind up in the bank.

Capricorn girls are generally very fond of family—their own, that is. With them, family ties run very deep. Never say a cross or sarcastic word about her mother. She won't stand for that sort of nonsense and will let you know by not speaking to you for days. In fact, you'd better check her family out before you decide to get down on bended knee, because after you've taken that trip down the aisle, you'll undoubtedly be seeing an awful lot of them.

With children, she's loving and correct. They'll be well brought up and polite.

ARIES MAN
AQUARIUS WOMAN

If you find that you've fallen head over heels for the woman born under the sign of the Water Bearer, better fasten your safety belt. It may take a while before you actually discover what she's like and even then you may have nothing to go on but a string of vague hunches. This girl is like the rainbow—full of all bright and shining hues; she's like no other girl you've known. There's something elusive about her, something delightfully mysterious—you'll most likely never be able to put your finger on it. It's nothing calculated, either; Aquarians don't believe in phoney charm. There will never be a dull moment in your romance with the Water Bearing woman. She seems to radiate adventure, magic, and without even half trying. She'll most likely be the most open-minded woman you've ever met. She—like you—has a strong dislike of injustice and prejudice. Narrow-mindedness runs against her grain.

She is very independent by nature and is quite capable of shifting for herself if necessary. She may receive many proposals for marriage and from all sorts of people. Marriage is one heck of a big step for her; she wants to be sure she knows what she's getting into. If she thinks that it will seriously curb her independence and her love of freedom, she's liable to shake her head and give you back your engagement ring—if she's let the romance get that far.

The line between friendship and romance is a pretty fuzzy one for an Aquarian. It's not difficult for her to remain buddy-buddy with someone with whom she's just broken off. She's tolerant, re-member? So, if you should ever see her on the arm of an ex-lover, don't jump to any hasty conclusions.

She's not a jealous person, and doesn't expect you to be, either. You'll find her pretty much of a free spirit most of the time. Just when you think you know her inside-out, you'll discover that you don't really know her at all.

Very sympathetic and warm, she can be helpful to people in need of assistance and advice.

She's often like a chameleon and can fit in anywhere without looking like she doesn't belong.

She'll seldom be suspicious even if she has every right to be. If the man she loves slips and allows himself a little fling, chances are she'll just turn her head the other way and pretend not to notice that the gleam in his eyes is not meant for her. That's pretty understand-ing. Still, a man married to a woman born under Aquarius should never press his luck in hanky-panky. After all, she is a woman—and a very sensitive one at that.

She makes a fine mother, of course, and can easily transmit her positive and big-hearted qualities to her offspring.

ARIES MAN
PISCES WOMAN

Many a man dreams of a Piscean kind of a girl—and an Arien is no exception. She's soft and cuddly, and very domestic. She'll let you be the brains of the family; she's content to just lean on your shoul-der and let you be master of the household. She can be very lady-like and proper; your business associates and friends will be dazzled by her warmth and femininity. She's a charmer, though, and there's much more to her, generally, than just her pretty exterior. There's a brain ticking away in that soft, womanly body. You may never be-come aware of it, that is, until you're married to her. It's no cause for alarm, however; she'll most likely never use it against you. Still, if she feels that you're botching up your marriage through incon-siderate behavior, or if she feels you could be earning more mon-ey than you do, she'll tell you about it. But, then, any wife would, really.

She'll never try to usurp your position as breadwinner of the family. She'll admire you for your ambition and drive. No one had better dare say one bad word about you in her presence. It's liable to cause her to break into tears. Pisces women are usually very sensi-tive beings and their reactions to adverse situations is sometimes nothing more than a plain, good, old-fashioned cry. They can weep buckets when inclined.

She'll have an extra-special dinner waiting for you to celebrate your landing a new and important account. Don't bother to go into the details, though, at the dinner table; she doesn't have much of a head for business matters, usually, and is only too happy to leave all that to you.

She can do wonders with a home. She's very fond of soft and beautiful things. There will always be a vase of fresh flowers on the hall table. She'll see to it that you always have plenty of socks and handkerchiefs in the top drawer of your dresser. You'll never have to shout downstairs, "Don't I have any clean shirts left?" She'll always see to it that you have. Treat her with tenderness and the relationship will be an enjoyable one.

She'll most likely be fond of chocolates. A bunch of beautiful flowers will make her eyes light up. See to it that you never forget her birthday or your anniversary. These things are very important to her. If you ever let them slip your mind, you can be sure of sending her off to the bedroom for an hour-long crying fit. An Arién with patience and tenderness can keep a Pisces woman happy for a lifetime.

She's not without faults herself, however, and after the glow of love-at-first-sight has faded away, you may find yourself standing in a tubful of hot water. You may find her lacking in imagination and zest. Her sensitivity is liable to get on your nerves after a while. You may even feel that she only uses tears in order to get her own way.

Pisces make strong, sacrificing mothers.

Woman—Man

ARIES WOMAN
ARIES MAN

The mating of Aries with Aries could lead to some pretty frantic fireworks, but it does not necessarily have to. As strong in her ways as he is in his, the Aries woman will make her Aries man happiest by supplementing his drives and dreams. An Aries woman can understand and respect a man born under the same sign if she puts her mind to it. He could be that knight in shining armor that Aries women are often in search of. Women born under the sign of the Ram are hard to please and are not interested in just getting a man. They know just what kind of a man he should be and usually do not settle for anything less than their ideal. They are particular. As far as love goes, neither of them shilly-shally with passion. They play for keeps. An Aries-Aries union could be something strong, secure, and romantic. If both of them have their sights fixed in the same direction and have mutual appreciation for each other, there is almost nothing they could not accomplish. It is a block-buster of a combination.

However, if the Aries wife chooses to place her own interests before those of her husband, she can be sure of rocking the boat . . . and perhaps eventually torpedoing it. The career-minded Aries woman, out to do better than her Aries husband, generally winds up doing herself in. He won't stand for it and your relationship won't stand the strain it will bring about. The Aries wife who devotes herself to teas and evenings of bridge will find that she's burned the one bridge she didn't intend to. The homeloving Aries man finds hastily scribbled notes on the dining-room table and TV dinners in the freezer equally indigestible. When you get home from that night out with the girls, he'll take his heartburn out on you instead of reaching for the Alka-Seltzer. If you want to avoid burps and bumps in your marriage, be on hand with his favorite meals, snacks, plus a generous amount of affection. The way to an Arien's stomach is through his heart.

Homemaking, though, should present no problems to the Aries wife. With her, it's second nature. With a pot of paint and some paper, she can transform the dreariest domicile into a place of beauty and snug comfort. The perfect hostess—even when friends just happen by—she knows how to make guests feel at home and this is what makes her Arien man beam with pride. Home is where some people hang their hat; for an Arien, it's where you hang your heart. It's his castle. Marriage can coast along royally for the Aries couple if the little woman keeps the home fires burning and wholeheartedly stands behind her man. This is no problem for the sensitive Aries wife.

ARIES WOMAN
TAURUS MAN

It is the Aries woman who has more than a pinch of patience and reserve who can find her dream-come-true in a man born under the sign of the Bull.

The steady and deliberate Taurean is a little slow on the draw; it may take him quite a while before he gets around to popping that question. For the Arien women who has learned the art of twiddling her thumbs and who doesn't care if her love life seems like a parody of "Waiting for Godot," the waiting and anticipating almost always pays off in the end. Taurus men take their time. Every slow step they take is a sure one—they see to that, especially when they feel that the path they're on could lead them to the altar.

Any Aries woman looking for a whirlwind romance had better cast her net in shallower waters. Moreover, most Taureans prefer to do the angling themselves. They're not keen on women taking the lead—once she does, he's liable to drop her like a dead fish. Once the Aries woman lets herself get caught on his terms, she'll find that her Taurean has fallen for her: hook, line and sinker.

The Taurus man is fond of comfortable homelife. It's as important to him as it is to the Aries woman. The Arien who centers her main activities on keeping those home fires burning will have no worries about keeping that flame in her hubby's heart aglow. The Aries woman, with her talent for homemaking and harmony, is sometimes the perfect match for the strong, steady, and protective bull. He can be the anchor for her dreams and plans, and can help her acquire a more balanced outlook and approach to her life and her goals. Not one for wild schemes, himself, the Taurean can constructively help her to curb her impulsiveness. He's the man who is always there when you need him. Taureans are rather fond of staying put, especially when it's near someone they love and cherish. When tying her knot with a Taurean, the Aries woman can put away all fears about creditors pounding on the front door. Taureans are practical about everything including bill-paying. When he carries you over that threshold, you can be certain that the entire house is paid for.

As a housewife, the Arien married to a Taurus man, need not worry about having to put aside her many interests for the sake of back-breaking house chores. He'll see to it that you have all the latest time-saving appliances and comforts.

The Aries mother can forget about acquiring premature gray hairs due to unruly, ruckus-raising children under her feet. Papa Taurus is a master at keeping offspring in line. He's crazy about his kids, but he also knows what's good for them. And although he may never resort to the rod, he'll never allow himself to spoil his child, either. Children respect Taurean authority and will usually do their best to make papa proud of them.

The Taurus spouse or lover is generous, patient, and easy-going. He's no slouch and it can lead to disaster if the ambitious Aries wife misinterprets his plodding ways for plain laziness. He knows where he's going. Make no bones about that. Stick with him even if sometimes he seems as slow as molasses on a cold day, and your marital life will be all sweetness and light.

The Taurus man is a steady-Eddy—the kind of man the Aries woman often needs. He appreciates her interest in his work, and pays heed to her helpful suggestions because they pay off. Taureans are faithful and never flirt. All his love and attention are riveted to the woman of his choice, as long as she shows that she's deserving.

ARIES WOMAN
GEMINI MAN

The Aries woman and the Gemini man are a twosome that can make beautiful music together. Perhaps that is due to the fact that they are alike in certain respects. Both are intelligent, witty, outgoing, and tend to be rather versatile. An Aries woman can be the Miss Right that Mr. Gemini has been looking for—his prospective better half, as it were. One thing that causes a Twin's mind and affection to wander is a bore, and it's highly unlikely that an Arien would ever be accused of that. He'll admire the Ram for her ideas and intellect—perhaps even more than her good cooking and flawless talent for homemaking. She needn't feel that once she's made that vow that she'll have to store her interests and ambition in the attic somewhere. He'll admire her for her zeal and liveliness. He's the kind of guy who won't pout and scowl if he has to shift for himself in the kitchen once in a while. In fact, he'll enjoy the challenge of wrestling with pots and pans himself for a change. Chances are, too, that he might turn out to be a better cook than his Mrs., that is, if he isn't already.

The man born under the sign of the Twins is like an intellectual mountain goat leaping from crag to crag. There aren't many women who have pep enought to keep up with him. But this doesn't fluster the spry Ram. In fact, she probably knows before he does which crag he's going to spring onto next. In many cases, she's always a couple of jumps ahead of him—and if she's the helpful wife Ariens usually are, she won't mind telling him when and how to jump. They're both dreamers, planners, and idealists. The woman born under the sign of the Ram, though, is more thorough and possesses more stick-to-it-iveness. She can easily fill the role of rudder for her Gemini's ship-without-a-sail. He won't mind it too much, either. If he's an intelligent Twin, he'll be well aware of his shortcomings and won't mind it if somebody gives him a shove in the right direction—when it's needed. The average Gemini does not have serious ego hangups and will even accept a well-deserved chewing out from his mate quite gracefully.

You'll probably always have a houseful of interesting people to entertain. Geminis find it hard to tolerate sluggish minds and dispositions. You'll never be at a loss for finding new faces in your living room. Geminis are great friend-collectors and sometimes go about it the same way kids go about collecting marbles—the more they sparkle and dazzle, the greater their value to him. But then in a day or two, it's not unusual to find that he has traded yesterday's favorites for still brighter and newer ones. The diplomatic Arien can bring her willy-nilly Gemini to reason and point out his folly in friendships in such a way that he'll think twice before considering an exchange of old lamps for new.

As far as children are concerned, it's quite likely that the Aries wife will have to fill the role of house disciplinarian. Geminis are pushovers for children, perhaps because they understand them so well and have that childlike side to their nature which keeps them youthful and optimistic. They have no interest in keeping a child's vigor in check.

Gemini men are always attractive to the opposite sex and vice-versa. The Aries woman with her proud nature will have to bend a little and allow her Gemini man an occassional harmless flirtation— it will seldom amount to more than that if she's a proper mate. It will help to keep his spirits up. An out-of-sorts Twin is capable of brewing up a whirlwind of trouble. Better to let him hanky-pank— within eyeshot, of course—than to lose your cool; it might cause you to lose your man.

ARIES WOMAN
CANCER MAN

It's quite possible that a man born under this sign of the Crab may be a little too crabby for the average Aries woman; but then, Cupid has been known to perform some pretty unlikely feats with his wayward bow and arrow. Again, it's the Arien with her wits about her who can make the most out of a relationship with the sensitive and occassionally moody Cancerian. He may not be altogether her cup of tea, but when it comes to security and faithfulness—qualities Aries women often value highly—she couldn't have made a better choice.

It's the perceptive Arien who will not mistake the Crab's quietness for sullenness, or his thriftiness for pennypinching. In some respects he can be like the wise old owl out on a limb; he may look like he's dozing but actually he hasn't missed a thing. Cancers often possess a storehouse of knowledge about human behavior; they can come across with some pretty helpful advice for those troubled and in need of an understanding shoulder to cry on. The Aries girl about to rush off for new fields to conquer had better turn to her Cancerian first. Chances are he can save her from making unwise investments in time and—especially—money. He may not say much, but he's capable of being on his toes even while his feet are flat on the ground.

The Crab may not be the match or catch for many a Ram; in

fact, he might seem downright dull to the ambitious, on-the-move Arien. True to his sign, he can be fairly cranky and crabby when handled in the wrong way. He's sensitive, perhaps more sensitive than is good for him. The talkative Arien who has a habit of saying what is on her mind had better think twice before letting loose with a personal criticism of any kind, particularly if she's got her heart set on a Cancerian. If she's smart as a whip, she'd better be careful that she never in any way conveys the idea that she considers her Crab a little short on brain power. Browbeating is a sure-fire way of sending the Crab angrily scurrying back to his shell, and it's quite possible that all of that ground lost might never be recovered.

Home is an area where the Aries woman and the Cancer man are in safe territory. Both have serious respect and deep interest in home life, and do their best to keep things running smoothly and harmoniously there. The Crab is most comfortable at home. Once settled in for the night or the weekend, wild horses couldn't drag him any further than the gate post—that is, unless those wild horses were dispatched by his mother. Cancerians are often Momma's boys. If his mate doesn't put her foot down, the Crab will see to it that his mother always comes first whenever possible. No self-respecting Arien would ever allow herself to play second fiddle, even if it is to her old gray-haired mother-in-law. If she's a tactful Ram, she may find that slipping into number-one position can be as easy as pie (that legendary apple pie that his mother used to make). She should agree with her Cancerian when he praises his mother's way with meat loaf, then go on to prove herself a master at making a super-delicious chocolate souffle. All Ariens are pretty much at home in the kitchen; no recipe is too complicated for them to handle to perfection. If she takes enough time to pamper her Cancerian with good-cooking and comfort, she'll find that "mother" turns up less often, both at the front door and in daily conversations.

Crabs make grand daddies. They're protective, patient, and proud of their children. They'll do everything to see that their upbringing is as it should be.

ARIES WOMAN
LEO MAN

For the Arien who doesn't mind being swept off her feet in a royal, head-over-heels, fashion, Leo is the sign of love. When the Lion puts his mind to romancing, he doesn't stint. It's all wining, dining, and dancing till the wee hours of the morning—or all poetry and flowers, if you prefer a more conservative kind of wooing. The Lion is all heart and knows how to make his woman feel like a woman. The Aries lass in constant search of a man whom she can admire, need go no farther: Leo's ten-feet tall—if not in stature, then in spirit. He's a man not only in full control of his faculties but of just about every situation he may find himself in, including of course, affairs of the heart. He may not look like Tarzan, but he knows how to roar and beat his chest if he has to. The Aries woman who has had her fill of weak-kneed men, at last finds in a Leo someone she can lean upon. He can support you not only physically, but also as far as your ideas and plans are concerned. Leos are direct and don't believe in wasting time or effort. They see to it that they seldom make poor investments; something that an Arien is not apt to always do. Many Leos often rise to the top of their profession and through their example, are a great inspiration to others.

Although he's a ladies' man, he's very particular about his ladies, just as the Arien is particular about her men. His standards are high when it comes to love interests. The idealistic Arien should have no trouble keeping her balance on the pedestal the Lion sets her on, so long as he keeps his balance on hers. Romance between these two signs is fair give-and-take. Neither stands for monkey business when involved in a love relationship. It's all or nothing. Aries and Leo are both frank, off-the-shoulder people. They generally say what is on their hearts and minds.

The Aries woman who does decide upon a Leo mate, must be prepared to stand behind her man with all her energies. He expects it, and usually deserves it. He's the head of the house and can handle that position without a hitch. He knows how to go about breadwinning and, if he has his way (and most Leos do have their way), he'll see to it that you'll have all the luxuries you crave and the comforts you need.

It's unlikely that the romance will ever die out of your marriage. Lions need love like flowers need sunshine. They're amorous and generally expect similar amounts of attention and affection from their mates. Fond of going out occasionally, and party-giving, the Lion is a very sociable being and will expect you to share his interest in this direction. Your home will be something to be proud of. The Joneses will have to worry about keeping up with you.

Leos are fond of their children but sometimes are a little too strict in handling them. The tactful Aries spouse, though, can step in and sooth her children's roughed-up feelings if need be.

ARIES WOMAN
VIRGO MAN

Quite often the Virgo man will seem like too much of a fuss-budget to wake up deep romantic interests in an Arien. Generally, he's cool, calm and very collected. Torrid romancing to him is just so much sentimental mush. He can do without it and can make that quite evident in short order. He's keen on chastity and if necessary can lead a sedentary, sexless life without caring too much about the fun others think he's missing. In short, the average Aries woman is quite likely to find him a first-class dud. His lack of imagination and dislike for flights of fancy can grate on an Arien's nerves no end. He's correct and likes to be handled correctly. Most things about him will be orderly. "There's a place for everything and everything in its place," is likely an adage he'll fall on quite regularly.

He does have a heart, however, and the Aries woman who finds herself attracted to his cool, feet-flat-on-the-ground ways, will find that his is a constant heart, not one that cares for flings or sordid affairs. Virgos take an awfully long time before they start trying to rhyme moon with spoon and June, but when and if they get around to it, they know what they're talking about.

The impulsive Arien had better not make the mistake of kissing her Virgo friend on the street—even if it's only a peck on the cheek. He's not at all demonstrative and hates public displays of affection. Love, according to him, should be kept within the confines of one's home, with the curtains drawn. Once he believes that you're on the level with him, as far as your love is concerned, you'll see how fast he can lose his cool. Virgos are considerate, gentle lovers. He'll spend a long time, though, getting to know you. He'll like you before he loves you.

An Aries-Virgo romance can be a life-time thing. If the bottom ever falls out, don't bother to reach for the Scotch tape. Nine times out of ten, he won't care about patching up. He's a once-burnt-twice-shy guy. When he crosses your telephone number out of his address book, he's crossing you out of his life for good.

Neat as a pin, he's thumbs-down on what he considers "sloppy" housekeeping. An ashtray with just one stubbed-out cigarette in it can be annoying to him, even if it's just two-seconds old. Glassware should always sparkle and shine. No smudges please.

If you marry a Virgo, keep your kids spic-and-span, at least by the time he gets home from work. Chocolate-coated kisses from Daddy's little girl go over like a lead balloon. He'll expect his children to observe their "thank yous" and "pleases."

ARIES WOMAN
LIBRA MAN

Although the Libran in your life may be very compatible, you may find this relationship lacking in some of the things you highly value.

You, who look for constancy in romance, may find him a puzzlement as a lover. One moment he comes on hard and strong with

"I love you," the next moment you find that he's left you like yesterday's mashed potatoes. It does no good to wonder "What did I do now?" You most likely haven't done anything. It's just one of Libra's ways.

On the other hand, you'll appreciate his admiration of harmony and beauty. If you're all decked out in your fanciest gown or have a tastefully arranged bouquet on the dining-room table, you'll get a ready compliment—and one that's really deserved. Librans don't pass out compliments indiscriminately and generally they're tactful enough to remain silent if they find something is distasteful or disagreeable.

Where you're a straight-off-the-shoulder, let's-put-our-cards-on-the-table person, Librans generally hate arguing. They'll go to great lengths just to maintain peace and harmony—even lie if necessary. The frank Aries woman is all for getting it off her chest and into the open, even if it does come out all wrong. To the Libran, making a clean breast of everything sometimes seems like sheer folly.

The Aries woman may find it difficult to understand a Libran's frequent indecisiveness—he weighs both sides carefully before committing himself to anything. To you, this may seem like just plain stalling.

Although you, too, greatly respect order and beauty, you would never let it stand in the way of "getting ahead." Not one who dilly-dallies, the Aries may find it difficult to accept a Libran's hestiation to act on what may seem like a very simple matter.

The Libra father is most always gentle and patient. They allow their children to develop naturally, still they see to it that they never become spoiled.

Money burns a hole in many a Libran's pocket; his Aries spouse will have to manage the budgeting and bookkeeping. You don't have to worry about him throwing his money around all over the place; most likely he'll spend it all on you—and lavishly.

Because he's quite interested in getting along harmoniously chances are he won't mind an Aries wife taking over the reins once in a while—so long as she doesn't make a habit of it.

ARIES WOMAN
SCORPIO MAN

Many find the Scorpio's sting a fate worse than death. The Aries woman quite often is no acception. When he comes on like "gangbusters," the average Aries woman had better clear out of the vicinity.

The Scorpio man may strike the Aries woman as being a brute

and a fiend. It's quite likely he'll ignore your respect for colorful arrangements and harmonious order. If you do anything to irritate him—just anything—you'll wish you hadn't. He'll give you a sounding out that would make you pack your bags and go back to mother —if you were that kind of a girl. Your deep interest in your home and the activities that take place there will most likely affect him indifferently. The Scorpio man hates being tied down to a home— no matter how comfortable his Aries wife has made it. He'd rather be out on the battlefield of life, belting away at what he feels is a just and worthy cause. Don't try to keep those homefires burning too brightly too long—you may just run out of firewood.

As passionate as he is in business affairs and politics, he's got plenty of pep and ginger stored away for romance. Most women are easily attracted to him, and the Aries woman is no acception. That is, at least before she knows what she might be getting into. Those who allow a man of this sign to sweep them off their feet, shortly find that they're dealing with a cauldron of seething excitement. He's passion with a capital P, make no bones about that. And he's capable of dishing out as much pain as pleasure. Damsels with fluttering hearts who, when in the embrace of a Scorpio, think "This is it," had better be in a position to realize "This isn't it," some moments later. Scorpio's are blunt. If there's not enough powder on your nose or you have just goofed with a sure-fire recipe for Beef Stroganoff (which is unlikely, you being an old hand with pots and pans) he'll let you know and in no uncertain terms. He might say that your *big* nose is shiny and that he wouldn't serve your Stroganoff to his worst enemy—even your mother. She might be sitting right beside him when he says this, too.

The Scorpio's love of power may cause you to be at his constant beck-and-call.

Scorpios often father large families and generally love their children even though they may not seem to give them the attention they should.

ARIES WOMAN
SAGITTARIUS MAN

The Aries woman who's set her cap for a man born under this sign of Sagittarius, may have to apply an awful amount of strategy before being able to make him say "I do." Although Sagittarians may be marriage-shy, they're not ones to shy away from romance. An Aries woman may find a relationship with a Sagittarian—whether a fling or "the real thing"—a very enjoyable experience. As a rule, Sagittarians are bright, happy, and healthy people and they can be a source of inspiration to the busy, bustling Aries woman. Their deep sense of fair play will please you, too. They're full of ideas and drive. You'll be taken by the Sagittarian's infectious grin and his light-hearted friendly attitude. If you do choose to be the woman in his life, you'll find that he's apt to treat you more like a buddy than like the woman he deeply loves. But it is not intentional; it's just the way he is. You'll admire his broadmindedness in most matters—including that of the heart. If, while you're dating, he claims he still wants to play the field, he'll expect you to do the same. The same holds true when you're both playing for keeps. However, once he's promised to love, honor, and obey, he does just that. Marriage for him, once he's taken that big step, is very serious business. The Aries woman with her keen imagination and love of freedom will not be disappointed if she does tie up with a Sagittarian. They're quick-witted, generally, and they have a genuine interest in equality. If he insists on a night out with the boys once a week, he won't scowl if you decide to let him shift for himself in the kitchen once a week while you go out with the girls.

You'll find he's not much of a homebody. Quite often he's occupied with far away places either in daydreams or reality. He enjoys —just as you do—being on the go or on the move. He's got ants in his pants and refuses to sit still for long stretches at a time. Humdrum routine—especially at home—bores him. At the drop of a hat, he may ask you to whip off your apron and dine out for a change instead. He'll take great pride in showing you off to his friends; he'll always be a considerate mate and never embarrass or disappoint you intentionally. His friendly, sun-shiny nature is capable of attracting many people. Like you, he's very tolerant when it comes to friends and you'll most likely spend a great deal of time entertaining people. He'll expect his friends to be your friends, too, and vice-versa. The Aries woman who often prefers male company to that of her own sex, will not be shunted aside when the fellows are deep in "man talk." Her Sagittarian will see to it that she's made to feel like one of the gang and treated equally.

When it comes to children, you may find that you've been left to handle that area of your marriage single-handedly. Sagittarians are all thumbs when it comes to tots.

ARIES WOMAN
CAPRICORN MAN

Chances are the Aries woman will find a relationship with a Capricorn man a bit of a drag. He can be quite opposite to the things you stand for and value. Where you are generally frank and open, you'll find the man born under the sign of the Goat, closed or difficult to get to know—or not very interesting once you've gotten to know him. He may be quite rusty in the romance department, too, and may take quite a bit of drawing out. You may find his seemingly plodding manner irritating, and his conservative, traditional ways downright maddening. He's not one to take chances on anything. "If it was good enough for my father, it's good enough for me" may be his motto. He follows a way that is tried and true.

Whenever adventure rears its tantalizing head, the Goat will ring up a No Sale sign; he's just not interested. He may be just as ambitious as you are—perhaps even more so—but his ways of accomplishing his aims are more subterranean or at least, seem so. He operates from the background a good deal of the time. At a gathering you may never even notice him, but he's there taking everything in and sizing everyone up, planning his next careful move. Although Capricorns may be intellectual, it is generally not the kind of intelligence an Arien appreciates. You may find they're not quick-witted and are a little slow to understand a simple joke. The Aries woman who finds herself involved with a Capricorn may find that she has to be pretty good in the "cheering up" department, as the man in her love life may act as though he's constantly being followed by a cloud of gloom. If the Arien and the Capricorn do decide to tie the knot, the area of their greatest compatibility will most likely be in the home and decisions centered around the home. You'll find that your spouse is most himself when under the roof of home sweet home. Just being there, comfortable and secure, will make him a happy man. He'll spend as much time there as he can and if he finds he has to work overtime, he'll bring his work home rather than stay in the office.

You'll most likely find yourself frequently confronted by his relatives—family is very important to the Capricorn, *his* family, that is—and they had better take a pretty important place in your life, too, if you want to keep your home a happy one.

Although his caution in most matters may all but drive you up the wall, you'll find his concerned way with money justified most of the time. He is no squanderer. Everything is planned right down to the last red penny. He'll see to it that you never want.

As far as children are concerned, you may find that you have to step in from time to time when he scolds. Although he generally knows what is good for his children, he can overdo somewhat when it comes to taking them to the woodshed.

ARIES WOMAN
AQUARIUS MAN

The Arien is likely to find the man born under Aquarius dazzling. As a rule, Aquarians are extremely friendly and open; of all the signs, they are perhaps the most tolerant. In the thinking department they are often miles ahead of others, and with very little effort, it seems. The Aries woman will most likely not only find her Aquarian friend intriguing and interesting, but will find the relationship challenging as well. Your high respect for intelligence and fair play may be reason enough for you to settle your heart on a Water Bearer. There's an awful lot to be learned from him, if you're quick enough. Aquarians love everybody—even their worst enemies, sometimes. Through your relationship with the Aquarian you'll find yourself running into all sorts of people, ranging from near-genius to downright insane—and they're all freinds of his.

In the holding hands stage of your romance you may find that your Water Bearing friend has cold feet that may take quite a bit of warming up before he gets around to that first goodnight kiss. More than likely he'll just want to be your pal in the beginning. For him, that's an important step in any relationship—even love. The "poetry and flowers" stage will come later, perhaps many years later. The Aquarian is all heart, still when it comes to tying himself down to one person and for keeps, he is liable to hesitate. He may even try to get out of it if you breath too hard down his neck. He's no Valentino and wouldn't want to be. The Aries woman is likely to be more attracted by his broadmindedness and high moral standards than by his abilities to romance. She won't find it difficult to look up to a man born under the sign of the Water Bearer—but she may find the challenge of trying to keep up with him dizzying. He can pierce through the most complicated problem as if it were a matter of $2 + 2$. You may find him a little too lofty and high-minded, however. But don't judge him too harshly if that's the case; he's way ahead of his time; your time, too, most likely.

In marriage you need never be afraid that his affection will wander. It stays put once he's hitched. He'll certainly admire you for your intelligence and drive; don't think that once you're in the kitchen you have to stay there. He'll want you to go on and pursue whatever you want in your quest for knowledge. He's understanding on that point. You'll most likely have a minor squabble with him now and again, but never anything serious.

You may find his forgetfulness a little bothersome. His head is so full of ideas and plans that sometimes he seems like the Absent-Minded Professor incarnate. Kids love him and vice-versa. He's tolerant and open-minded with everybody, from the very young to the very old.

ARIES WOMAN
PISCES MAN

The man born under the sign of Pisces, may be a little too sluggish for the average Aries woman. He's often wrapped up in his dreams and difficult to reach at times. He's an idealist like you, but unlike you, he will not jump up on a soapbox and champion a cause he feels is just. Difficult for you to understand at times, he may seem like a weakling to you. He'll entertain all kinds of views and opinions from just about anyone, nodding or smiling vaguely, giving the impression that he's with them one hundred percent. In reality, that may not be the case at all. His attitude may be "why bother" to tell someone he's wrong when he so strongly believes that he's right. This kind of attitude can make an Arien furious. You speak your mind; he'll seldom speak his unless he thinks there'll be no opposition. He's oversensitive at times—rather afraid of getting his feelings hurt. He'll sometimes imagine a personal injury when none is intended. Chances are you'll find this sort of behavior maddening and may feel like giving your Pisces friend a swift kick where it hurts the most. It won't do any good, though. It may just add fire to his persecution complex.

One thing you'll admire about this man is his concern and understanding of people who are sickly or who have serious (often emotional) problems. It's his nature to make his shoulder available to anyone in the mood for a good cry. He can listen to one hard-luck story after another without seeming to tire and if his advice is asked he's capable of coming across with some very well-balanced common sense. He often knows what is bugging a person before that person knows it himself. It's amost intuitive with a Pisces, it seems. Still, at the end of the day, he'll want some peace and quiet and if his Aries friend has some problem or project on her mind that she would like to unload in his lap, she's liable to find him rather short-tempered. He's a good listener but he can only take so much.

Pisces are not aimless, although they may often appear to be when viewed through Arien eyes. The positive sort of Pisces man is quite often successful in his profession and is likely to wind up rich and influential—even though material gain is never a direct goal for a man born under this sign.

The weaker Pisces are usually content to stay put on the level they find themselves. They won't complain too much if the roof leaks and the fence is in need of repair. He's capable of shrugging his shoulders and sighing "that's life."

Because of their seemingly free-and-easy manner, people under this sign, needless to say, are immensely popular with children. For tots they play the double role of confidant and playmate.

ARIES

YEARLY FORECAST: 1989

Forecast for 1989 Concerning Business and
Financial Matters, Job Prospects,
Travel, Health, Romance and Marriage
for Those Born with the Sun
in the Zodiacal Sign of Aries
March 21–April 20

You of Aries, the sign of the Ram, ruled by the energetic and adventurous planet Mars, should hit the high spots this year. Challenges will be faced resolutely. Aspirations will be high and important goals sought. You seem determined to concentrate on getting on in the world, through career or profession. In some way you will be seeking the limelight that goes with success and another triumph racked up. It follows that your resources will be tested to the full. This you can relish, not wishing to stand still since that means retreat to you. Heavy demands will be made on you before you can begin to appreciate the power and authority at your finger tips. A number of you will achieve greatness. Many more will establish themselves at the top of the tree and stay there for years to come. So much will depend on your flair, perseverance, respect, imagination and willingness to stand up and be counted. Practical success will have a bearing on material assets and resources. Your personal income can continue to be boosted for part of the year. You will develop along sound and sensible lines till you feel you are clear of any financial shortcomings. Your attention will be drawn to the opportunities to grasp or be created in advertising, public relations and a general livening up of personal know-how. You will wish to develop your ability to communicate if aspirations are to be fulfilled and your position strengthened. Later on in the year, there should be an opportunity to develop an interest in property. This can affect your business life as well as making personal affairs much more interesting. Professional success often depends on the quality of homelife. Both are highly important this year. You may

124

look farther afield in your search for recognition. Jobs may be changed. In all probability you have worked up to this point in your life through examinations and acquired technical ability and status. Now you will feel you can look around for the best offer. It is not in your nature to stay in a rut, especially when you feel you now have the choice of the market. Attention to basic details may keep you more at home than abroad. Traveling to distant places may not suit you, but you appear to have plenty on your hands in a local way that will keep you on your toes. For some, their greatest achievement will lie through romance. For others, the material goals will give the greatest thrill. The strong desire to take initiative will open the doors to a new life-style that may center around the home and family. It is not a year you will trifle with your affections or the affections of the one you love. Whatever you do will have essential meaning.

Now you should feel in charge of your destiny. Business life will never be dull. You realize this is a year to make your mark, but the challenges you face will not always be in one direction. Insight will play a major part in your arrival. Your intuition is excellent. You know what you are after and can go for it. Up to about March 10 do all in your power to build up financial and material resources. If you employ labor, see that you have good relations with staff and that their welfare is fully catered for early in the year. During the period between March 11 and July 29, considerable time and money may be spent on advertising, publicizing and making contact with new customers. In consequence, you could be busy and mobile. Your own knowledge and appreciation of basic needs, likes and dislikes of the community will grow. Have your business house in order. Your enthusiasm, in the first three weeks or so of the year, may win you support, but can also stir up opposition. Those already in authority at the top may take a dim view of a personal crusade. There is time and place to show your drive in a more constructive or cooperative way. Between October 23 and December 17 you may be in a position to spread out. A merger or major contract with a large firm or corporation can form part of your plan to develop. Here again your enthusiasm may overstep the mark. You could take a chance on a small scale, particularly after November 4. It will be up to you to match your natural talent for individual progress against the responsibilities you are now taking on. You could get top-heavy and be unable to control efficiently all you seek to gather around you. Speculation can bring damaging results. While it is essential you stay above the run-of-the-mill member, you should be careful not to alienate the conventional strength of the business community. Honesty will always pay off. Added to this, you know you are in the driver's seat and responsible for your own actions.

Finances should be sufficient to see you through in whatever direction you wish to develop. From the beginning of the year till March 10, you should be able to add to your resources, provided you are considerate and do not trust to your good luck too much. Make hay while the sun shines in this period. There may be a temptation between January 19 and March 10 to get rid of as much as you gain. If you take a long-term view of your chances, and consider why you should be making money, your natural good sense could make you redouble efforts to make rather than to squander the essential funds. Obviously with career prospects at a high, you could be earning quite well. In order to keep this position secure, you must use money wisely. During the period between April 29 and June 15, you could be laying out money on property or land. This may be a good investment or it could be overhead you would be better without. However, later on, between July 30 and the end of the year, an interest in land or property could make you money. This may mean buying or selling to your advantage. Security will be important during this period. From June 16 to August 2 you may want to consider speculation. Be guided by the conservative aims you have in mind. Make good use of any funds you invest and avoid get-rich-quick schemes. Too much is at stake to be careless with your resources or your reputation. Between August 3 and September 22, you may come to realize the importance of making money work for you and the need to keep your nose to the grindstone in order to earn a living. Salary increases and bonuses will be earned through your application and hard work. Look after any joint holdings, insurance and taxation matters that affect your finances between October 23 and November 21.

With added responsibility coming your way, you will take the normal routine of work in your stride. The desire to make progress may mean you change jobs in order to achieve promotion and a larger salary. It is not your usual way to look back, except to build up momentum for the future. Qualifications and skills developed in the past few years may now be put to good use. You are not likely to sell yourself short. So there may be a move to self-employment for many. This is a natural way of life for you who must do your own thing. Some may start up in a small way, working from home, between July 30 and the end of the year. Employers or suppliers can be particularly cooperative between August 23 and September 22.

Health seems to bring no problems. You may be keyed up and too eager to get on to be slowed down by any illness. Chronic ailments are likely to disappear or be pushed to the background. Modern or different treatment should help you who need medical attention. Pressure of work or business may be wearing at times, but you are noted for your spirit so you will soon recover. You will drive yourself hard between January 1 and 18 and August 3 to September 18. Be sure you can stand the strain. See that you are nourished. Take care when driving between March 11 and April 26. You could do a lot of local trips during the year and this can be a time when you have more than you wish.

Traveling any great distance, whether for business or on vacation, is best undertaken between November 22 and the end of the year. There may be an added impetus to a break from about December 20. You could have a particular purpose for this journey. Otherwise, a great deal of your time, especially between March 11 and July 29, can be taken up in local travel, keeping in touch with relatives and generally developing bread-and-butter connections in order to sustain and build up your growing reputation. These apparently minor essentials are all part of the greater picture of your growth into a more complete person.

The home should have some significance during the year. You will need to set up house or develop the potential of home in some way after July 30. If your hopes have been realized through marriage, your first home will be quite an adventure. You are not living in a fairyland world and will have your feet firmly on the ground. So to start a home of your own or, if you are married, begin to build up the family structure, will give you a great boost. For some, the pressure of business or personal aspirations may cancel out much love life. If sweethearts or partners miss your company, there could be some problems. You will have your priorities sorted out and should be able to achieve understanding or acceptance of your personal viewpoint. Be considerate of your partner between September 19 and November 3; otherwise there could be some fireworks. During the period between March 11 and July 29, you could have little time for romance, being on the move quite a lot. Personal interest in the other sex may reach a peak from mid-June to about August 3. During this period, in the first three weeks of July, there could be proposals or marriage. Between February 3 and 26, you could be enjoying the social whirl to some extent. Relationships started up then may develop as the year progresses. Your personal desires will probably be at their strongest between March 23 and April 15. You could be the center of attraction. No relationship made this year is likely to be trivial. You are going places and will want no excess baggage. You can appreciate someone who will go all the way with you.

DAILY FORECAST

January–December 1989

JANUARY

1. SUNDAY. Sensitive. Although this will be a pleasant enough day for the most part on which to start the New Year, your pleasure will be somewhat marred. It will be the result, to a certain extent, of arguments that are likely to break out between you and your spouse at home. Disagreements are most likely to be over money or the lack of it! You should make a serious attempt to cut down on expenditures now the holiday season is over. You seem to have been drawing on your reserves to a considerable extent of late. It is best not to take anything for granted or to assume that people understand more than they do. Relatives or neighbors could make unwelcome appearances if you are unprepared.

2. MONDAY. Sensitive. It is important that you get your priorities straight. You may have some difficulty in getting down to work of a routine nature. After the recent festive period you will have to exercise quite a lot of discipline if you are going to deal with desk jobs. Otherwise, you could make silly mistakes that would result in your having to do the work all over again. Research current business ventures. Try to find ways to cut expenses. Today should be good for dealings with the heads of large business firms and corporations. Later on, the day may contain some problems connected with joint financial affairs. Partners may be disgruntled and make extra demands on you.

3. TUESDAY. Difficult. It is still rather difficult for you to settle down at your place of employment. Readers who recently undertook new positions in offices or stores may find that working colleagues are not altogether friendly. However, by sheer grit and determination, you should be able to win your superiors around. The important thing is to show that you have the driving force to win

128

through. It is important that you show that you are the kind of person who does not stand for being pushed around. At home you should be able to make good progress with any joint financial ventures that you have undertaken in conjunction with your mate or partner. It is important to check over taxation and insurance matters.

4. WEDNESDAY. Important. Not very much will go wrong with today! You will feel that you can afford to take on more work. Heavy schedules are not likely to be a problem for you. Aries-born people can race ahead of their competitors now. Show people who are in the position to grant you pay raises and promotional opportunities that you have the stuff that leaders are made of. Second-best will definitely not be good enough for you today. Make a fresh and brisk start to the day. People at or from a distance may be instrumental in bringing about the fulfillment of a secret wish or dream. Today will be good for all business financial negotiations.

5. THURSDAY. Rewarding. It will be favorable for obtaining official or government approval for major business mergers. You are not likely to have any difficulty in obtaining interviews with people who are in a position to be of assistance to you. The important thing to remember today is to lay your cards on the table. Associates will appreciate your honest and fresh approach. This is also a helpful day for dealing with publishers and large publishing houses. Writers born under the sign of the Ram may be able to have their novels or short stories accepted for consideration. Today is also good for undertaking travel and for taking up new positions abroad.

6. FRIDAY. Disquieting. Aries-born women who are left alone to manage the home are likely to become easily bored and distracted. You will be fed up with the same old round of household chores. This is one of those days when you could easily give in to extravagance. But the important thing is to try to keep the impulsive side of your nature in check. This is a helpful day for buying office equipment, though. You may be able to pick up some bargains in the sales. Professional reputations need careful guarding. Do not lay yourself open to the gossip and rumormongers. Unconventional actions on your part could lead to reprimands by your boss.

7. SATURDAY. Mixed. This should be quite a good day for contacting influential people. They have proved to be somewhat vague and elusive away from the business scene. This is one of those days when business and pleasure are likely to mix rather well. Be sure that you keep your requests simple and clear-cut, though. Earning additional respect and prestige in the business world today will be favored. It is important for you to show that you are a reliable person. Do not do anything that could undermine your position at work. All research and investigations are worthwhile pursuing. Good, too, for handling money on behalf of others. Patience is essential.

8. SUNDAY. Inactive. The chances are, this will be a pleasant and easygoing day. You will be able to take stock of the progress that you have been able to make during the first week of the New Year. It would not seem that you have to deal with anything of particular importance today, however. Quite a lot of your time is likely to be spent in seeing to the needs of loved ones. Do what you can to make your mate or partner feel happy and contented. Be sure that you include your opposite number in any social occasions that you are asked to attend this Sunday. Don't speed when behind the wheel of your car, as this could lead to fines and brushes with the law; worse, to accidents and injuries.

9. MONDAY. Tricky. Don't be in so much of a rush. It is essential that you do not take on more jobs today than you can reasonably expect to handle. Give plenty of attention to desk jobs. There would seem to be quite a lot of paperwork that you will have to handle before you can make any new starts. Although you are keen to make more money, you will not be able to do this unless you conduct thorough investigations into all facets of business ventures. Aries people may find it difficult to get the working week off to a good start. Friends could be in trouble and may require a helping hand. Social or activities related to friendships may prove to be rather disappointing this evening. No one is to blame.

10. TUESDAY. Useful. Aries can carry generosity to a fault this morning. You must try harder to put more money to one side. Hard-luck stories that people relate to you may understandably touch your heartstrings. But you must not deplete your reserves too drastically in your attempts to assist others with their financial difficulties. People in charge of clubs or societies may back down or break their promises. This can be an exciting day for romance, however. Someone who has been little more than a friend to date could become quite a lot more than that now. This would be a good time for springing a surprise or two on close relatives.

11. WEDNESDAY. Productive. Make an early start. There will be plenty to keep you meaningfully occupied during your waking hours today. Do what you can to make a good impression on your boss. Do not wait for superiors to give orders. Come to grips with little chores that associates may have been shirking. Work through your lunch hour, or even after office or store hours, in order to catch up. This is a favorable day for concentrating on furthering developments behind the scenes. Secrecy can be the key to success. More roundabout and diplomatic methods are likely to succeed where the direct approach would be bound to fail. Out-of-court legal settlements can save a waste of time and money.

12. THURSDAY. Mixed. Some behind-the-scenes maneuvering can help to make money-making ventures more lucrative. An influential person may be willing to give you the financial support that you need. But this benefactor will probably want to remain anonymous for the time being. It is important that you respect such wishes. This would be a good day for the Ram to raise money for charitable causes that mean a lot to them. Aries may gain through the generosity of anonymous donors. People who reappear out of the past can bring a new ray of sunlight into your life. But there can be a sense of being trapped or restricted. Evening could see you spending more time at home.

13. FRIDAY. Sensitive. It is important not to skim over business or career affairs. There is a greater risk of deception in this area of your life than in any other. Do not part with the cash to back risky ventures. Influential people will not live up today to promises of support that were made to you earlier in the week. It would be a good idea to spend more of your spare time attending to home and family affairs. If you do not, there will be arguments with your mate or partner who is likely to feel imposed on. Minor errors at the office or work place that are allowed to pass undetected can throw whole ventures out of whack. The company and conversation of close friends can be especially congenial.

14. SATURDAY. Tricky. On checking up on the state of your bank account, you may well find that you are not as well off as you had first thought. Perhaps you forgot to make allowances for some rather large expenditures. It will be helpful to discuss with your close family members ways in which extra savings can be made. Brushes with the law should be avoided if at all possible. Be sure that you obey the laws of the road if you are driving today. Police or government officials may take exception to the brusque manner of the Aries-born, even if you do not mean to be rude. It is important to do nothing to earn the enmity of influential people.

15. SUNDAY. Changeable. Pace yourself today. It is a good day for attempts to place financial affairs on a more solid and long-term foundation. Loved ones will be more amendable to your ideas for cutting back on expenditures. The important thing to remember today is to keep all discussions you have about savings both logical and low-key. Avoid, at all costs, allowing emotions to creep in. You won't need to spend a great deal of money to extract the best that this day has to offer. It should be a good day for catching up with your letter writing. Be sure to write and thank people who sent you Christmas presents, but who you have not seen since the festive season ended.

16. MONDAY. Mixed. The advice of friends may be well-intentioned, but nevertheless unreliable. When dealing with financial matters it would be best to go by what professional people have to say to you. Listening to your close associates could get you into unnecessary trouble and possible losses. This can be a fortunate day for your career. Aries may receive sums of money without having to work at all hard for the privilege. Don't be extravagant. Spare time should be used constructively and not in the company of people who have more time on their hands than is good for them. The health of loved ones may give you cause for concern. You may have to make a trip later on in the day in connection with the affairs of an older relative.

17. TUESDAY. Productive. Get out and about more. Aries-born who have plenty of spare time today can use it to good effect. Get in touch with old friends early in the day; you may be able to arrange meetings with them. This would be an excellent time for trips to places of historical interest. This is also a good day for study and self-improvement activities. Aries should be able to add to their circle of acquaintances through trips they have made. New contacts can give you a new slant on life and provide valuable information in the bargain. Today is good for all means of communication, correspondence and telephone included. It is also favorable for furthering mental and creative endeavors.

18. WEDNESDAY. Demanding. People may be trying to wring favors from you in roundabout ways. Do not fall for the old friends act. Do not part with money to back ventures that may turn out to be very risky indeed. This will probably be a somewhat slack day from the work point of view. You may find that you have more time to attend to hobbies and second-string jobs. Time and money spent on traveling around could be wasted. Getting in touch with people by phone later will probably be just as effective, if not more so. It is important not to take glamorous people and situations too seriously. Romantic affairs can be disappointing and downright deceptive.

19. THURSDAY. Difficult. Try to get yourself into better shape physically. You ought to be paying much more attention to your health now. If you have been putting on quite a lot of weight since Christmas, you had better take yourself in hand. It would be wise to get more fresh air. Domestic upsets could interfere with your plans for the day. You and your mate or partner are likely to find yourselves locked in some fairly rough arguments. Discussions over cash, or the lack of it, could become rather heated. Emergencies may arise in connection with other family or household members. Sudden developments can turn property negotiations upside down. Aries may have to do some basic rethinking.

20. FRIDAY. Tricky. This will be another day that will have you worrying. Little things are likely to go wrong. You must watch your temper. Do not take out your anger on loved ones just because you are feeling frustrated and dissatisfied at this point. Health problems will not be easy to resolve. But it is a more favorable day for handling real estate affairs. Aries who have been trying to sell property for sometime may get a definite offer that they find acceptable. Tax rebates may be received. But influential people, possibly government officials, can clamp down on the financial activities of Aries and impose restrictions on their usual money-making ventures.

21. SATURDAY. Demanding. This will be a difficult day for you to get ahead with the new projects you would like to launch. It is not going to be easy for you to win the support of those people who are in a position to assist you. This is not a day for taking gambles of any kind. You may think it is worthwhile to have a fling in order to supplement your income. You are more than likely, however, to come to grief badly if you speculate. Listen to the advice of older relatives; they are not likely to put you on the wrong track. It is necessary to use a great deal of caution where your funds are concerned. It is important also not to be bullied or hurried into decisions by people who give you no time for reflection.

22. SUNDAY. Fair. The Ram is likely to be rather pleased to have the opportunity to take a break from the rigors of the workday week. There is not likely to be anything occurring today to send you to panic stations. But children can be quite a handful for the Aries parent. Offspring will be demanding more of your time and attention. You may not be able to attend to outside affairs as much as you would like. Pleasure plans may have to be canceled altogether or postponed. However, there is likely to be plenty to keep you meaningfully occupied within your own home. It is best to avoid any overexertion in sporting activities.

23. MONDAY. Demanding. This is another day that warns against taking risks or gambles of any kind. You will have to keep the impulsive side of your nature in check. Tips that are passed on to you about gambling should be investigated thoroughly. It seems highly unlikely that you will be able to make money the easy way. People in the theatrical or entertainment business may break their word. Aries who are in show business could be in for a letdown. This is not going to be an easy day to find employment for those of you who are without a job at the moment. It is important not to give in too much to the demands of children. Discipline continues to be the most important way in which to teach them.

24. TUESDAY. Lucky. It is about time for the breaks to go your way. At last, you should be seeing the gray clouds tinged with a silver lining. Loved ones will be easier to get along with. Your mate or partner will be taking more of a live-and-let-live attitude toward life. Ties of affection can be strengthened. Trust will be greater between loving couples. Health is likely to be considerably improved over recent weeks. You should find that you can carry out more tasks successfully without feeling tired or drained. Perseverance in routine occupational activities can pave the way for future promotion. Last-minute changes in plans can boost earnings.

25. WEDNESDAY. Sensitive. This midweek day could see you rethinking your schedule. It seems that Aries will have to make changes in the way they handle routine work. Otherwise, they are going to have trouble keeping up to the schedule that has been set for them by influential people. It may even be necessary to start work earlier in the day. You will have to make it clear to loved ones that they cannot expect their selfish demands to be fulfilled by you. Repetitious chores will be less of a drudgery and more of a pleasure. You may feel that you are at last earning the respect of those in authority for what you are trying to achieve. Aries can derive extra satisfaction from the smallest of things.

26. THURSDAY. Mixed. Professional reputations must not be endangered. You must not do anything that could affect your status at your place of employment. Do not get involved with people who have a history of being troublemakers. Those of you who are hoping for promotion soon must try harder to keep up with their work and in line with regulations. It is important not to divulge too much to friends. It is also wise to keep your secret hopes and dreams to yourself for the time being. Today should be favorable for all partnership negotiations. There will be a good opportunity for obtaining advice in connection with legal affairs. Quick thinking on your part can help you to get out of some tight spots.

27. FRIDAY. Tricky.   Don't take things at face value today. This is a day when people may be out to trick you. Keep your wits about you when you are engaging in business discussions. Do not allow yourself to be bullied or browbeaten. Any terms offered to you to sign new contracts should be studied carefully. They should be turned down if they are below the going rate for the same job that friends of yours are getting. Be sure that you put a fair price on your talents. This is a day that demands extreme care in the handling of routine business affairs. Aries cannot be too wary of deception and underhand dealings. Mates and spouses are unlikely to sympathize with your compassionate and charitable urges.

28. SATURDAY. Upsetting.   This could be a rather stressful day. You may be feeling the effects of pressure that you have been under of late. Loved ones will not be very helpful. You may feel that you are being asked to take on more than your fair share of the household duties. Romance is likely to be playing an important role in your life. A relationship that you have come to look upon as permanent could be turning sour. You might discover that you do not have as much in common with a member of the opposite sex as you had first imagined. It is important to remain impartial and unemotional when making important business or career decisions. Otherwise, personal desires can interfere with results.

29. SUNDAY. Mixed.   You may be disappointed early at the outcome of a telephone conversation. If you are a parent, children could be getting on your nerves just now. If there is any disciplining to be done, it is probably best to leave it to your partner. The day will become quite interesting for unplanned social activities. Friends and acquaintances may drop in. But nothing should be taken for granted. Life contains more secrets and surprises than we can conceive of. Overspending can become a problem, especially if liberties are taken with joint funds. There is the likelihood of merriment in many Aries people's homes this evening, particularly if more than one person born under this sign is involved. There could be an impromptu party.

30. MONDAY. Difficult. You may know that an associate could help you, but still have trouble in obtaining his or her cooperation. This could happen between husbands and wives. The other person in the twosome is likely to be quite stubborn until you find the right way to handle the impasse. This is a period when you are likely to put in a great deal of effort at your place of employment for very insignificant results. Minor financial affairs related to taxation, insurance, alimony or pensions may prove to be especially time-consuming. News of a death can create sadness or depression. Thinking may become obsessive and have to be controlled. You will only make matters worse if you act hastily.

31. TUESDAY. Important. The last day of the first month of the year finds you in a bright and breezy mood! Your optimistic outlook is likely to have a beneficial effect on people that you come into contact with. This is an excellent day for teamwork. This will be especially true if there are a number of routine chores that you want to push out of the way before January comes to an end. The morning is particularly good for communicating with people and friends at a distance. This would be a good time for obtaining the advice or recommendations of influential people. This can be a lucky day for romance. Career activities can lead to finding new and exciting attractions.

FEBRUARY

1. WEDNESDAY. Rewarding. Some interesting news is likely to come through this morning. You may receive a telephone call or a letter that makes you feel more optimistic about current affairs. It is a day when you will have the opportunity to advance career matters. Actors, writers, and singers among you will welcome the opportunity to have in-depth discussions with agents and producers. The day will be favorable, too, for dealings with publishers. Teachers can be particularly helpful, as well as other professional people. Friends may provide valuable introductions to influential people with power and authority. New contacts made in the business world can lead to the forming of new friendships.

2. THURSDAY. Easygoing. Although there is not likely to be much exciting action today, this is an important period for getting caught up with desk jobs. There still seem to be a number of matters connected with last year's accounts that you have not brought up to date. You will find it easier to concentrate on jobs that you have to attend to on your own as there will not be so many interruptions to distract you. This will be a fairly relaxed and unstressful kind of a day. Aries are advised to take advantage of conditions to rise above petty emotional difficulties. They should make every effort to view affairs from a broader perspective. You will be keener to better yourself in any way that you can.

3. FRIDAY. Mixed.   Press ahead with your business and career activities. It is really up to you to call the shots today. Try to come to grips with jobs that broaden your artistic bent. Hobbies can be turned into alternative sources of income. Do not be afraid to stretch your imagination. Obvious determination will impress people who have any sort of authority over you. Spare time should also be used for paying bills and looking for ways to make extra savings. People will be more likely than usual to grant favors. But bankers are not apt to be helpful. This is not the right time for putting in requests for loans or for allowing yourself to overdraw on your account.

4. SATURDAY. Excellent.   This will probably be one of the most exciting days so far this year. You will have plenty of energy. You should be able to wind up jobs that you do not want to have hanging over your head during the weekend. Loved ones will show greater understanding for what you are trying to achieve. Romance will be much on your mind. Aries who are dating for the first time should be very pleased at how things go. Aries-born people will tend to be more alert than ever. Their mental abilities and agility can be used to particularly good effect. The day will be favorable for furthering routine business transactions. Travel should yield good results whether over long or short distances.

5. SUNDAY. Sensitive.   There are likely to be minor irritants that prevent your getting full enjoyment from the day. What will get your goat is the fact that friends and certain relatives will be making demands on your spare time. This will cut back your relaxing and unwinding as much as you would like to. However, you must be firm with people who try to put pressure on you. This could be a good day for tackling major career or professional problems. See what you can do to overcome obstacles related to earnings and income. For the self-employed, it can be a particularly good day for laying the foundations for success in the weeks and the months to come.

6. MONDAY. Difficult. Concentration will be difficult to attain and maintain. Your mind will be more concerned with having fun than it will be with work. But you may find that you can afford a special treat that you have long been denying yourself. On going over your accounts, you might discover that you can purchase a luxury article for the home. Today should be good for shopping expeditions and for bulk buying. But friends can be disappointingly unreliable and create some disillusion in Aries men and women. This is not a day for taking risks in business financial affairs and ventures. More time will have to be spent at home this evening if you are going to avoid serious arguments.

7. TUESDAY. Rewarding. You won't feel that there are quite as many restrictions placed upon you today. You will have greater freedom at your place of employment to experiment with your ideas to improve the work flow. It may be possible to use more imagination to brighten up jobs that have become somewhat dull and routine. Efforts to promote teamwork in order to get some of the more mundane jobs done fast will be successful. Professional Aries people may find behind-the-scenes maneuvering especially effective in promoting business or financial affairs. A more diplomatic approach may prove to be the key to success. Today should be good for reunions with people known from the past.

8. WEDNESDAY. Challenging. Be on the lookout for opportunities to advance your business interests this midweek day. The rewards are likely to be worth aiming for. If you can make an earlier start with your work, all well and good. Do not allow yourself to be sidetracked by friends who have more spare time on their hands than is good for them. It may be possible to make reservations for a summer vacation today. It would be best to pay in advance or to make a down payment for pleasure activities if you possibly can. The day is favorable for secret dealings and confidential negotiations. Public images can be boosted through skillful promotional work.

9. THURSDAY. Productive. This is a particularly pleasant and auspicious day for romance. Things may not have been going too well for you in your love life, but all that should change today. It is important that you act with more confidence where members of the opposite sex are concerned. Try to converse in a free and easy manner with people whom you find attractive. Secret hopes and wishes can come a lot nearer to fulfillment. But it is important that Aries keep a tighter control over the more reckless and less tactful side of their nature. Otherwise, they can endanger their good names. This is a favorable day for travel, especially in connection with business. You may be able to return on the same day.

10. FRIDAY. Mixed. Influential people are more likely to go along with the personal desires and wishes of the Ram today. You should be able to get your request for time off granted if you wish to attend to matters of a personal nature. This would be a good day for visiting friends and loved ones who are sick or lonely. Do what you can to cheer up dear ones who have been having a particularly rough time of it of late. You won't have so many personal worries to depress you. Valuable cooperation can be obtained that will enable you to promote team effort. Your past experience in dealing with difficult people is likely to stand you in good stead.

11. SATURDAY. Manageable. The week comes to an end on a fairly optimistic note. It is true that you have had your ups and downs during its course. You should be feeling fairly well pleased with the progress that you have made, however, both in your career and in your personal life. Once again, you will be thinking quite a lot about romance. Frank discussions with your partner may help you to clear the air and to straighten out problems. Money matters should also be discussed. You should be able to voice your worries to influential people. Talk about your hopes for the future in business. Aries people may need to bluff somewhat.

12. SUNDAY. Changeable. Today will be equally as good for sports people among you as it will be for the keep-fit fanatics. You will enjoy any pastimes that involve the awakening of a team spirit. It is important that you spend some time away from the domestic environment today. You and your close family members will get on each other's nerves if you spend too much time together in a confined space. It is important not to attempt or to condone anything that is illegal. Friends can land Aries in trouble with the authorities. Heavy fines may result that will have to be paid. Increased membership costs of clubs and societies could be prohibitive. Later in the day you are likely to be in a more cheerful and optimistic frame of mind.

13. MONDAY. Easygoing. You will be grateful for the fact that you are able to ease quietly into this working week. There is not likely to be any pressure placed upon you at your place of employment. Quite a lot of your time will probably be spent dealing with letter writing and putting your business affairs in better order. This is one of those days when success or failure could depend very much on how you channel your energies. Motivation is likely to have to come from within. Pointless running about would lead to nothing but mental and physical exhaustion. Today should be favorable for catching up on the latest neighborhood news and gossip. The latter need not necessarily be harmful or spiteful.

14. TUESDAY. Important.   Keep long-term objectives in mind and plan for the future. Give particular attention to your career. Aim at making better progress where you are by expanding your responsibilities. Do not go looking for a new job due to discontent or restlessness. This is a mind-stretching day in which there may be opportunities to gain new knowledge or further your education. Keep your eyes and ears on the alert for valuable tips and pieces of information. It is important not to overestimate the amount of available spending money you have. Taxation and other overheads can account for much of it. By teaming up with groups, you will have the chance to make new friends.

15. WEDNESDAY. Confusing.   This will be a difficult day for getting along with people with whom you live. Loved ones will be struggling with emotional problems that may upset the balance in the household. It does not seem that there is a great deal you can do to help some people. They just do not appear to be willing to assist themselves in any way. At your place of employment, influential people can be downright irresponsible. You could find they will not be above abusing their power to further their own selfish ends. The more that you can rely on yourself today, the better it will be for you. Aries people may feel virtually deserted by loved ones and friends alike.

16. THURSDAY. Productive.   Keep on your toes! There is a risk of deception when dealing with financial matters. Be sure to check all figures related to earnings very carefully. You may find that more has been deducted from your wages or salary than should have been. This is not a time for taking anyone or anything for granted. It is also important not to endanger reputations by mixing with people or organizations of dubious repute. Listen to older people whose advice has been proven right in the past. This can be a good day for investing in property. Work that is finished ahead of deadlines may earn the Aries native useful bonuses.

17. FRIDAY. Lucky.   You will welcome the letter or telephone call that you receive today. It will set your mind at rest over a problem that has been bothering you for some time. Some news from a distance will certainly be cheering. It may be that a good friend or a loved one is coming home after spending a considerable amount of time away from home. You will certainly be pleased to see and welcome this person home again. Aries people who are in the farming or horticultural business will discover that this is an excellent period for buying or selling products of the earth. Today will also be good for going ahead with property development or with plans to add another room or work area to your home.

18. SATURDAY. Harmonious. The week comes to an end on a quiet note. You will be happy to take life at a steady pace today. You will find you have the opportunity to deal with lots of little odd jobs. You may have had to leave these to one side earlier in the week due to work pressures. You will be able to spend more time with loved ones. Make it up to family members if you feel that you have been neglecting them too much of late. There will be plenty of entertainment on hand this evening. Even more to the point, it is not likely to cost you a lot of money to have a really good time. Today will be favorable for sporting activities, though they should not be the very strenuous kind!

19. SUNDAY. Difficult. Don't take on too much this Sunday, whether work or play. This is the simple message to all people born under the sign of the Ram. You may get a lot of invitations to go out, but you should be just a little bit choosy. Don't forget, either, to consult with other members of the family. Any decisions that would involve travel on their behalf should have their approval. The temptation to overspend must be resisted. There will be heavy winter bills presenting themselves soon and you should make adequate provisions for these. Children should not be talked down to or patronized as this will tend merely to make them more rebellious. This could be tricky, so handle with care.

20. MONDAY. Mixed. It will not be easy for you today to get back into the routine of work. Aries people who hold down factory and office jobs may rebel inwardly. They find the chores they have to cope with are even more monotonous than usual. However, you must stop your mind from wandering when you are dealing with accounts and other paperwork. Mistakes made now could prove to be expensive. It would be best to keep a low profile. Words or actions contributed by you can easily be interpreted as a challenge to authority. Superiors may impose extra workloads and responsibilities without so much as a word of explanation. The self-employed can make good headway under their own steam.

21. TUESDAY. Excellent. This will be one of the best days that you have experienced so far this month, if not this year. People will be much easier to get along with than usual. You will have the opportunity to make an important breakthrough at your place of employment. Loved ones will show greater understanding of your problems. You may, for instance, have to spend more time than usual away from home in order to tackle career matters. Research projects and all investigative procedures will go well for you. Some Aries-born may have been feeling rather poorly of late. They should find now that they are over the worst of their illness. Their health should begin to improve at once. Work done today will help to increase economic security.

22. WEDNESDAY. Important.   Another positive and optimistic day comes along. You should find once again that the atmosphere at work is conducive to making good progress. Have a talk with superiors if there are important questions about the future that you wish answered. Lay your cards on the table. If you are straight with your bosses, it is more than likely that they will be straight with you. Influential people may make entirely unexpected moves which will favor or support the Aries person. Approaches to people who wield power and authority behind the scenes can be surprisingly productive. Business companies may agree to sponsor charitable or other worthwhile projects.

23. THURSDAY. Mixed.   Aries-born, who have started on new jobs only recently, may find that they are beginning to break the ice at last at their places of employment. Firm friendships can be formed with co-workers. These will make you feel a good deal happier about what the future holds for you. Better liaison with business colleagues and partners will help to make ventures more lucrative. More money can also be made by Rams who are able to work from their home bases. There will be fewer interruptions to disturb their concentration. But legal problems, if ignored, could turn into much more serious matters. It is important to adopt a down-to-earth, realistic attitude. It can only work to your benefit.

24. FRIDAY. Easygoing.   Any Aries people who are left alone to cope at home may find that this is a somewhat disturbing day. It will be extremely difficult to stave off boredom. It is important that you find better ways to fill in any additional time you may find you have on your hands. It is pointless to dwell on mistakes of the past that you cannot do anything to alter now. Children may be somewhat troublesome. You will have to discipline yourself not to lose your temper with unruly youngsters. This would be a good time for lending a helping hand to colleagues or associates who have more to contend with than Aries. You are likely to have less room to maneuver or to implement your personal plans.

25. SATURDAY. Rewarding. Sports enthusiasts among you should find that there is plenty to occupy your time today. This will be an exciting period for travel. It will be especially true if journeys are made in connection with your favorite hobby or pastime. Some extra research conducted into current business ventures is likely to be extremely useful. It should indicate the best course of action with surprising accuracy and simplicity. This is a favorable time for all matters connected with business mergers and dealings with large firms and companies. You will get on particularly well with authority figures. Business and pleasure activities will mix in rather well. Later will be good for informal gatherings.

26. SUNDAY. Changeable. Personal relationships may become somewhat strained today. The Aries-born person could have communication problems with their mates or partners. The best way to overcome domestic difficulties is to try to organize outings that all members can derive some pleasure from. This may mean that you have to put the interests of others before your own. Suspicions can arise as to the true motives of acquaintances and so-called friends. Romantic companions can break their word or fail to honor promises. Some time today should be favorable for the handling of financial and related matters. You should have better luck in formulating a budget and sorting out tricky money matters.

27. MONDAY. Demanding. You will have great difficulty in getting yourself into high gear. This is one of those Mondays when you may become bogged down with boring and rather mundane jobs. It would be a good idea to work at a slow and steady pace, however. If you try to rush through your chores, you will only find that the work has to be done all over again. That will be due to errors that you make. Aries people cannot afford to be neglectful in following the instructions of others. This applies to the handling of money or property. You may be held personally responsible for any professional errors that you make. The amount of taxation that you are likely to pay can be honestly underestimated.

28. TUESDAY. Strenuous. The month comes to an end with your feeling somewhat worried and disturbed. Perhaps life is not going as well as it should with your loved ones. You and your mate or partner will have difficulty in seeing eye-to-eye. This pertains especially in financial matters. You should think again before you make any new purchases for the home. Official or government grants for study may be withdrawn or suspended. Appeals for permission to travel abroad may be turned down. Aries travelers may be held up by obstructive government officials. Important decisions would be best postponed as it will be difficult to see things in their true perspective.

MARCH

1. WEDNESDAY. Inactive. The third month of the year gets off to something of a lackluster start. You may be a little disappointed that you are not able to come to grips with new projects that you are keen to promote. The main reason for this delay is the fact that you have a lot of little odd jobs to be dealt with first. These include dealing with accounts and catching up with a backlog of correspondence, none of which can be put aside any longer. Aries natives may be relieved of some of their duties that might have earned them extra money. This would be a good opportunity for using spare time to further self-improvement or academic pursuits. Study a subject that could help you get ahead.

2. THURSDAY. Exciting. One of the most important things about today is your attitude. You are probably feeling in a much more optimistic and positive frame of mind. Outlook is a very important factor for the Ram at this point. It is essential that you do more than you have been doing to maintain your standard of living. You may feel that your earnings have not been keeping pace with inflation. In that case, it is about time for you to have a chat with your boss about this state of affairs. Personal friends may prove to be of considerable assistance today. They may volunteer to help Aries further business and career interests. But surprises can be in store, so it is best not to become too glib or confident.

3. FRIDAY. Mixed. An early start would help you out today. This is a good period for coming to grips with any work that you have had to put to one side. Pressures over which you have not been able to have much control have interfered. Loved ones will be more understanding about what you are trying to achieve. This will be a helpful day for handling the taxation and insurance problem of business and professional affairs. This can also be a day that will test the stamina of Aries people who are engaged in business or professional areas of work. Competitors may be resorting to unfair means to get even with you for real or imagined past conflicts. Romance can add excitement to the evening's activities.

4. SATURDAY. Successful. This will be an especially good period for the Ram. Much of what you have been trying to achieve all week is likely to come together at once. People will be easier to get along with. It will be possible to promote teamwork to get rid of jobs that you do not really like having to handle on your own. Do what you can to forge ahead with career and related matters. You may otherwise find you are wasting it, doing little or nothing that is constructive. Later in the day can bring you some good luck in love. Romance is highlighted, especially with people much younger or older than yourself. New financial or business opportunities are likely to prove to be most worthwhile.

5. SUNDAY. Sensitive. Although things should go fairly well for you today, you are likely to hold even higher expectations. Perhaps you would be wise not to spend too much money on pleasure and entertainment. Otherwise, at the end of the day, you may feel that friends and loved ones have taken advantage of your hospitality. It would seem as if they took it for granted. Small, intimate gatherings are likely to work much better than large parties. Friends can become a positive nuisance, especially if they have too much to drink. They could very well make a mess of your home by either burning the carpet or damaging some valuable item. It may be difficult to deal with close associates both politely and firmly.

6. MONDAY. Mixed. Business financial affairs need to be handled with a lot of care. Before you make any new investments you had better go over your accounts fairly thoroughly. You may not have quite as much capital as you thought and need to make exciting starts with projects. Influential people might not be as helpful as they had promised they would. The backing that you had been hoping for from them may not be forthcoming. It could become necessary to channel business profits back into current developments. That would preclude your taking them as personal earnings. Aries can be skillful in turning uncertain or confused situations to their own advantage.

7. TUESDAY. Important. It is about time that you forced yourself into high gear! You do not seem to have been making as much use as you can of your natural talents. Try much harder to achieve the success in your career that you know, deep down, you are capable of. Loved ones will be an inspiration to you. They will also do much to encourage you to go farther. Secret investigations or research can dig up facts that would not normally come to light. It may be necessary to work longer hours than usual, but it will be most worthwhile to do so in the long run. Today should be good for arranging out-of-court settlements. Alimony affairs are best settled on amicable terms rather than through litigation.

8. WEDNESDAY. Changeable.   Opportunities or propositions received from unlikely sources are worth investigating. They could prove to be especially lucrative. This is one of those days when something happens on the spur of the moment that is likely to work very much to your advantage. Some quick thinking is apt to be called for on your part. Influential people may be on the verge of taking you into their confidence. But you must be very careful that you do not overstep the mark with those in authority. Do not get too familiar with people who you know can change moods very quickly indeed. There will be a good opportunity for raising funds for worthwhile charitable causes.

9. THURSDAY. Fortunate.   You will have less difficulty today in knowing what you want out of life. What is even more important is that you will know how to go about getting it! Loved ones will be very much on your wavelength. This is quite a good day for shopping around for bargains for the home. You may be able to get the very article that you have been looking for but at a marked-down price. This is an important period for carrying on with odd jobs in and around the home. They can add quite considerably to the value of it. Long-term gains can be won through greater use of diplomacy and behind-the-scenes maneuvering. Personal friends in the business world may prove to be especially helpful.

10. FRIDAY. Mixed.   This is not an especially favorable day for making journeys. The long kind will be particularly poor. Trips that you set out on may not bring you the happiness you have been hoping for. Moreover, they could prove to be more expensive than you may have imagined. The advice of friends might be well-meaning, but it is quite likely to be unreliable. People who try to tell you how to handle problems related to your personal life are likely to be way off the mark. But romance may be flowering for the single reader. You are likely to find that you spark off an immediate rapport with people whom you meet at parties. Quick thinking on your part can lead to worthwhile financial gains.

11. SATURDAY. Exciting.   Romance continues to look very promising. Some Aries people may attend parties or intimate gatherings today. They might even get a chance to meet and talk to someone whom they have long admired and wanted to get close to. You can show off your personality to very good advantage today. Your natural qualities of leadership are likely to be very much to the fore now. Travel undertaken on the spur of the moment can yield especially constructive results. Friends will be willing and able to do favors for you. There should be a good chance for greater involvement in community affairs and for doing what you can to help others.

12. SUNDAY. Disconcerting. Perhaps you will awake rather like a bear with a sore head today! Whatever the reasons for your bad temper, you must try not to take it out on loved ones. Any bad atmosphere that is created in the home is likely to be very much the result of your bad temper, so beware! Your mate or partner will be expecting you to attend to domestic affairs. Some Aries people may have spent a good deal of the week that has just come to a close away from the home base. They should therefore try harder to satisfy the desires of their nearest and dearest. Travel plans can be interrupted by unexpected developments. It is important to choose words with more care.

13. MONDAY. Uncertain. There will be a so-so beginning to this week. You may have a touch of the Monday blues early in the day. It might be that you are feeling a little depressed that you have not made as much progress in your career as you feel you should have. Perhaps your patience is running out with associates who said they would do favors for you. Have you ever thought that perhaps you yourself should be doing more to get ahead. Romantic affairs can cause some anxiety. Aries may feel there is something wrong without being able to put their finger on the trouble. Or romantic companions may simply be unavailable and impossible to get in touch with.

14. TUESDAY. Undemanding. Don't push yourself too hard. The message would seem to be loud and clear for the Aries native that they have been overdoing things. More attention to your diet and your health is essential. You are going to require much-needed energy to make the hoped-for good progress in your career. This is likely to be a fairly relaxed and undemanding day. This will be especially good for those of you who have the opportunity to operate from your home base. There is likely to be less friction between you and your loved ones now and you should do what you can to build on this. Family or household members will give you a hand with routine chores that can be shared.

15. WEDNESDAY. Tricky. Beware of taking anyone or anything for granted this midweek day! People who offer you support may not be sincere. The more you can rely on yourself and your own talents, the better you will get ahead. This advice is something you should keep in the back of your mind at all times. Aries may also find that they are suspected of having committed actions for which they are definitely not responsible. Family members cannot be trusted to tell the whole truth. Property deals would best be postponed. This is not the greatest of days for real estate practices. There are just too many unknown factors involved to make it wise to proceed at present.

16. THURSDAY. Important. The chances are you will be back to something like your old self now. Your judgment should be right on target. Go with your intuition; it will not play you false. This is a favorable day for adding the finishing touches to artistic or creative work. Give free rein to your natural talents. Today would be good for buying new furniture or decorations for the home. Entertaining influential people today will be very successful. You may be able to clinch a lucrative deal under pleasant social conditions. An intimate atmosphere is recommended. It will make a better impression on those who are in a key position to give you the help you require.

17. FRIDAY. Rewarding. Carry on in the same vein as yesterday. Do all that you can to get a good rapport going between yourself and those who can give you help. They have the influence and power to aid you in getting ahead. Your realistic and no-nonsense attitude cannot fail to impress those who can assist you. Romance will be very much on your mind. Some of you will be coming to important decisions about the future. A matter of the heart will be resolved and you will feel much better about this area of your life. Put more exertion into furthering artistic endeavors. It's a favorable day for all promotional work. Those of you who are in advertising should be full of good ideas.

18. SATURDAY. Misleading. This can be a rather disappointing day for pleasure seekers among you. Outings that you undertake are not likely to be as successful as you may have hoped. It might be best not to spend too much money on pleasure and entertainment. Trips can go wrong; it may be that you would run out of funds. The speculators and gamblers in your midst could incur heavy losses. Tips that are passed on to take a fling on the dog or the race tracks are likely to come to a miserable conclusion. But when it comes to creative work, the intuitive abilities of Aries peo-

ple may be heightened. This will enable them to spot hidden opportunities. Today should be favorable for visiting.

19. SUNDAY. Mixed. Spring-cleaning chores will be looming
large for some of you. If you feel at loose ends today, this is as
good a time as any to start. You could have a good clearing out of
closets. Get rid of unwanted clothes and other superfluous articles.
You may have something for which you have no further use. But it
could be of great assistance to a charitable organization or to people who are not as well off as you are. There are likely to be distractions later in the day. These could prevent your dealing with
certain domestic issues, paperwork and other desk jobs. You may
have unexpected callers to whom you cannot be abrupt or uncivil.
Be prepared for disruptions.

20. MONDAY. Important. This is an especially important day
for making new starts. Do not stand for any nonsense from people
who try to interfere with your work. It is vital that you show
influential people that you put your career first. There will be good
opportunities to earn bonus payments if you are prepared to put
your shoulder to the wheel. All in all, this can be an auspicious
beginning to the working week. Aries' sixth sense will enable them
to cut unnecessary corners while satisfying superiors that everything is still safe. The day is particularly good for all forms of imaginative work. Doctor-prescribed drugs can alleviate uncomfortable
or downright distressing symptoms.

21. TUESDAY. Disconcerting. Perhaps you are expecting too
much of today. Your confidence in making progress in your career
is likely to receive an unexpected setback. You will have problems
in getting superiors to agree to any changes that you wish to make
in working methods. It might just be best to go along as you are.
Keep your more way-out ideas to yourself for now. Wait for a
more auspicious time to arrive for you to go off in a different direction. This will not be such a helpful period for dealing with routine
desk jobs. You are likely to find that concentration on paperwork
is difficult, due to constant interruptions. It would be unwise to
risk overdoing.

22. WEDNESDAY. Changeable. People in positions of power
and authority may be genuinely willing and eager to help Aries.
They will be unwilling to do so, however, for purely formal reasons. This will be a tricky period for dealing with friends who want
to borrow from you, too. You would like to help a good pal who is
in distress, of course. But you may feel that it simply would be

throwing good money away were you to give any financial assistance. Business colleagues may lose Aries clients for them, though ill-advised actions. It would be best for you not to delegate your responsibilities today. Calling emergency meetings for discussions can help to solve what appear to be insuperable problems.

23. THURSDAY. Ordinary. This can be quite a favorable day for doing your own thing. You should tread lightly. This is not a time for being forceful of for trying to get your own way. This applies particularly if you know it will clash with the hopes and aspirations of others. You must try harder to curb spending. This is the time of the year when you should be attempting to put more money to one side to meet income tax and insurance payments. It may be necessary to lecture young people for whom you are responsible on the merits of savings. You cannot expect to win the unqualified approval or undivided attention of your colleagues. Tact and diplomacy will be all-important.

24. FRIDAY. Inactive. There is a greater need than usual to cater to the desires of others. People will be looking to you for support and for sympathy, you must not be found wanting. You may find yourself in the position where you have to prove that you live up to the same high principles you are always championing. Pressure should be eased up at work; your boss may be busy with reorganization or he may even be absent for a large part of the day. Fellow workers can be relied upon to give you a hand if you have any last-minute rush jobs. Loved ones will genuinely appreciate your kind and thoughtful gestures this evening. Give your mate or partner a special treat then.

25. SATURDAY. Mixed. A mixed bag seems to be in store for you on this last day of the week. You may not be able to bring to completion as many of the chores that you were hoping to. Influential people may wish you to give more attention to rather mundane matters than you want to. But this would not seem to be the day for arguing the issue with authority figures. Today should be good for secret research and investigations. It will also be favorable for dabbling in esoteric knowledge and the occult. Aries may be able to find a thread of common sense. This is a particularly auspicious day for forming new romantic alliances. You might get lucky enough to meet your future mate.

26. SUNDAY. Happy. This will be an important day for cementing new relationships. These have come to mean quite a lot to you suddenly. You and your mate or partner are likely to be entering into an even more important stage in your relationship now. Some free time today would be useful for handling joint monetary affairs. See what you can do to cut back on expenditures. All additional savings that you can make now will help you meet the heavy bills that are bound to be coming in shortly. During the latter part of the day, happy reunions with people you have not seen for a long time may take place. It will be good for visiting loved ones and friends who are sick or under medical care.

27. MONDAY. Difficult.   You may awaken this morning feeling rather depressed. And you will be unable to put your finger on exactly why you are feeling so low. The best way for you to overcome this depression is to busy yourself. Deal with matters that will take your mind off personal problems. These may have been enlarging all out of proportion in your mind. See what you can do to alleviate the pain and suffering of people who are far less well off than yourself. Count your blessings. This is not a particularly favorable day for long-distance travel. Plans can easily go wrong, possibly due to bad timing. But influential people at a distance will tend to be more helpful than ever.

28. TUESDAY. Easygoing.   This can be a somewhat upsetting day for romance. Aries people who have been expecting a call or a letter from a loved one who is far away may be greeted only with silence. Do not get too depressed about this silence. There could well be delays in the postal service. Faults with engineering may have put distant telephone lines temporarily out of order. Pressures from routine work and duties are likely to be fewer than usual. This should allow more time for concentrating on study and reading. Today will be favorable for drawing up tentative plans for the future. People at or from a distance may provide you with some especially valuable information.

29. WEDNESDAY. Mixed.   Professional Aries people need to maintain strict impartiality. You may be asked to preside over a fight between two people at work. So you must be careful that you do not overrule on one side in favor of the other, due to favoritism. You will need to keep your wits about you when dealing with members of the younger generation today. Children will see how far they can go and may require some extra disciplining. This is a good time for Aries who are involved in advertising to discover new publicity angles. Routine business affairs can be subject to ups and downs later in the day. You will want to spend more time with your loved ones this evening.

30. THURSDAY. Demanding. Watch that temper of yours! You could easily say something to a loved one that you would later regret. Show more compassion for people who you know have been having a trying emotional time recently. Listen with sympathy to the hard luck stories of friends. You will be doing them a great favor by hearing them out and showing you care. This can be a rather tiresome and frustrating day at your place of employment. Delays and setbacks can interfere with the smooth running of routine affairs. But large business corporations can lend a helping hand. It is best to avoid snap decisions and risk of deception.

31. FRIDAY. Inactive. There will not be much taking place on this last day of the month. But you are not likely to have any objection on this score. You will find that influential people are extremely helpful if you are having difficulty in winding up with chores that you are keen to get rid of today. The expertise of elders will be invaluable to you. Aries men and women can probably afford to take things easy in their private lives. As far as romance is concerned, this is no time to attempt to push others into making important and life-changing decisions. Today should be particularly favorable for spending more time in the congenial company of close friends.

APRIL

1. SATURDAY. Difficult. This is not at all an easy day for the Ram to end the week and start the month on. In fact, this would appear to be a day of great change for you. Some of these changes in your life will be most welcome. But some of you will be trying to fight, especially the emotional ones, to little or no avail. Special requests that are made to the Aries native should be examined most carefully. Flattery could be particularly dangerous as it can conceal an intent to deceive or exploit. This will be particularly enjoyable day for socializing and for friendship activities. It should be favorable for travel, especially if it has been suggested by in-laws. It could indicate full trust and approval.

2. SUNDAY. Disconcerting. Money problems are likely to loom large. You may have been a little free and easy with your cash of late and this could be the day of reckoning. On going over your accounts, you are likely to discover one or two serious gaps. Perhaps you have forgotten to pay a bill, but thought that you had settled it. One way or another, you and your nearest and dearest are probably going to have to make some cutbacks. These, of course, are going to entail a certain amount of self-sacrifice. This is another day when it is not necessarily your best option to give other people the benefit of the doubt. When your suspicions are aroused, try to remember that there is no smoke without a fire.

3. MONDAY. Sensitive. You are probably recovering from a somewhat topsy-turvy weekend. You may not be ready yet to make the new starts that you were hoping to put into practice today. On this first day of the working week, it would be in your best interests to stick to what you know and understand. Some behind-the-scenes maneuvering can enable professional Aries people to increase the security of their positions, one way or another. You will find that private discussions with superiors may mean that you can ascertain just what they see in the future for you. This is likely to be anything but a gloomy picture. Today might be useful for promoting charitable or other worthwhile causes.

4. TUESDAY. Good. This is an important day for implementing changes in and around the home. They are the kind you have been feeling are necessary for some time. It will be a good day for shopping expeditions. You may be able to pick up articles in the shops that you have long been searching for at bargain prices. It will be easier to agree with other members of the family in exactly what areas savings can best be made. There will be a good opportunity, too, for discussions with superiors and other influential people. Greater understanding on everybody's part can come from it. Today should be favorable for making applications for special travel allowances.

5. WEDNESDAY. Useful. This will be a promising day as long as you do not allow yourself to get sidetracked. Do not allow interference with what you consider to be your priorities. You should work out a plan of campaign and stick to it. You will have to be firm with loved ones who may try to take up your time. You know you should be giving all of it to career matters. There may even be fights about the amount of time you spend away from your home base. But you know, deep down, that this is for the best of those people who rely on you. Aries people could be somewhat mystified by certain goings-on today. These seem to have specific connections with their career and professional affairs.

6. THURSDAY. Easygoing. There will not be a lot taking place today. But the slow and steady pace can be used to good advantage by people born under the first sign of the Zodiac. There is not likely to be any pressure on you to hurry your chores. The day would be especially fortunate for account work for starters. It would also be good for anything that you have not yet attended to this week that requires special attention to detail. This is a period when people may do favors for you without even being asked. Friends will be helpful in little ways that you will find deeply touching. You may find that there are loyalties that you did not know existed. Personal aims can be furthered with little or no effort.

7. FRIDAY. Sensitive. You can make some important progress today, as long as you do not reach too high. This is only likely to be on a small scale, however, both in your personal and your public life. A bright idea that comes to you suddenly could help you solve a business problem. It has been hanging over your head for some considerable time now. This would be a very good day for the recovery of debts. Be sure that you go after the people who seem to have conveniently forgotten that they owe you money. Taxation and insurance matters should be checked carefully to ensure they are fully paid up to date. You may owe a penalty if you are late.

8. SATURDAY. Quiet. This will, in all likelihood, be a calm and peaceful weekend in general. Little will take place to interrupt or to interfere with what you may have arranged for today and tomorrow. You are not likely to have any difficulty with rounding off chores at your place of employment. Teamwork will be easier to promote than is usually the case. Associates will not be putting as many difficulties in your way as they may have been doing earlier in the week. It would be best to use your time constructively rather than seeking distractions. Free time should be good for dealing with paperwork of every kind. Attempt to further your financial affairs by getting your accounts into better order.

9. SUNDAY. Useful. This will be just the sort of Sunday that you are likely to welcome. You will have the opportunity to spend more time with people whom you may be feeling guilty about having neglected. This is especially true for the Aries business or career woman. You will find it easier to get along with members of the younger generation. It would be best not to waste your time in pointless running about today. You may have been contemplating embarking on long-distance travel on the spur of the moment. But that would appear to be a complete waste of time and money. Telephone calls can be useful for contacting people whom you have not heard from for a long time. A fast reply is assured.

10. MONDAY. Important.   The morning is a good time for obtaining an audience with influential people. You will be given the opportunity to air your complaints about the way work and business matters have been run recently. People in positions of power and authority are likely to take note, and may even act immediately on what you have to say. There will be a good opportunity for dealing with all forms of official correspondence. Professional people will be helpful with the advice that they offer on income tax and insurance matters. Today will be favorable for writing up reports for submission to superiors. Later in the day could be especially good for romance and love.

11. TUESDAY. Demanding.   You may become upset because a silly squabble turns into something far more serious. You and your mate or partner may find that you are disagreeing on lots of little matters. This is especially true for Aries who have been having problems with offspring. You may not be able to agree about just how strongly youngsters should be disciplined. Major self-sacrifices may be demanded if walkouts are going to be avoided. You may even have to cancel an outing with friends that you had been looking forward to making for sometime. Errors committed in routine business affairs may lead to disruption. Even worse, you may be getting behind with your schedule.

12. WEDNESDAY. Difficult.   There may be some strong criticism from the parents of Aries-born people about the choice of romantic companions. It might be best not to bring home sweethearts with whom you have only recently become involved. Wait awhile, at least until you can let older relatives become more resigned to the idea. Do what you can to keep the peace rather than bringing sensitive matters to a head. You will gain nothing by a show of temper. Other household members can be curt to the point of rudeness. Too much seeking for perfection can result in the actual ruining of artistic or creative work. This is not a particularly favorable day for home entertaining.

13. THURSDAY. Mixed.   You are not out of the woods by a long shot yet. But this will be a day when you can certainly do a lot to improve close personal relationships. Start by acting with greater tact and diplomacy. There are still likely to be problems with youngsters who may refuse to listen to reason. It might be best to try the silent approach with youngsters who are acting in a particularly strong-willed manner at the moment. They may soon learn the error of their ways then. The Ram could be guilty of making some fundamental miscalculations. You should not put too much trust in your judgment when it comes to speculative or gambling propositions. There could be many reasons for this.

14. FRIDAY. Difficult. This does not appear to have been the most exciting of weeks, overall. And today is quite unlikely to prove to be the exception. In fact, you may be looking forward to Saturday now to change the picture. At least, it would seem that you will then have more control over your life and the decisions that you are able to make. There appears to have been an underlying current of dissension within the home. This is not a day for going over old differences, even if they have not been completely resolved. It would be better by far to build on the good points of relationships. This is another day that poses great risks to speculators, as heavy losses can be incurred.

15. SATURDAY. Enjoyable. It will probably be the best day of the week. You will feel somewhat relieved that you can choose, to a great extent, what plans you wish to follow. The pressure within your home is certainly sure to have eased. Older Aries will find that their relationships with members of the younger generation has greatly improved. Superiors may grant extended vacation or weekend leaves and there is not likely to be a drop in your pay check, either! Recreational or sporting activities may bring you twofold benefits. You could come into contact with people who are in a position to do you a lot of good in practical ways. This will also be a propitious day for romance.

16. SUNDAY. Manageable. Health may be somewhat below par, but at least you should have the chance to indulge yourself with extra rest. Take more care of any coughs, colds or similar ailments that are troubling you. Otherwise, if you do not, they could easily turn into something more serious. Eat substantial meals rather than going along with snacks. Do not pick at your food. But on the other hand, you must also guard against overindulgence. This should be a good day for tackling routine chores in and about the home. You may have neglected these recently, due to outside pressures. Short trips can be helpful, mainly for advancing money-making ventures. The evening can be unusual and interesting.

17. MONDAY. Manageable. This is not a day for overdoing anything. In fact, you should not push too hard when it comes to attempting to win the support of influential people. Superiors will be fairly easy to get along with. But be careful that you do not put in too many requests for time off of for additional payment. Any extra work that you do will be rewarded, even if perhaps not right away. You must curb impatience at all times. This might well be translated as a lack of trust by the people in authority. It is also important to heed the early warning signs of impending ill-health. Driving needs more care. Do not speed or take any other silly risks while on the highway.

18. TUESDAY. Sensitive. Business and financial negotiations can negate the suspicions of the other people involved. Discussions can help break the ice and overcome others' resistance. You may be able to advance a project that is very close to your heart today. You should be able to rely on the support of people who can wield power and influence to your advantage. But new financial commitments should not be made without first consulting bankers or accountants. Partners can be in a strange and unpredictable mood. It would be best not to make any arrangements on behalf of your loved ones without checking first to see that they are agreeable. Sometimes we tend to see only what we want to.

19. WEDNESDAY. Demanding. Beware that you may be misjudging your overall financial situation. It is quite likely that you will receive some money today for a job that you completed some time ago. It is important that most of this windfall is put into some savings plan. Or you could invest it in Treasury bonds or your regular savings account. There may be a need for income tax payments later in the year. They are likely to be higher than you would imagine at the moment. So it would be prudent of you to make provisions for them now. Aries people could be treading on dangerous ground without realizing it. It is important to check that your activities are in no way breaking the law.

20. THURSDAY. Disconcerting. Partnership or matrimonial problems may have been souring a relationship lately. It is one that is very important to you and it should be cleared up now by some frank talking. Discuss problems openly with other members of the family. You have probably had some difficulty up to now in bringing them out into the open. It should be easier for you to talk more frankly about your secret hopes and desires. Your opposite number may discover he or she can do the same. Today will be favorable for promoting all teamwork and cooperative endeavors. It will also be good for clarifying legal complexities and for dealing effectively with red tape.

21. FRIDAY. Productive. In all likelihood, this will not be an absolutely stunning day. But you can make some good progress as long as you are willing to put your nose to the grindstone. Deal with the jobs that can be boring and sometimes even frustrating. You can do yourself a good turn by proving to influential people just how reliable you can be. Although you may not get a pay raise immediately, do not assume that your efforts will go unnoticed. The day should be good for attempting to extend contracts with business firms or corporations. But in the romantic area of your life, emotional strains may begin to show. You may feel that unfair demands are being made on you by your partner.

22. SATURDAY. Tricky. Give others a fair hearing. Do not judge situations. The Ram should be prepared to hear the truth. Do not try to dominate people who have their own ideas and opinions. Aries parents who have children approaching their mid-teens should give youngsters greater freedom to make up their own minds about important issues of the day. You will gain greater respect if you allow members of the younger generation to stand on their own two feet. Discussions with partners over joint finances are not likely to reach any definite conclusions. There is a danger of your becoming over-materialistic. Advertising strategies may lure you into wanting things you do not really need.

23. SUNDAY. Difficult. It is important for you to keep yourself meaningfully occupied. This can be a fairly fulfilling day as long as you do not slip into lethargy. Take up with part-time jobs that bring you some artistic satisfaction. If you have too much spare time on your hands, you could give in to overindulgence or extravagant spending. Do not allow friends to dictate how you should spend your leisure time. Forceful personalities must not be allowed to prescribe terms today. But investigations of religious, philosophical or related subjects may lead to an unbelieving or skeptical conclusion. This is not a particularly favorable day for starting out on long journeys.

24. MONDAY. Inactive. There will not be a great deal taking place that will excite you today. You will be rather pleased, in fact, that you can work at your own pace. New starts can be made with jobs that require a lot of groundwork. Not before then can you really get interest from influential people to back them. Go over accounts carefully. It would be a good idea to check up on just how much money you have on deposit so that future planning is realistic. But Aries who think they can implement schemes directly are likely to be disappointed. The advice of professional people and experts will be worth following in minor affairs. In-laws can be helpful as well, if they feel in the mood.

25. TUESDAY. Fair. This will be a frustrating day for Aries people who are trying to make progress with artistic jobs. They have been working on them on their own. Publishers and producers may not even give scripts or manuscripts a second glance. You may feel that all the hard work that you have put in on a pet project has been for nothing. You must not allow your outlook to become soured, however. Try to learn something from your experiences today. Travel can involve delays. More time should be allowed for journeys if you have important appointments to keep. This is quite a favorable day for dealing with financial matters as well as professional affairs.

26. WEDNESDAY. Sensitive. Taking a more flexible approach to routine business and career affairs would be helpful. Do not prejudge situations. Even though there may be differences with influential people, these can be overcome. You must take a more reasonable approach. Show that you are prepared to give way on matters that really seem to be worrying superiors. There is the possibility of some deception at your place of employment. Old enemies may deliberately be plotting and scheming. The day is favorable for all research work. Romance can contain some truly magical and delightful moments. You could find that you are more in love than has been the case for some time past.

27. THURSDAY. Important. This will be one of the most important days of the month. You will have excellent opportunities to make progress in your career. Try to get into the social scene. Accept any invitations that will bring you into contact with influential people who can do you some good in your career. You will find that friends will be extremely helpful with the kind of introductions they can arrange for you. Make a concerted effort to boost returns from routine business transactions. Quick thinking and astuteness can stand Aries in good stead. This would be a favorable time for dealing with correspondence of a financial nature. It would also be helpful for dealing with publicity matters.

28. FRIDAY. Mixed. It is important that you do not allow yourself to be too easily led by friends who live by their wits. Such a course of action could easily lead you into brushes with the law. These you could well do without. Schemes that are presented to you for making some easy money could become severely flawed. Stick to regular ways to boost your income. Pay bills on time. Do not use money that you have on deposit in savings to supplement riotous or luxury living. Influential people can be resolutely opposed to business financial schemes and ventures. It will be another favorable day for all publicity and advertising.

29. SATURDAY. Restful.   Although this will be a rather quiet day, you are not likely to have any complaints about the lack of activity. There will be plenty of jobs for you to deal with at home. Get caught up with accounts for the month. Do not leave work to pile up for Sunday that could keep you apart from members of your family. They are undoubtedly planning to make demands of a personal nature on your time then. You will enjoy the social scene. Friends may come up with some ideas for going out that will appeal to you greatly. There will be opportunities for meeting new people in pleasant surroundings.

30. SUNDAY. Mixed.   The Ram is likely to be surprised at how much can be accomplished on this, the normal day of rest. You will be able to get through a greater work load by carrying out jobs in seclusion. Team effort may not bring the results that you were hoping for, though. Discussions with associates could lead to very little satisfaction. On the social side of your life, old acquaintances could make some welcome but unexpected appearances. A telephone call or a ring on your doorbell may herald the arrival of a chum from distant parts whom you have not seen for ages. There will be good opportunities for casual and informal meetings with influential people. But Aries can embarrass themselves and others with their verbosity.

MAY

1. MONDAY. Important.   You will be full of good ideas today. What's more, you will have better opportunities to put them into practice. Influential people will be most helpful. They will encourage you to go even further in making more use of your imagination on the job. The drive and confidence of the Ram will be valuable for getting new operations off the ground. The day will be favorable for deepening personal relationships. You should be able to get closer to someone whom you have only worshiped from afar to date. There should be a good opportunity, in particular, for making friendships with people who operate from behind the scenes.

2. TUESDAY. Mixed. Don't waste any time this morning. If you decide to postpone work on regular jobs that it is imperative for you to complete today, you will probably find you will have to put in a lot of overtime. People may stand in the way of Aries people but they are likely to grow stronger from the opposition they encounter. Remember that nothing of any significance is ever achieved without a struggle. Later on today, influential people will show a greater willingness to help you. This evening will be a good time to meet with friends with whom you are really close. None of you feel that you have to put on any kind of an act for the others. Your friendship is sincere, based on mutual trust and sincerity.

3. WEDNESDAY. Easygoing. This will be a first-class day for getting yourself better organized. Make a concerted effort to deal with any backlog of mail that has been building up. It is important that you work out a schedule for today and stick to it. You should have plenty of time to include all the little chores you had meant to complete before the month of April came to a close. There are unlikely to be any problems within your own home to slow you down if you are operating mainly from your own base. Aries can become adept at getting people to cater to their desires and to fit in with their plans. Those of you who set their sights too high will be disappointed. But it is better to aim too high than too low.

4. THURSDAY. Lucky. Consider this an important day. You will have a much better idea of what to aim for in life. What is more important, you will know how to go about achieving your aims. Your relationship with your boss is likely to be very much improved. The best way to get superiors to grant favors is to follow their instructions to the letter. This holds especially true when dealing with new rush jobs. Your backing will help to boost their confidence. Remember that people older and more experienced than yourself can sometimes have secret, nagging doubts about their own judgment. The day will be favorable for putting more exertion into furthering financial affairs.

5. FRIDAY. Fortunate. This day finds you smack in the middle of a first-class time frame. Be sure that you make hay while the sun shines. Push home any advantage that you have been able to gain over competitors. See what you can do to make influential people hold true to their promises. Superiors will probably be more willing to stick to their word when it comes to promotion and bonus payments. You should be able to continue to make a good impression where it counts. Any extra money that comes in now should be put safely away in rainy-day savings. The morning can be a particularly good time for implementing financial plans. It will also be good for making new acquisitions, possibly for the home.

6. SATURDAY. Important.   Mundane, routine chores can be taken care of without too much fuss or bother. You do not seem to be worried by the petty criticisms of others now. In fact, you seem to be able to rise above that sort of thing very adequately. This is a particularly favorable day for Aries people who live by their wits. It should also be good for getting backing from wealthy people who are in a position to assist you. Your driving force, coupled with your natural charm, could go a long way toward assisting you in getting what you want. Quick thinking and astuteness may prove invaluable in seizing worthwhile opportunities before it is too late. It is a good time for the signing of documents.

7. SUNDAY. Upsetting.   It would seem as though you are now paying for the pace of the last few days. You are probably feeling somewhat tired and drained. Although you appear to have made certain gains, this would not appear to make up for your depressed state today. There are likely to be problems in and around the home that will not help out. You and your opposite number seem to be going through a difficult and uncommunicative stretch at the moment. It is more important than ever to be in the right place at the right time. Aries who spend the day running around pointlessly will become infuriated at the opportunities they have missed. There is a risk of devaluation of stocks and shares.

8. MONDAY. Difficult.   A somewhat shaky start to the working week would appear to be in store for Aries-born readers. It would seem to be rather important that you do not make any silly mistakes today with money. Do not rush into new investments. Glib-talking associates may be trying to get you to back speculative schemes and other dubious ventures. You would be well advised to give such propositions a very wide berth, indeed. Emergencies can occur involving the home. It is best to be on call, just in case. You may have to interrupt working schedules to make trips in order to see the needs of loved ones in distress. This could create a crisis situation with your work load.

9. TUESDAY. Mixed.   You may still be having some trouble in overcoming problems that arose right at the beginning of this week. You may be lacking in energy and driving force. Do not allow depression to color your long-term thinking. It would be best not to plan too far ahead. Try to solve only problems that you are capable of taking positive action on. It would be wise to avoid the company of depressing people. At your place of employment, associates could be cold and indifferent. Aries may have their patience tested to the utmost. Nothing should be done to offend against convention. There may be a good opportunity later on for entertaining influential people at home.

10. WEDNESDAY. Buoyant. This midweek day sees you bouncing back as only the Ram can! With plenty of energy at your disposal, you should soon be able to catch up with chores that got left undone for one reason or another. Influential people will be very impressed by your grit. More flexibility when dealing with financial affairs will enable you to finish jobs well ahead of schedule. The day might be good for adding to collections of antiques or other beautiful objets d'art. You may be able to make some handy money on the side by giving more attention to a second-string job or hobby. Conditions will be favorable for beautifying the home with new furniture or redecoration of some key rooms.

11. THURSDAY. Changeable. This need not be a difficult day as long as you take a positive outlook. Much will depend on your personal attitude toward what is going on around you. One thing seems certain: you cannot make things happen. You will have to exercise a good deal of patience if you find that you are not getting on as fast as you had hoped with your money-making schemes. Influential people may be difficult to track down, but strong-arm tactics simply will not pay off when you are dealing with superiors. Do what you can to work on artistic endeavors in your own time. You should not expect to see results right away, though. Travel will be helpful for implementing pleasure or entertainment plans.

12. FRIDAY. Difficult. Children may land their Aries parents or teachers in trouble with the authorities. There will be one thing that will really irritate you today. It is that you will probably have to spend a long time straightening out difficult situations that are really not of your making. Superiors may cancel leave or postpone it, due to a heavy backlog of work that they feel must be caught up with. You are likely to have to change your plans at the last moment. You are undoubtedly going to find this state of affairs extremely frustrating and irritating. Influential people in the business or economic world are unlikely to sponsor speculative or risky ventures. You may have to approach them with a proposal.

13. SATURDAY. Mixed. This is a favorable day for putting in some overtime at your place of employment. If you are honest with yourself, you will own up to the fact that you have probably been backsliding. Do not attempt to cut corners. Such an attitude would only backfire on you at a later date. Good progress can be made with desk jobs, and you will not be averse to a little heavy manual labor, either. You should be able to end the week making up for any damage that you have done to your reputation in the eyes of influential people. Aries business people may be able to achieve greater independence and freedom. Today should be good for doing odd jobs in and around the home.

14. SUNDAY. Easygoing. It will be just the sort of a Sunday that the doctor ordered! You will be able to laze around your home and take things at a leisurely pace. This is a period when Aries men and women may need and deserve some extra relaxation. Try to prepare yourself for what is likely to be a fairly hectic start to the working week. Aries people will be able to handle all sorts of domestic duties without having to push themselves too hard. Some of you may have been feeling a little under the weather lately. You should have the opportunity to get more sleep and give additional attention to your diet. Overexertion should be avoided, as rest is essential.

15. MONDAY. Difficult. You may find yourself feeling boxed in and be unhappy. The Ram will probably have less leeway than usual for implementing personal plans. One of the main problems for you today will not be in knowing what you want. Rather, what it will be is how to persuade other people to help you get it! It would be best not to be too pushy. More time should be given to matrimonial and partnership plans. Do not ride roughshod over the desires of your opposite number. Nothing should be done to rock the domestic boat. Loved ones will take exception to any additional time that the Ram uses for attending to public affairs. This results in keeping them away from the domestic environment.

16. TUESDAY. Disconcerting. This is going to be an extremely sensitive day for all financial matters. It would seem that the best advice that can be offered to you today is not to invest in any schemes. It applies even if they come to you with the recommendation of others. Be firm, no matter how strongly you are advised that you should get a piece of the action. Fights can develop very easily between you and your mate or spouse. You are both likely to be blaming the other for extravagance and the resulting lack of available cash. It is best to try to remain calm and unemotional or these fights could end in walkouts. Business enemies could be attempting to stir up trouble by testing your loyalty.

17. WEDNESDAY. Tedious. Boredom could easily set in. This will not be a very satisfactory day from many angles. You will be feeling lethargic. Most likely there will be ways open to you to make money. But you are unlikely to have the inclination or the energy to push yourself hard enough. Your thinking about financial affairs could be a little blurred. It would be wise to sit tight and not to make any new investments. It would also be best to think twice before taking the plunge with new partnership investments. But current cooperative or teamwork endeavors can be productive. Evening is a time for recharging your energy and taking it easy. Take your mind off work problems and enjoy some leisure.

18. THURSDAY. Difficult. Now is the time for Aries-born people, who have come to the end of their tether at taking orders from above, to branch out on their own. You could try to set up private businesses. You can afford to be a mite more daring. You may be able to win the support of a person who will give you financial backing. You must be wary of any strings that are attached to loans, however. Professional people will be helpful in explaining the ins and outs of contracts and complicated legal documents. But this can be a day when the past catches up with the Ram! You may have to pay the price for sloppy workmanship at an earlier date. Good names can be endangered.

19. FRIDAY. Routine. This would be a good day for taking advantage of what is likely to be a lull in normal activities. Come to grips with pet schemes and hobbies that you have sadly neglected. Aries people who operate from their home base will have the opportunity of one or two hours of uninterrupted study. There will be good opportunities for all investigative procedures. Investigations should be made now into operations that you will probably want to carry out next week. You may be thinking of making one or two new investments. Discussions that you have with professional people are likely to bring interesting new facts to light. This might be a favorable time for the handling of joint finances.

20. SATURDAY. Difficult. You could call this a look, listen and learn day. Don't be in too much of a hurry to tell other people how they should conduct their affairs. Don't speak up too quickly when influential people are asking for original ideas. You can learn a great deal from the mistakes of eager competitors. This is not an especially auspicious day for travel. Trips are not likely to work out very well. Check that you are really needed in other towns or cities before you set out. Otherwise, you may go to a great deal of expense for nothing. Even travel in the immediate vicinity could turn out to be a complete waste of time. Aries may be confronted by a dilemma regarding domestic affairs.

21. SUNDAY. Harmonious.   Communicating with people at a distance could lead to misunderstandings. It would be better by far to deal with matters nearer to home today. Loved ones will not be too difficult to get along with. Time can be meaningfully spent going over ways to turn hobbies into second-string jobs. You should certainly be seeking opportunities to make extra money. Thinking may be rather impractical at this time. Forward planning in connection with regular career matters would be best postponed. But this can be a particularly fortunate day for romance. Flirtations may lead to the forming of new love attractions with especially compatible partners. You will welcome new scenes and faces.

22. MONDAY. Routine.   This may be one of those irritating days when you have to wait on the goodwill of other people. Without it, you cannot make any important moves in your career. Unless you find matters of the moment to occupy yourself with, you could become extremely frustrated. Influential people will not be available when you want to see them. This will probably be an easier day for the self-employed and for Aries who are more in control of their own destinies in other ways. Reading and study of all kinds will be favored today. Aries who will soon be sitting for examinations should be able to enhance their chances of passing by whatever knowledge they are able to retain.

23. TUESDAY. Mixed.   There are likely to be some added new challenges to face today. Aries business and career people are likely to welcome this switch. They appear to have been going through a particularly frustrating period since before the weekend. In fact, you will be champing at the bit. It is important not to overreact with excitement to favorable new developments. If a new contract is dangled before you, it might be best not to accept the terms that are offered to you. You may be able to get more money by playing a waiting game. It should be a good day for dealings with large business companies and corporations. It could also be good for discussions about the future with influential people.

24. WEDNESDAY. Boring.   Don't allow boredom to overtake you. There is no good in sitting and waiting on ceremony. If you want to achieve anything of significance, you will have to be the one to make the first move. This is a day when you may realize that you have been sitting on the fence for too long. Get back into the mainstream of life. You can no longer afford to wait for people to approach you. Go all-out to make a good impression on the people who are in a position to help you to get ahead. You will welcome all the help you can get in your chosen field of endeavor. It is up to the Ram to get a move on, rather than waiting for others to take the initiative. Nothing should be rushed, though.

25. THURSDAY. Excellent. This may probably be the best day of the month that you have experienced so far. You are likely to feel much more in control of your own situation. People at your place of employment will have more respect than is usual for your opinions. This is an excellent time for all business financial transactions and negotiations. The advice of colleagues and acquaintances will be well worth following. New contacts can be made, some of them possibly with people occupying positions of considerable power and authority. Today should be good, for readers who are interested in humanitarian projects, to promote these. Why don't you be the one to initiate this?

26. FRIDAY. Fortunate. Carry on the good work. You seem to have made excellent progress yesterday. You are getting people to accept what is very important to you as far as your career is concerned. Continue to build on the goodwill and rapport that have been established between yourself and an older, influential person. Show that you are neither scared nor unwilling to put more energy into jobs that are physically demanding. Extra energy that is at your disposal should be channeled in positive ways. This is a helpful day for advancing publicity ideas and promotional ventures. Secret hopes and wishes with regard to romance have a better chance of fulfillment.

27. SATURDAY. Sensitive. After what appears to have been quite a spurt over the last two or three days, you are likely to start feeling the pace. Some of the jobs that you have to tackle may not be altogether agreeable. But tackle them you must if you wish to round off your week successfully. Attempts to get hold of information before it is officially released may lead Aries into trouble with the authorities. Whatever you do, you must try to keep on the right side of the law. The cooperation or assistance of influential people is likely to have some strings attached. Behind-the-scenes maneuvering can lead to major breakthroughs in business or career affairs. Evening is a good time for sharing with loved ones.

28. SUNDAY. Productive. A pleasant day would appear to be in store for you and yours. You will be pleased if you can spend more time within your own four walls. You and your mate or partner will have quite a lot to discuss, especially when it comes to finances. Additional ways must be found now for making extra savings. Secrecy and roundabout methods may be successful when straightening out neighborhood problems. There might be a good chance for unearthing plots or intrigues. Then you must take the necessary measures for self-protection. But travel plans could easily misfire. This is not a good day for making trips. Talk to older relatives by phone if you can save yourself a journey by doing so.

29. MONDAY. Changeable.   This is a make-up-your-mind kind of day. Decisions will have to be made about family affairs. Domestic problems may be affecting your marriage negatively. Your relationship with a loved one may need some straight thinking. Face up to reality; it will help you to reach the right conclusion. As far as work is concerned, quick thinking can put the Ram where he or she likes to be: among the leaders and winners. But ideas or plans may simply be too futuristic for general consumption. Friends and professional people will be helpful. Romantic ventures should be happy for the single Aries. A free exchange of ideas at home will do much to clear the air this evening.

30. TUESDAY. Productive.   Get out on the golf course or tennis court with professional acquaintances. Try to mix with people who have special knowledge and are not averse to sharing it in a related situation. Aim to spend some hours out-of-doors, especially if you are employed all week in a sedentary occupation. Wide-open spaces and the wind in your hair will make you happy. But you must at all times do what you can to ensure that no harm is done to your professional reputation. This time of year is favorable for promotion work and advertising campaigns. Relatives can be helpful with personal problems. You should be careful, however, not to reveal too much information.

31. WEDNESDAY. Rewarding.   The month comes to an end on quite a high note. The morning can be particularly auspicious for romance. You may receive a letter or telephone call that sends your heart into a flutter. Arrangements that you are able to make for early next month will please you. It is a good time for writing love letters, too, and for contacting romantic partners by other means. New attractions may be formed while you are traveling. Do not allow your responsibilities to keep you in one place for too long. You will have much more success and satisfaction today if you keep on the move. Friendship will be important; knowledge and information can be picked up in lighthearted conversation.

JUNE

1. THURSDAY. Mixed. Go with your intuition; it will not play you false! Hunches that you get today are more than likely to be correct. It would be better to act on your own judgment, rather than allow yourself to be persuaded by forceful associates. Financial gain is possible. An attitude of self-sacrifice in relation to family members will benefit the Ram in the long run. A fine sense of discrimination will be helpful to your plans in the long run. Career plans can be eased with the help of professional people. Take advice on monetary matters from your accountant or bank manager. This may be a time to ease up on extravagant tendencies. Try to work out some formula for spending.

2. FRIDAY. Important. The day will be favorable for financial negotiations, especially with the income tax department. If you feel that you are being charged too unfairly by government agencies, you should bring the matter up for discussion. You may have to be a little more forceful with professional advisers. Be sure at all times that your interests are well represented. This should be a good day for travel in connection with routine and practical matters. Some of you may be discussing the finer details of a property deal just now. It may be that some good progress can be made in this area. Aries can use their mental abilities to particularly good effect. This might be a good time for gathering facts and information. Shoppers may be able to pick up a useful bargain or two.

3. SATURDAY. Rewarding. You should be rather pleased with your progress during these very early days of the month. This will be a pleasant day. Loved ones will show greater understanding about your prior commitments. You may feel that you have to give more attention to work than has been necessary recently for a Saturday. You will have a chance to tie up the loose ends of jobs that are usually associated with the month of May. Aries' alertness and ability to prolong concentration are likely to be at their peak. Today might be good for furthering all mental and creative endeavors, particularly writing projects. It will also be favorable for handling of official correspondence.

4. SUNDAY. Special. This will be a good day for getting out and about more. Remember the old adage that all work and no play makes Jack a dull boy, or girl if that is the case! Give your loved ones a special treat. Find ways to express to your mate or partner all that you feel you owe to them. Aries parents should find they are drawn closer to offspring than has been the case for some time past. You may find it possible to have a special chat with members of the younger generation. Single Aries can make new romantic conquests. Flirtations can lead to the forming of especially compatible relationships. This could be a favorable time for engagement and marriage proposals.

5. MONDAY. Difficult. Although you will be extremely keen to get new projects off the ground today, some caution is necessary. Do not invest a lot of money in a venture that has not yet really proved itself to be a workable proposition to you. This is rather a sensitive start to the working week. It might be best to get involved in routine matters that do not have a chance of backfiring on you. Go over your accounts. You may discover that one or two bills have not been paid. Perhaps you have made a mistake in your accounting. You may not be as well off as you may have thought you were. Family or household members can be forgetful and neglect to perform important chores or duties.

6. TUESDAY. Changeable. Mixed trends are indicated for you this second weekday. As long as you are prepared for sudden changes in working conditions then all will be well. Your boss may be in a changeable mood. Schedules are likely to be updated with very little notice given. You may be able to gain something of a head start over your competitors by being quick to take advantage of the changes. Don't try to bring differences out into the open. The direct approach is not likely to lead to success in the long run. Far more subtle and covert methods will be required. Nothing should be done to provoke or irritate household or family members. Today should be good for shopping expeditions.

7. WEDNESDAY. Tricky. You will have to draw upon your inner reserves of strength to fight back. This is an extremely difficult day for home life and for work. Business and personal affairs will not mix together very well. You will have to be strict with loved ones who bother you with private matters while you are at your place of employment. Superiors will show little understanding of what you are attempting to achieve and of the delicate balance that you are trying to maintain. Romantic affairs contain a greater risk of separation or estrangement. Loved ones can resent the natural tendency in their Aries partner to judge them and to see them in terms of the past.

8. THURSDAY. Productive. A complete reversal of yesterday's somewhat dismal trends appears likely. You get off to a good start at home. Some news that you receive first thing is likely to cheer you up considerably. A letter or telephone call will set your mind at rest. You have been worrying about a matter that has caused you a few sleepless nights. This will be a day when influential people will be more helpful. This is the best day of the week, so far, for putting in special requests for time off or perhaps an advance on your salary. Teachers or professors may write impressive recommendations that will help the younger reader to get a job. It will be favorable for romance.

9. FRIDAY. Productive. You should be able to carry on today with any jobs that you were attending to yesterday. You will like this period just before the weekend a very great deal. The fact is that you will have the chance to please yourself about the pace at which you work. With more driving force at your disposal, you should have both the energy and the inclination to make good progress. This, of course, will assure that you earn more money. You are likely to discover, as well, that superiors have enough trust to leave you to cope with routine matters as you see fit. They recognize your abilities so do not interfere. But there would be little point to drawing up pleasure plans for the weekend just yet.

10. SATURDAY. Useful. Aries may be promoted to positions of prestige and authority. A long-held ambition is likely to move closer to coming true. Your advice is also more likely to be valued by people around you. Influential people will continue to be helpful and friendly. You will probably be feeling much more contented with your present job and with what the future holds for you. The day should be favorable for using spare time for charitable deeds and service. Any work that you intend doing at home will probably be best carried on entirely in seclusion. This is a good time for checking up on matters related to pensions and retirement. Later, health could suffer because of overindulgence.

11. SUNDAY. Important. Aries-born people should be able to look back at the first third of the month with a considerable degree of satisfaction. Although you have had to suffer one or two setbacks, overall, the thrust seems to have been a forward one. There are likely to be many important matters that are related to home and family affairs that you can deal sensitively with today. There is not likely to be any problem in getting loved ones to agree with home-front improvements that you wish to make. It will be favorable for doing odd jobs in and around the house yourself. Be more of a handyman. You will get pleasure from fixing something yourself. You will also save yourself money in the process of doing so.

12. MONDAY. Demanding. The chances are that you will have trouble getting along with colleagues. The differences at your place of employment are likely to start early in the day. You may be late for work and not call in. Or there could be some other distraction that causes a rift between you and the people whose support you need to make progress with team jobs. Misunderstandings will easily occur. A note of sourness could creep into relationships. Marital affairs may contain disagreements over domestic and family issues. Business partnership ventures might produce disappointing results. Compromises are likely to be called for. Unless each person concedes, nothing will be achieved.

13. TUESDAY. Uncertain. This is likely to be one of those days that is marked by its lack of activity. All in all, you are going to be slogging away at the details of routine matters. However, this is not to say that it will be a wasted interval: far from it. You will be pleased to have the chance to catch up with lots of minor affairs. You knew you would have to turn your hand to them sooner or later. In this case, sooner will be much better than later. Get to the real cause of legal matters and problems. Discussions with lawyers will help you to obtain a greater understanding of where you stand in the eyes of the law. It would be a good time for discussions or negotiations with influential people.

14. WEDNESDAY. Confusing. Beauty and attractiveness are now always the best or most accurate guides to character. You would do well to remember this piece of advice today. You may be charmed by someone whom you meet later on. But you would be foolish to put a long and happy relationship in jeopardy in order to grasp at some fleeting pleasure. Do not jump into anything feet-first. Legal matters are likely to take up more time and attention than you were anticipating. Family members should be given more of a chance to speak their minds. Research work can lead to the unearthing of new and exciting facts. Don't put any pressure on loved ones who may be feeling overtaxed as it is.

15. THURSDAY. Productive. This is an excellent day for dealing with large business firms or corporations. Aries who are involved in industry should be very pleased at what takes place today, especially at boardroom level. It seems that your intuition will be on a very high plane. You may be able to anticipate what people are thinking. This gift, if used correctly, can win you many new friends. Business and pleasure will mix together rather well. Further investigations made into current ventures are likely to set Aries' minds at rest. Other people will remember acts of kindness performed by you. But taxation and insurance problems are likely to arise later on. These should be handled right away.

16. FRIDAY. Rewarding. Aries-born people who handle money or property on behalf of others should be able to produce substantial gains. These would accrue both to themselves and to their clients. This is a starred day for those of you who earn a living through money made on a commission basis. Recent hard work that you have put in on publicity and advertising campaigns could begin to bear fruit now. This will be a helpful day for property investors. It will be easier for Rams to get their own way in joint financial affairs. It's a good time for making attempts to close outstanding transactions. This evening older relatives are likely to play an important role in your life.

17. SATURDAY. Easygoing. There is likely to be a slackening of pace for you today. You probably won't have too many objections to this state of affairs. You seem to have been working under a lot of pressure all week. You will certainly be pleased at the progress that you have been able to make. But it would appear that both your mind and your body do need some relaxation as well as some distraction from money-making matters. The sort of jobs that you do have to handle now will be routine and are not likely to be particularly taxing. Day-to-day activities can be dealt with in a minimum of time. There should be a good opportunity for all self-improvement endeavors.

18. SUNDAY. Difficult. The more time that you can spend in and around the home base, the better it will be. This is not a good day for travel. Trips that you make are not likely to be worth the time or the money involved. Aries involved in higher education or special training courses may find their enthusiasm waning. But it is best not to make decisions now that are not forced on you as you might later regret them. In-laws may start throwing their weight around in an irresponsible fashion. You will have a hard time getting along with the relatives of your mate or partner. They seem determined to make life difficult for you. Unless you put a stop to this right away, you may become embroiled in constant fights.

19. MONDAY. Demanding. One thing is sure, you won't be in the mood to handle the more mundane tasks that come up on this first day of the working week. Some mothers and housewives among you will find that your boredom level is low. Youngsters are likely to get on your nerves. This is more than likely to be due to your own mood. You are accustomed to the temper tantrums that they are likely to throw. It will not be easy to get along with associates at your place of employment, either. You may find that superiors will be difficult to track down. You may have been hoping to have interviews with them today. Circumstances or conditions can change at a moment's notice, though. Nothing and no one should be taken for granted.

20. TUESDAY. Disturbing. Recognition for original or inventive work is likely to be given reluctantly, if at all. This is not the best of days for bringing your natural talents to the notice of superiors. Keen as you are to make progress with hobbies and second-string jobs, you must restrain your natural Aries impulsiveness. Aries people will be more aware than anyone else of the problems confronting them. These occur in connection with regular business affairs. This is another day when it will be very difficult for you to concentrate for long spells on jobs that you feel almost anyone could do. The desire to break out will be strong. But do not throw up your regular job when you have nothing definite to go to.

21. WEDNESDAY. Tricky. You may be feeling rather disappointed with the little progress you have been able to make at your place of employment so far this week. But being something of a realist, you will be willing to accept most of the responsibility for this state of affairs. In any case, this is no time for apportioning blame. Do what you can to patch up any differences that have recently arisen between you and your colleagues. It will then be easier for you to get caught up with day-to-day chores. Until you straighten out routine matters it will be very difficult to make headway in other areas. No risks should be taken with business finances. Speculation would probably lead to heavy losses.

22. THURSDAY. Difficult. Unless you keep close watch on youngsters, they could cause you trouble. You may find that the calls of domestic duty are particularly heavy today. You will not have as much time to pursue hobbies as you would like to. Perhaps you will have to control your temper a little more effectively. If you do try to discipline members of the younger generation, you should do it calmly and with authority. Do not give way to sudden outbursts of temper. This would appear to be the last of a stretch of a few bad days. During this time, Aries are likely to have had to contend with continual frustration of their plans and their desires. Social activities may have to be canceled due to lack of funds.

23. FRIDAY. Lucky. This would be a particularly favorable day for getting on better terms with influential people. If you have any special requests to make, do this on a social basis rather than standing on ceremony. You and your immediate boss are likely to be able to get on a much better wavelength now. Home entertaining can be a good way of getting your employer's guard down. You will be pleased at the attitude of your mate or partner. Loved ones will be doing all they can to back you up. You will also have good reason to be proud of a member of the younger generation. You seem to feel some special responsibility for this youngster. This will be a challenging day for Aries business people.

24. SATURDAY. Sensitive. Maintain a low profile. It would be best for the Ram to operate from a position behind the scenes today. Do not make a big song and dance about changes in working methods. In order to achieve these successfully, you should just proceed quietly. In this way, you will avoid unnecessary opposition from people who may be feeling jealous of you. The less that you talk about your schemes, the more likely they will be to succeed. Words need to be chosen with more care as it is easy to give the wrong impression and possibly cause offense. Influential people can make strange and incomprehensible demands. Try to find out the reasons for these without incurring their wrath.

25. SUNDAY. Important. The chances are that you will be somewhat pleased that the week has come to a close at last. Although no absolute tragedy has taken place, it does appear that you have been through a fairly draining period. You will enjoy home and family life very much. Any differences that you and your mate or partner have experienced lately can soon be forgotten. Do not hark back to the past. It is best to look to the future with confidence. It would be a good day for putting the finishing touches to holiday plans. This is a favorable period for spending more time alone with romantic companions. It will also be especially favorable for picking up the pieces of old romances.

26. MONDAY. Mixed. Be straightforward. This will be the best way to win people's confidence and to overcome their suspicions. Some rumors may have been spreading around about you. Although they may not be based on the truth, you are going to have to work quite hard to dispel them. The morning can be a fast-moving and successful time for Aries people. Risks can pay off. It should be good for putting more exertion into furthering creative endeavors. Frankness and directness will make it difficult for people to turn down your requests. But nothing should be done to arouse unfair prejudice. If you appear flashy, you could alienate those colleagues from whom you want to gain some support.

27. TUESDAY. Sensitive. This is a particularly favorable day for doing what you always love most: self-promotion. You will be enjoying yourself if you have the opportunity to take center stage. Aries who are attending interviews or auditions should do particularly well. This would appear to be a very good period for those of you who are in show business. This also goes for those who catch the public eye in any other role: sports, for instance. There will be more opportunities for putting personal ideas over with force and conviction. The day will be good for all promotional and publicity work. But in romantic affairs it will be necessary to use a mite more discretion than usual, plus gentleness and tact.

28. WEDNESDAY. Fair. Influential people can be especially cooperative. This is a helpful day for attending to personal matters that you have not been able to straighten out recently. Your boss is likely to allow you some time off to attend to family affairs that may have been taking your mind off your job. Have a frank talk with superiors. You are not apt to regret it if you open your heart to them. Real estate affairs can be improved. You may be able to clinch a deal that puts more money into your bank account. You will be able to impress those who matter by showing your ability to meet deadlines consistently. But old money problems could rear their ugly heads. You may have forgotten a debt that is overdue.

29. THURSDAY. Routine. Domestic discord could interfere with the smooth running of your home life. But if you make an attempt not to be critical of others, you could in all probability find the peace that you are looking for. This is a time when you should be taking a very much live-and-let-live attitude. Try to reconcile differences early, preferably before going to work. Rifts left unhealed are apt to widen as the day progresses. This is not likely to be a very demanding day at your place of employment. You will have the opportunity to attend to matters connected with the monthly accounts. But Aries people should try not to slip into habits, good or bad, that make their lives a ritual.

30. FRIDAY. Buoyant. This will be quite an exciting and stimulating sort of a day. The sort of people with whom you have the chance to mix are likely to spark off some bright ideas in your head for making extra money. It will be a particularly good day for all attempts at self-expression, particularly through writing and other creative endeavors. The chances for getting on good terms with children and other members of the younger generation will be better than ever. You should be able to find ways to put savings plans into practice, probably with the support of your mate or partner. The day will be favorable for getting out and about more and meeting new people from different walks of life. The search for pleasure should not be allowed to lag.

JULY

1. SATURDAY. Uncertain. It is just as well that this month starts on a Saturday. You will not have the opportunity today to make as many new starts as you would like to do, as the second half of the year gets under way. Much of this weekend will be taken up with duties relating to undone chores. Also, loved ones will be making extra demands upon you. Relatives should be given the benefit of the doubt. In any disputes, positions should be surrendered gracefully. This is a favorable day for travel, particularly with regard to meeting people and gathering information. Shoppers may be able to pick up summer bargains at greatly reduced prices. But nothing is truly a bargain if you don't need it.

2. SUNDAY. Difficult. Health may not be up to snuff. Those of you who were hoping to involve yourselves in some energetic pastime or sport may have to cancel at the last moment. It will simply be because you are not feeling up to it. This is a period when you should be taking it easy. Try to come to grips with accounts. Money problems will not go away just because you are ignoring them. Other family and household members should not be imposed upon too much. They may well be feeling the need to treasure their independence and privacy. Do-it-yourself work can lead to botched jobs. The latter part of the day can be more favorable for entertaining influential people than an earlier time.

3. MONDAY. Quiet. You can expect a slow-moving start to the working week. You should not be in too much of a rush to make new starts. Check over details before you invest money in any venture in which there is an element of risk. This will be a fairly uneventful period at your place of employment. Perhaps you should wait awhile before you approach superiors with your new ideas. You have been updating current ways of handling jobs, making them more streamlined. Small incidents are likely to arouse strong memories and make Aries people feel nostalgic. Today will be favorable for closing outstanding affairs and transactions before the start of more important enterprises.

4. TUESDAY. Happy. Some news that you receive early on in the day is likely to cheer you up. This is an important period for getting things done. You are likely to have more driving force and energy at your command. You should do all that you can to channel it in a meaningful and purposeful way. There will be greater understanding between you and your mate or partner. This will mean that you are not likely to face any opposition from within the home about what you have in mind. Bankers can be particularly cooperative and may approve a loan for homes or home improvement. Later in the day will be particularly favorable for romance and the search for pleasure.

5. WEDNESDAY. Disconcerting. Some debt that you had forgotten all about may have to be paid rather quickly. You will probably receive notice from a person to whom you owe money that payment must be made immediately. If you do not meet whatever is the deadline, there is likely to be some form of legal action. This would only put you to additional expense in the long run. It may be necessary to dip into reserve funds to get yourself straightened out. Or you may even have to approach your bank manager for a loan. You are certainly going to have to face up to more responsibilities. Gambling urges will be stronger, but you must resist them totally. Children may get out of hand if allowed too much freedom, but they will surely chafe if not given enough.

6. THURSDAY. Mixed. Aries-born people who like to have a fling should beware of propositions that seem suspiciously attractive. Even more important is that you do not invest your savings in anything that could put you in jeopardy with the law. Remember that you would have no recourse to the courts if things go wrong and you were mixed up in anything even slightly illegal. But this can be a lucky day for Aries salespeople and agents. Sales can be boosted very significantly. Travel is likely to bring first-class results. Writers can gain renown for their new ideas. Nothing should be said or done to arouse the ire of Scorpio people! If you are fearful of a confrontation, avoid them completely.

7. FRIDAY. Changeable. It would look as though you have had a fairly frustrating start to the month. You should lower your sights. It is no good trying to promote original ideas if you do not seem to be able to arouse the enthusiasm of superiors. It may be best to attend to routine affairs. Try to be more resigned to jog along until conditions change. Aries people may be able to demonstrate their reliability and their efficiency in routine work affairs. Their efforts are likely to be noted with approval. Keep slogging away and you may get the promotion that you have been angling for sooner than you thought. It would be a good time for dealing with pension and related matters.

8. SATURDAY. Demanding. Thinking can be erratic and not accurate. Too much frankness may lead to alienation. It is all very well to be straightforward with loved ones, but sometimes it would be best to hold back information. You would know best what is going to upset them. If there is no way that they can improve the situation by having the knowledge that you possess, why bother? Do not gossip or get involved with people who are catty and back-biting. Excesses or indulgences can endanger your health. Drinking and driving are a dangerous combination, to say nothing about the illegality. Lapses of concentration when behind the wheel could be the cause of accidents. Routine affairs and obligations should not be neglected or treated lightly.

9. SUNDAY. Difficult. You are likely to feel rather depressed on this day of rest. The state of your mind will not necessarily be due to any one particular factor. There may perhaps be a combination of things. You might feel that fate is conspiring against you at this time. Feelings of frustration, because you are not able to express yourself freely, will undoubtedly be present. You must keep calm. This is just one of those times when you will simply have to sit tight and sweat it out. It is therefore unlikely to be a weekend that will leave Aries with much peace or respite. Tension in marital or partnership relationships can build, perhaps causing some unpleasant scenes. Do your best to work out solutions.

10. MONDAY. Sensitive. Some improvement in relationships is indicated, but you are not going to take the world by storm today. But neither will there be any violent quarrel. It will be a far more pleasant interval, though. The Aries native will be delighted to get back into the old routine. Surprisingly, you will be happy to deal with the more mundane jobs. The weekend seems to have been a difficult time for personal relationships. This could be a good day for teamwork. Get together with like-minded people in your spare time. Try to do what you can to be more creative. You could form some kind of club within the work force. It could be a sports-oriented one or one for socializing.

11. TUESDAY. Useful. This will be another day that will give you an opportunity to join forces with other people interested in artistic projects. Give free rein to your natural talents. Allow the artist in you to speak. You will probably want some monetary reward for your efforts at some point, if only to cover your expenses. But it should not be money that is uppermost in your mind. Achieving the artistic heights that you know you are capable of will be far more important to you. It seems that you have something quite important to prove to yourself today. The signing of property or other financial agreements today is advisable. But there is a greater risk of deception than usual in routine business and career activities.

12. WEDNESDAY. Important. Contracts that are coming up for renewal can be extended. You can do yourself a lot of good by getting involved in discussions with superiors. Hold out for terms that you feel are reasonable. Do not undersell your natural talents. There may be some Aries who are in the public eye because of their sporting prowess. They should remember that they only have a limited amount of time at the top. They must take that into consideration when agreeing to new terms. Do not depend on anyone else to give you a good break, necessarily. Nothing should be taken for granted if handling money or property on behalf of other people. Instructions need to be followed to the letter.

13. THURSDAY. Excellent. Good news: your luck seems to be changing with a vengeance today! Letters and telephone calls that you receive should leave you with feelings of joy and well-being. It looks as if you will be moving nearer to the fruition of a secret wish or dream. Both private and public life seem to be very much improved. This is a day when influential people will be particularly helpful if approached in the right way. Use that Aries charm of yours to the best possible effect. Do not suffer fools gladly. Bankers are more likely to be cooperative with your ideas. Local officials will understand the intricacies of your home and real estate affairs and may grant loans without lengthy delays.

14. FRIDAY. Easygoing. It should be a good day for entertaining people at home, but only on a small scale. Arrange an intimate dinner party or have a few business colleagues come in for cocktails. Business and pleasure will mix in rather well for you today. Some valuable information or advice can be obtained through speaking with people who come from distant places. Devoting more time to drawing up plans for future business goals would be both practical and realistic. This is also the right day for putting the final touches to vacation plans. If you have not yet decided on your summer holiday for this year you should devote serious thought to it. Attempts to improve work efficiency can be introduced at your place of employment.

15. SATURDAY. Excellent. Looking back over this past week, about to end, you should be fairly pleased with your overall progress. It might even be your best week so far for this year. Contracts that you have had in your possession for some time can now be signed. It would appear that you cannot really improve on the offers that are now being made to you. The time is favorable for dealings with publishers and literary agents. This is a good day for the Aries writer. It is also true for those of you who earn your living by making special use of your imagination. The day will be favorable, too, for distant travel, whether for business or for pleasure. Good for putting more exertion into academic pursuits.

16. SUNDAY. Disturbing. The point at which you will become bored will be particularly low today. Concentration will be a weak spot. You will not really enjoy attending to desk jobs and account work. Lapses in concentration could prove to be expensive if you are going over income tax matters. You will also have quite a few interruptions to contend with from other members of the household. Your mind is likely to be wandering all over the place. This will avail you nothing at all. It will be a day when more honesty with yourself, as well as with others will surely be required. Neighbors can be selfish and irresponsible. Plans for the future that are drawn up today may later prove to have major flaws.

17. MONDAY. Disconcerting. This is not a day for rushing into new agreements too quickly. You will regret it if you sign legally binding documents because of feelings of insecurity. It would be a good idea to check that you have got your facts straight before you take on influential people. Don't go to court without engaging the best possible legal advice you can afford. Aries can be rather mystified at the goings-on around them today. Extra responsibilities may be imposed upon them for no understandable reason. But although the fulfillment of ambitious urges may seem to be a long way off, this is likely to be only a matter of perspective. Difficulties should be taken as challenges, not as a cause for despair!

18. TUESDAY. Difficult. This is almost certain to be a somewhat stressful day, not only for Aries but for everyone around them, as well. There is likely to be trouble within the home early on. Disagreements that are only over silly little affairs could develop into something much more serious later on. In the turmoil of activity it may be rather difficult to get people to listen to reason. Influential people may demand the temporary suspension of lucrative business ventures. You will find it difficult to understand the reasoning behind their actions. But later in the day, you may be able to get these same superiors to realize the error of their ways. Try to make it clear that the negativism of their present thinking can only be detrimental to their business interests.

19. WEDNESDAY. Tricky. Perhaps you will find it difficult to settle down this midweek day. The chances are, you are expecting too much to take place. Set your sights just a little bit lower. You will not achieve your aims by riding roughshod over the wishes of associates. Acting like the proverbial bull in a china shop will win you only enemies. Friends may be in a difficult spot. They undoubtedly need and deserve any extra time that Aries can spare for them. Business financial affairs would best be handled with less recourse to the advice of partners and colleagues. The results of research work that you may have recently carried out are likely to be rather disappointing. They may have lacked supervision.

20. THURSDAY. Changeable. This will be a run-of-the-mill sort of a day. That is not to say that anyone or anything should be taken for granted; far from it. Too many people may be trying to give you advice and this will annoy you. Although friends and associates will mean well, you probably sometimes wish that they would simply mind their own business. Too much trying on the part of the Ram can actually remove them farther from the realization of their secret hopes and wishes. Friendship obligations may interfere with romance. You may not have the chance to see your loved ones this evening and this you will find extremely irritating. Risks should be taken only after a great deal of consideration.

21. FRIDAY. Rewarding. This is a much better day. You seem to be back on the track of something that you were chasing last week, but which suddenly became elusive. Aries-born natives will suddenly have a clearer idea of what they want out of life. Just as important will be their idea of how to go about getting it. Approaches that you make to influential people should be well received. You and your superiors should be getting along in a much better way. It will be easier for the Ram to understand the motives of their boss. There will be a good opportunity for concentrating on furthering developments behind the scenes. It will be a day when more discretion and diplomacy in business and professional affairs can produce especially good results.

22. SATURDAY. Satisfactory. You are likely to have plenty on your hands today. Rush jobs may mean that you have to rearrange your schedule. But Aries like a challenge. You will probably confound your critics and please your supporters by displaying super-human reserves of energy. Influential people are likely to be very pleased with you. You will undoubtedly be rewarded for any overtime that you put in. But this is not a good day for trying to extract promises from other people or commitments about the future. Marriage and engagement plans would best be left in abeyance for now. Travel arrangements may go wrong leading to disappointment. Airlines are apt to be affected by weather, but highway travel can be dead-slow.

23. SUNDAY. Enjoyable. It is important that you plan carefully for today. Don't leave yourself at loose ends. Otherwise you could find yourself spending quite a lot of money on entertainment and similar pleasure-seeking activities. These really do not give you good value for your money for the most part. The best way to have a good time this day of rest is to get together with friends with whom you have a lot in common. You can also enjoy a certain amount of solitude. There do seem to be problems that you need to spend a few quiet moments thinking about. Only you can work out the best course of action. The day should be good for discussions, particularly with children. Aries will be able to state their desires and requests clearly and concisely.

24. MONDAY. Lucky. This could be a day when gambles may pay off. Tips that you receive on having a fling should be investigated thoroughly. You may be able to make money the easy way, but be warned any cash that you do make from such methods is likely to be a small amount. So do not go in for the big kill. This should be a good day for overcoming most obstacles and for dealing with difficult people. It could also be a good time for making new romantic conquests. Aries may be able to capitalize on their artistic abilities with particularly good results. It will be favorable for sporting activities. You are likely to win the applause of your colleagues. You might even persuade some of them to join a team.

25. TUESDAY. Fair. As long as you are not too pushy, all will be well. Take an easygoing attitude toward work. This is not to say that you should be sloppy in your performance, far from it. Simply do not allow yourself to be drawn into arguments that are being waged by others. By carrying on along normal routines in the background and sticking to your duties, you could easily catch the attention of influential people. The health problems of loved ones that may have been causing some real concern for you are likely to be lessened. You may feel that you do not have to take on quite so much responsibility for your nearest and dearest. The advice of people who have given you good tips in the past is likely to be overly speculative.

26. WEDNESDAY. Difficult. This is not a day for taking risks of any kind. Don't be a sucker for the old-pals act. Such people may be trying to wheedle money out of you. Be sure that you take your responsibilities toward your loved ones seriously. Children may cause damage that Aries parents will subsequently have to pay for. Romance can contain stormy arguments. Pleasure and entertainment plans may have to be abandoned due to the heavy costs involved. When checking up on the state of your finances, you may find that you are inexplicably in the red on recent transactions. Skimping on insurance payments could cause you some regrets later on. Be sure you are covered where it counts.

27. THURSDAY. Sensitive. It will be a day when Aries workers will have to struggle to keep their minds on the job in hand. Distractions should be avoided if at all possible. Be polite, but remain firm with people at your place of employment who egg you on to take time off. You will probably have to exercise a great deal of self-discipline now. It would be entirely too easy to succumb to one of the many temptations that are likely to be dangled before you. Messages to or from loved ones may go astray. It would be best not to deal through a third person if you can possibly help it. The more that you can rely on yourself the better it will be. This advice applies in almost every area of your life. Health may be suffering because of your overindulgence.

28. FRIDAY. Rewarding. This is a helpful day for Aries people who have to live by their wits. There will be opportunities to make more money. This could be a good time for giving your spare time over to secondary jobs. You will be grateful for any extra money that you can possibly put your hands on. This is an important period for Aries who operate from their home base. You are likely to make an important breakthrough with any projects that you have been experimenting with. There may be a good opportunity for taking children on all-day sightseeing excursions. It will be favorable for all mental endeavors, and particularly so for furthering writing projects. Signing of all formal agreements and contracts is also recommended at this time.

29. SATURDAY. Changeable. Funds that are held in joint names must not be tampered with by the individuals concerned.

Only by mutual consent can any good come from withdrawing this money. Tidbits of advice or information that are dropped casually by people can be the seeds of something important. Aries should not dismiss anything provocative they hear or read about without further investigation. Your love of excitement must not be allowed to outweigh the need for discretion. Wrong company should be shunned like the plague. Today should be good for travel, though. Trips are likely to be fun, especially those undertaken later in the day. But there could be an unpleasant surprise before bedtime.

30. SUNDAY. Enjoyable. It will be one of the most enjoyable days that you have spent for quite awhile. You will certainly know how to enjoy yourself and to get the best out of other people, too. You will undoubtedly find that your company is very much in demand. There are likely to be quite a few invitations to choose from on the social scene. But you should be sure that you do not try to spread yourself too thinly. Also, you must not ignore the wishes of other members of the family. However, you seem to have enough energy and drive to keep yourself, as well as everyone else, satisfied. Routine chores and work affairs can be a pleasure to perform. This would be a good time for deepening romantic involvements with people much younger or older than yourself.

31. MONDAY. Happy. Improvements can be made in the wake of changing conditions. This is a favorable day for shopping expeditions or for buying in bulk. It will be especially true if you are in the company of family or other household members. You may be able to pick up bargains at any summer sales that are currently running in your shopping area. This is a good day for formulating new plans and establishing connections abroad. As many activities as possible should be carried into new areas. The emphasis of your thinking may be on social welfare and the well-being of others. Keep in touch with professional people who are handling any legal or income tax matters for you.

AUGUST

1. TUESDAY. Productive. Self-improvement interests are likely to be uppermost in your mind on this the first day of the month. You will have fun at attempts to master new hobbies and sports. Some time spent in the company of friends who can demonstrate specialized knowledge for you will not be time wasted. Influential people will show a greater willingness to back speculative projects. But first you will have to prove to them that there is a better than even chance of handsome profits being made. This is a favorable day for deepening current romantic involvements. Someone with whom you have only recently fallen in love is likely to be talking seriously about the future. The advice of relatives will be well worth tuning in to.

2. WEDNESDAY. Challenging. New starts can be made. This is an important day for working at home and for business. Do what you can to demonstrate your natural talents. Get the attention of people who are in a position to lend you a helping hand. You and your superiors will find that relationships are extremely cordial. Any teamwork that you can promote with influential people should bring you in extra profits and some benefits. Aries who are traveling in connection with their job should have plenty to keep themselves stimulated. The ingenuity of Aries people can help them in furthering their creative or spare-time interests. The day will be favorable for transactions or negotiations with people who have connections with show business.

3. THURSDAY. Excellent. This month certainly seems to have gotten off to an excellent start for those people born under the sign of the Ram. Carry on the good work. There does not seem to be anything that can stop you from making progress, as long as you are not impulsive. The morning is a good time for putting in an early appearance at work. Your performance during the early part of the day can lead to an important breakthrough. It is in the period up to and including midday when you will be most likely to catch your competitors asleep at the switch. Promotion plans may be in the pipeline for you. Personal problems can have an unexpectedly simple solution. This is a happy day for your love life.

4. FRIDAY. Demanding. Some news that you receive first thing is likely to bring you to a full stop. Letters and telephone calls that come through could result in your having to rearrange your schedule. You may have to make a sudden and unexpected journey. Professional people will be making additional demands upon you. Bills that come in are quite apt to be for greater amounts than you had budgeted for. Routine work that you must deal with will be somewhat time-consuming. Aries who have to take on extra responsibilities are unlikely to see any tangible returns. Superiors may have taken off on vacation at a time that is most inopportune, at least for you.

5. SATURDAY. Sensitive. A lot of your time is likely to be taken up with your regular activities. You will also be attempting to straighten out certain matters connected with your job. You do not want to have to think about these over the weekend. Aries men and women may find it difficult to anticipate the motives and intentions of partners and loved ones. The more that you can rely on yourself the better it will be for you. Come to grips with home decorating plans. You should be able to save yourself quite a lot of money by attending to odd jobs yourself. Matrimonial affairs contain a greater risk of misunderstandings or outright deceptions. But later on in the day, recreational pastimes or entertainment will enable Aries to get on good terms with influential people.

6. SUNDAY. Manageable. It is unlikely that this will be a very active day. There will probably not be many objections to this state of affairs from the Ram, however. In fact, you are likely to be feeling fairly drained after what appears to have been a rather hectic start to the month. It may be difficult for you to understand what your mate or partner wants from life at the moment. But it would be best not to press loved ones too hard. Committing themselves to a definite course of action at this point is doubtless out of the question. This is quite a good day for Aries-born people who are setting off on their vacations or who are putting the finishing touches to their plans for them.

7. MONDAY. Easygoing. There will not be a lot going on at your place of employment. The same could be said to be true for any of the Aries-born people who are spending their time attending to situations at home. However, as long as you do not set your sights too high or expect to make a great deal of money, then all will be well. It might be best to maintain a low profile. Don't be over-explicit with others about your long-term desires and intentions. Although vagueness is not really your way, it would be wise to play a close hand at this stage. Attempts to get other people to cater to your personal desires are likely to fall through. Compromises can be useful from a purely tactical point of view.

8. TUESDAY. Mixed. Much more exertion should be put into routine occupational affairs. Don't be satisfied doing just enough to get by. It would be better by far to push yourself even harder. By doing so you can make an excellent impression on your boss. Do all that you can to strengthen your future employment prospects. Contracts that were running out may be renewed or extended. But you want to be a bit more careful about real estate matters. Property investments may seem more attractive than they really are. You may find that you become personally involved in some way looking after the affairs of younger family members. Try to reason with them and urge them to be sensible.

9. WEDNESDAY. Satisfactory. So far, you do not appear to have been able to make the progress you were hoping for this week. Nothing you can pinpoint seems to have gone particularly wrong for you. But the leads that you had been hoping to follow up are not likely to be very productive. It might be best to carry along quietly in the background. This does not appear to be the best of times to launch important new publicity campaigns. Heads of large business firms and corporations can be unyielding, once they have taken a stand. No amount of persuasion is likely to get them to change their minds. But this is a good time for all attempts to improve economic security by introducing budgetary systems.

10. THURSDAY. Inactive. Although this will be a fairly easy-going day, it may well be more significant than you had thought at first. There will be a good opportunity for rising above petty emotional differences and gaining a clearer perspective of things as a whole. It is not so much actions as attitudes that will count for most. Try to be more sympathetic to members of the younger generation. They seem to be going through an emotional time at the moment. Try to recall what it was like to be the same age yourself. Aries may find that they have better luck when making attempts to shake off lingering doubts or inhibitions. These may have stopped them from throwing themselves into a new romance.

11. FRIDAY. Demanding. Perhaps you are in too much of a rush today. You will not achieve anything of significance if you try to go too fast. Some chores require special attention to detail. Your relationship with your superiors may leave rather a lot to be desired. You will not be getting along very well with your boss. It would be wise not to put in any requests for special favors to be granted. Work on your own as much as possible. Teamwork is not likely to bring you the results that you may have been hoping for. Communicating with people at a distance can lead to serious misunderstandings. Aries may have to face accusations of which they are innocent. They must remain steadfast in their denials.

12. SATURDAY. Uncertain. Loved ones may be down in the dumps. It could be up to you to lift the atmosphere at home. Family members are likely to be in an emotional frame of mind. Try to suggest outings that would not cost a great deal of money but that would at least brighten the day. You yourself must take steps to assure that your outlook is not soured. You might be affected because you are in close proximity to people who are depressed. Count your blessings. If you think about it, you have much to be grateful for at the moment. Chances are, health problems will require attention. Visits to the doctor cannot be ruled out. More attention to occupational interests will be helpful.

13. SUNDAY. Changeable. It is really up to you to make this day a pleasant one for you and yours. Members of your family will be looking to you to take the initiative and make suggestions for pleasure seeking. It might be a good idea to make arrangements to see a close relative or friend who you have not been in touch with for sometime. You should make attempts to get out of the usual Sunday rut. Trips will be pleasant and need not cost you a great deal of money. Despite its being a day of rest, this would be a good one for furthering routine employment activities. For those who are self-employed, or able to put in some overtime, quite a bit of particularly good work can be done.

14. MONDAY. Rewarding. This should be an excellent day. It will be good for money-making purposes. You may be able to supplement your income in a way that does not interfere with your regular job. Superiors will be understanding. They will grant time off if you have any important domestic problems that cannot wait until evening to be attended to. All in all, there will be a favorable start to the working week. Aries business and career people will be on top of the world and will be able to make the best of existing opportunities. By adapting yourself to the mood of the moment, you will be able to make faster headway. Later in the day is favorable for romance. A personal matter is likely to be resolved then.

15. TUESDAY. Important. Business and financial affairs should be given priority. Do not allow people to take up your time with incidentals. You must try to forge ahead with paperwork. There will be a good chance for board meetings where future policy will be discussed. You will be able to air your point of view without fear of rebuttal. Influential people will be taking notice of what you have to say. You should be feeling much more confident in the way you express yourself now. There will be fewer complications and distractions to contend with. Today is favorable for all attempts by the Aries boss to boost morale among employees. This would be a good chance to spend more of your leisure time with close friends.

16. WEDNESDAY. Disconcerting.   Health may not be all that it should be. You will have to be stronger-willed and think more about your diet. This is the right time to start an exercise course. If you have been feeling the pressure a bit lately, it could mean that you have been backsliding when it comes to looking after yourself. Get on the scales regularly. You may be surprised at how much over your best weight you actually are. This can be a tense and frustrating period. Other people will also tend to be on edge. It will mean that there is less chance of any constructive work being done. This would be a favorable time for entertaining select groups of people at home. But later you may be feeling tired.

17. THURSDAY. Fair.   Some noticeable improvement in your physical condition is indicated. But you are still likely to be feeling some strain a bit. There are, however, plenty of jobs that you can deal with that will not exert too much pressure upon you. This is quite a good day for experimenting with ways to streamline routine jobs. They have become somewhat dull and mundane probably due to repetition and little challenge. Influential people will give you more leeway. You can make additional use of that vivid imagination of yours. Aries people who earn their living through writing could be well pleased with the progress they are able to make.

18. FRIDAY. Tricky.   Don't adopt a jaded and depressed outlook on life. Perk up your ideas. You are not likely to achieve much if you are depressing company among associates at your place of employment. You will be shunned if you are continually looking on the gloomy side of things. You may have missed one or two seemingly good career opportunities of late. But it would be pointless to cry over spilt milk. Do not grieve over what you are powerless to change. Aries may suffer from insomnia with the consequent impairment of concentration during the day. Any special efforts you make to get caught up with routine work are likely to be ignored or not even noticed by superiors. It may take some innovative cost-saving ideas to make any impression.

19. SATURDAY. Disconcerting.   This will be an unsettled kind of a day. You may have had very definite ideas worked out about how you hoped to spend your leisure time. Your plans were well defined. Unfortunately for you, you are not going to be able to fulfill these plans without stiff opposition from loved ones. If you want to avoid all-out confrontation, you are going to have to compromise. Aries could well be exaggerating their need for freedom and independence. There is no point in making other people feel so uncomfortable. Your mate or partner may have had a very trying week. You should at least try to do what you can to make them feel happy and contented.

20. SUNDAY. Easygoing. This will be just the sort of a day that the doctor ordered! You will be able to get more rest than usual. You can deal with all the jobs that have been piling up and have been a constant source of irritation to you. Answer letters and pay bills. Aries readers who are keen on the outdoor life will be able to spend a lot of time in the garden. Loved ones will not be quite as demanding, so you will have more spare time to deploy as you think fit. People will be happier than usual to cater to your desires and to make life more pleasant for you. As far as personal plans are concerned it is best to keep them modest and unpretentious. Small beginnings can lead to great things.

21. MONDAY. Excellent. There is no doubt about it: this will be one of the best days you have experienced so far this month. Aries-born people may have been down in the dumps. Their career has not been going very well of late. Now they are likely to hear news that brings tears of joy to their eyes! Those of you who are involved in the arts are likely to do particularly well, if attending auditions or submitting work for approval. Act with confidence. You should have influential people on your side. Hobbies can be turned into commercial propositions. Fame and renown may be won for creative work. Children can make Aries parents particularly proud. Today would be good for channeling funds into home-improvement schemes.

22. TUESDAY. Mixed. It would be a good idea to get on with the job as early in the day as possible. It would also be a propitious time for the Ram to tackle routine affairs first thing. There are likely to be many interruptions later on. These will tend to make it hard for you to deal with matters that you prefer to deal with in solitude. Personal earnings can be increased substantially if you try to squeeze more activity into your waking hours. There will be greater opportunities for using your initiative. That would be especially true if you have the chance to hold meetings with influential people in other towns and cities. But Aries' neglect of taxation and insurance matters can catch up with them.

23. WEDNESDAY. Productive. This midweek day could find you fairly embroiled with your attention on accounts. Go over your bank statements with care. Try to get a clearer picture of your financial standing in its totality. Employment affairs are not likely to contain any problems for you. The sort of jobs that you are required to handle will be well within your capabilities. Influential people will grant you plenty of time off. You may have trouble with concentrating, though. You must try harder to keep your mind on the job as any lapses could cost you. This would be a good time for attending to routine medical checkups. You are likely to get a clean bill of health.

24. THURSDAY. Mixed. This is not a day for overdoing. Take your time with jobs that would require you to use a good deal of physical energy. There could be some interruptions to cope with. The demands of loved ones could result in your getting behind with routine matters. Driving needs much more care. Do not speed, whether on long journeys or short ones. Do not take any silly risks behind the wheel that might get you into trouble with the law. Unexpected offers of promotion may be received. This can be a rather frustrating and disappointing day for romantic affairs. Plans that you had for future happiness are likely to be dashed by the lack of cooperation of loved ones.

25. FRIDAY. Mixed. This is not a particularly favorable day for the signing of contracts or other important documents. In fact, you want to be a bit wary of just what you are putting your signature on. Take the advice of professional legal people if you do not fully understand the small print of any documents that you are asked to study. The idea is that you will become a party to the project. Travel plans may have to be altered, if not put aside for the day altogether. Trips are not likely to work out as successfully as you would have hoped. Usually reliable people may let you down. This evening would be good for entertaining superiors at home. Plan for a small supper party or ask your boss in for a drink.

26. SATURDAY. Misleading. Trust yourself and your own judgment rather than relying too much on the advice of others. Tips that are passed on to you to gamble are not likely to bring you in the much promised returns. You should also check over your bank balance and any other holdings that you have. Perhaps the money that you have on deposit is not earning you as much interest as it could or should. Aries people will need to keep a clear head today if they are going to avoid getting bogged down in intrigue and deception. Complications can arise, in relation to accommodation or homes, which demand considerable discretion. Loved ones may not be expressing their feelings frankly.

27. SUNDAY. Misleading. Try to get more rest on this day of rest. You seem to have had quite a lot on your plate toward the end of the week that has just come to a close. Slow down a bit. Do not allow yourself to be put upon. This is a time to put your feet up and please yourself as to how you spend any spare time you might have. Discussions with partners or loved ones about the future might not be very constructive. You may not be able to get your opposite number to agree with your ideas for making additional savings. Relationships can develop into power struggles. People will keep on changing their minds and this will be extremely irritating for you. You like to have everything buttoned up.

28. MONDAY. Lucky. You can expect an excellent kick-off to the working week. You will have more energy at your disposal and this will enable you to tackle new jobs with relish. Superiors will be very helpful. You are not apt to have any problems with those who hold authority over you. Trips are likely to work out especially well. This is a starred day for Aries who are starting vacations. Trips that you make, especially if you are going abroad, are sure to be real eye-openers. There will be opportunities for mixing work with pleasure. Influential people, employers included, can be especially attentive. They will give you time off if you need it to attend to personal situations.

29. TUESDAY. Rewarding. A very good day has arrived for most people born under the sign of Aries. Love affairs are likely to advance to the marriage stage. Even more engagements will be announced. Numerous single Aries men and women will be leaving home and branching out on their own. Compatible people will be joining forces. This is also a starred day for shopping expeditions. You may be able to pick up an article for the home that you have been looking for. It might even be on sale at a reduced price. It may also be some cooking utensil or other household appliances that you require. Today will be good for all routine work and other occupational affairs.

30. WEDNESDAY. Important. There could be some break-fast-time confusion for married folk about arrangements for the day. You would be wise to check all details if you are planning to meet later. Tell your mate to allow extra time for traveling to appointments. A poor aspect for the Aries person could produce a delaying factor. Business deals can be clinched with especially good profits. Friends will be lucky for you. This is a favorable day for making moves in the direction of becoming self-employed. Aries may be given the opportunity of doing more, or even all their work, in the comfort and convenience of their own homes. Superiors are more likely to act with your long-term interests paramount in their minds.

31. THURSDAY. Mixed. Plans for vacations in distant places and for visits abroad should be set up without delay. If you have not had your summer vacation yet you should try to make any necessary reservations immediately. If you leave it any longer, you are not likely to be able to find accommodations where you want to go. As far as work is concerned, this is the right time for furthering research projects and investigative work. Employment prospects continue to look quite bright. There may be definite opportunities for improving future economic security. But overworking is neither desirable nor necessary. This is not a good day for trying to arrange a loan from a large financial institution.

SEPTEMBER

1. FRIDAY. Difficult. This would appear to be an extremely difficult day on which to start the new month of September. You will have many new jobs thrown at you. What you would prefer to be dealing with are the chores left over from August. Loved ones will be difficult and may be making emotional demands that you find rather selfish. Partners may insist on doing things their own way. That will result only in confusion and disorganization. Teamwork or cooperative efforts will require drastic changes, of course. There will not be much room for change at your place of employment. People will be less willing to honor commitments and keep their word. This could impose a hardship for you if it leaves you in the lurch.

2. SATURDAY. Uncertain. Discussions with loved ones or spouses are likely to bring you somewhat better results. Talk over the financial situation. It is important that you begin to make provisions for the heavier winter bills that you will be receiving during colder months. These will comprise a financial drain toward the end of the year. Some definite advance planning is essential. This is not a period when you should be taking a live-for-the-moment attitude to life. Self-employed Aries and those of you who work by special contract should be prepared for some slacking off, due to the current economic situation. There should be a good chance for developing more informal relationships with influential people. Take advantage of any opportunity that comes your way.

3. SUNDAY. Sensitive. This will be an auspicious day for romance. Plans for meetings with lovers and sweethearts are likely to be carried off without a hitch. You could find yourself more in love than ever before. This is a pleasant day for attending forms of entertainment that take you away from your home base. Current romantic involvements can be strengthened. Some confusion that has been giving you concern for the future should be straightened out to your satisfaction now. This could be quite a good day, too, for meetings with top brass. But they would best be carried out under informal conditions. This should also be a particularly easy-going day for the married Aries. Actions and gestures will be more important than words. Be sure that you do not leave yourself open to charges of hypocrisy!

4. MONDAY. Lucky. An excellent start to the working week is indicated. You should be able to tackle new challenges without any problems. There will be opportunities to show off your natural talents to superiors. Be firm. Act with confidence as this will be the best way to insure promotion and be delegated more responsibility. The day should be favorable for researching current projects. Aries may make some surprising discoveries or devise some time-saving devices. Bankers can be unexpectedly helpful. This is also quite a good day for attempts to secure loans to back new ventures. Success in joint financial affairs may lead to improved reputations. Business partners may feel greater confidence in sharing ventures with you.

5. TUESDAY. Useful. Taxation, insurance and all related matters should not be ignored. You should not attempt to wriggle out of your responsibilities in this particular area of your life. You will only be storing up trouble for yourself at a later date. Take the advice of professional people like accountants and lawyers. If you insist on taking a live-for-the-moment attitude, you will doubtless have a very tricky start to the winter. Pension or retirement schemes may require closer investigation. Superiors and other influential people will be particularly helpful if only you will consult them. Employers may make comments which increase the Aries' optimism about their future occupational prospects. Keep doing your job with your usual, positive approach to show you like the work and are eager to get ahead.

6. WEDNESDAY. Easygoing. There will not be much taking place today. There will be opportunities to attend to duties that have been put to one side since before the weekend. This will not be a particularly active or demanding day. It's a good period for coming to grips with hobbies that give free rein to your natural talents. Allow the artist in you to speak. Research can go quite well. An important breakthrough can be made with pet theories and projects. Circumstances permitting, this can be a good day for delving into matters in greater depth than would usually be possible. It will also be favorable for drawing up budgeting plans on the basis of recent figures showing expenditures. Take your time in calculating income versus outlays. Mistakes can be costly.

7. THURSDAY. Demanding. The people with whom you are dealing may not be straightforward. It would be best to delay signing important documents. Wait until you have had better opportunities to investigate details. Do not allow pushy associates to dictate the future to you. Stand up for your rights. Don't you allow yourself to be pushed around by self-appointed bosses now. This could set you back in your hopes to gain promotion or a position of greater trust and responsibility. This is a helpful day for obtaining the advice or assistance of professional experts and consultants. It will be good, too, for communicating with people at or from a distance. These may be business associates on an assignment or relatives who are traveling abroad.

8. FRIDAY. Confusing. Aries people may feel somewhat under the weather. The chances are your health will not be up to snuff. You are very likely to find that your work performance at your place of employment is affected. Your output will be poor because of your physical condition. Some rearrangement of schedules is likely to be necessary. It will be difficult to put all the exertion that you would like to into your activities. Routine work affairs can become a drudgery. The Aries-born who are left to cope at home are likely to be overtaken by boredom and even some mild depression. In-laws may create some trouble for you. Aries workers will have a particularly difficult time in adapting themselves to new procedures. Try to forget your resentment and decide another way will be easier.

9. SATURDAY. Disconcerting. The week comes to an end with your having a lot more to cope with in connection with your regular job than you like. You must not try to launch any new projects just now. This is not the time to get your artistic ventures off the ground. Attempts to make new business moves will also meet with stubborn opposition. People are unlikely to approve of Aries' original schemes. There seem to be plenty of desk jobs for you to cope with. You are more than likely to find such routine affairs one big yawn. Fast reflexes are important, especially when dealing with stiff competition. Domestic chores may have to be left unfinished for awhile. This may be irritating to you, but it is not a threatening situation. Just forget them for a bit.

10. SUNDAY. Important. Arrange to have off-the-cuff meetings today between yourself and influential people. They are likely to go off rather well. Try to track down associates who hold positions superior to your own. They have proved to be rather elusive all week. Use your initiative. Aries who do some home entertaining should be rather pleased with the way things go. This will be especially true if you mix business with pleasure. You should find that you are complimented on what a good host or hostess you are. You should not find that you have to spend a great deal of money to get the best that this day has to offer. Extra work that you deal with today can boost your reputation considerably. But family members may start throwing their weight around and demanding more of your time and attention.

11. MONDAY. Tricky. It is important to remain rational and not to be swayed by your emotions. Do not allow people at your place of employment to get your goat. Watch that temper of yours. People may be out to pick arguments with you just for the sake of it. It is important that you show your boss just how well you can cope under pressure. There may be difficulties in keeping up to schedule. Jobs that you had earmarked for today may take longer to get finished with than you had allowed for. Any hint of prejudice or favoritism on the part of Aries professional people can be seized upon. Competitors and enemies will be all too eager for just such a slip.

12. TUESDAY. Uncertain. Romantic affairs may have to be given second place in today's activities. It may be difficult to get loved ones to understand that it is imperative for you to give more time to your job. But this can be a favorable day for the signing of business agreements that will make the future more secure. You should still be trying harder to put more money to one side, however. Regular bills that will be coming in shortly are likely to be greater than you would have imagined. It is important to read the small print of contracts and other legal documents. There are likely to be hidden clauses that could be detrimental. Closer liaison with business partners can produce improved results. Pay attention to any health problems. Ignoring them is not a wise choice.

13. WEDNESDAY. Happy.   There do not appear to have been any great disasters in your life. So you may be feeling somewhat disappointed that you have not made the progress that you know you are capable of. This may not really be your fault as you have certainly had some difficult external conditions to cope with. Unexpected developments that have been brewing behind the scenes, unknown by you, are now likely to come to the fore. Aries can be the first to know about them. They can also be the first to take advantage of them if they are quick off the mark. This can be a pleasing and exciting day for romance. Aries will feel more secure in their relationships, and will also experience a greater freedom and independence.

14. THURSDAY. Enjoyable.   This will be still another important day. Follow up on any leads that you got yesterday. Aries will have the opportunity to be where they most like to be: in the driver's seat. Push much, much harder to get the results that you know you are capable of. You will have better chances of winning the approval and the support of superiors. Your special talents are likely to be very much in demand. This is an important day for making money for those of you who hire their services out for specific tasks. The morning can be a highly nostalgic time. Small incidents can bring up happy memories. It will be good for going ahead with home development or extension schemes. Later on, it will be favorable for entertaining intimate friends. Keep the group small and the conversation sparkling.

15. FRIDAY. Disconcerting.   Do not listen to rumors or gossip. Do not believe everything that you are told, either. It would be best to rest on your laurels and to take up a position behind the scenes. The more that you can keep your opinions to yourself at your place of employment, the better it will be. Superiors will be tricky. This is not the day to introduce new methods without getting the approval of your boss first. There is a greater risk of deception in financial matters. Even loved ones may not be above resorting to dishonesty. On checking your bank statements, you may find that you are not as well off as you thought. All in all, this can be a day of some stress. Your best bet is to sit tight and let the chips fall where they may. Then start putting things to rights.

16. SATURDAY. Tricky. Expect another day when it may be necessary not to believe everything that is said or claimed. Business competitors may be resorting to intrigue. Or they might use unfair means in their battle for improved returns or better reputations. The important thing for you today is to try to maintain any special relationship that you have with your boss. Keep all of your dealings strictly open and aboveboard. The best way to counteract the devious methods of others is to show that you do not stoop to that level. Discussions with loved ones about plans for the weekend could lead to arguments. Be sure to include your mate or partner in any outings that you may be planning. Otherwise, there is bound to be a fight and unhappiness.

17. SUNDAY. Happy. After what appears to have been a week of considerable emotional swings, you will be pleased to take a break for the weekend. This will be a pleasant, happy day. You will have better than usual opportunities for doing your own thing. Loved ones will not be so demanding. Jobs that require a certain amount of solitude can be dealt with speedily and efficiently. Facts that have been eluding you are now likely to come to light. There are some important issues that you can straighten out before you go back to the workaday routine. The morning can bring some added excitement. It will be good for attempts to gain greater financial independence. Building or repairing electrical machinery would be a good way to relax and take your mind off any worrisome problems.

18. MONDAY. Harmonious. There will be opportunities to make unexpected financial gains. Those Aries who have the chance to handle second-string jobs will be able to boost incomes. Your specialist talents will be very much in demand. All in all this will be an excellent beginning to the working week. Workloads finished ahead of deadlines can win the Aries-born substantial bonuses. Products of the earth can fetch better than expected prices in the market place. But insurance or accounting problems can rear their ugly heads. This is a favorable day for strengthening current romantic involvements. Loved ones will show more caring and affection. If you reciprocate their feelings, be sure to make that clear.

19. TUESDAY. Manageable. This will be a pleasant, if not very exciting day. You should rely on yourself more than others to make any progress at work. Associates are likely to be enjoying a somewhat lethargic mood and it will therefore be difficult for you to get them to join you in making any team effort. Employers may grant pay raises, but these are only likely to be on a small scale. Do not ask for any special favors to be granted, though. The more that you can show that you are keen to get ahead, the better. Show that you will even work late or through the lunch hour. The more you do, the more it will improve your standing in the eyes of those who matter. Aries professional people can become acknowledged leaders in their fields, with consequent benefits to income. Leave yourself some time for socializing. Life should not be all work.

20. WEDNESDAY. Rewarding. Now you can afford to pull out all the stops. Go for what you really want! Grab at any chances you get to show off your talents. To date, you have not had the opportunity to parade them in front of influential people. Journeys are likely to have a successful outcome for you. Trips that you make in order to do any buying or selling should be an unqualified success. There are not likely to be any problems in your personal life. Romantic involvements will bring you pleasure and satisfaction. Interesting new attractions can be formed with people met through work or business. Bankers will tend to be more sympathetic and friendly than they usually are. Take advantage of this.

21. THURSDAY. Tricky. Plans are quite likely to receive a setback today. Schemes that you were keen to put into operation are likely to be delayed through no fault of your own. Unfortunately, you seem to have to rely rather heavily on other people when dealing with speculative propositions. Some of the people are not likely to be true to their word. Aries may be late to work, due to no fault of their own. But superiors, pressed for time, are likely to be angry, nonetheless. Health may be somewhat below par. It would be easy to overdo. Nerves will be on edge. Emotions will be very close to the surface. Employers may separate Aries-born people from their favorite workmates.

22. FRIDAY. Sensitive. There will be plenty to keep you meaningfully occupied today. None of it, unfortunately, will be the sort of work that could bring you a great deal of money. There will be a number of incidentals in connection with income tax and insurance matters. You may have to go over your accounts once again. There is a chance that income tax inspectors will want more details of your accounts. It will be especially true if you have been submitting rather large claims for expenses. Property moves may suffer severe setbacks, but a stroke of good luck can pull Aries through. Nothing should be done to lay the harmful foundation for future misunderstandings with romantic companions.

23. SATURDAY. Difficult. This will be a very tricky day on which to end the week. People and circumstances appear to be conspiring against you. There seem to be so many jobs that you were hoping to complete before you took a break from the office or store. But they will have to be left to one side until after the weekend. This is a better day for tackling odd jobs around the home than it is for going out to earn a few dollars. Partners and spouses will be quite sensitive. They will tend to take offense at words that were spoken in all innocence. Romantic affairs may be going through a period of major upheavals. Hidden feelings of resentment will start to come to the surface. Driving needs more care, especially late at night. Cut down on speed and give other drivers plenty of room.

24. SUNDAY. Mixed. Try to overcome minor ailments that have been slowing down your progress at work. Do what you can to put yourself into better shape physically. A new diet or a keep-fit course may be the answer. Exercise more self-discipline. Do not succumb to minor whims or fancies. It will be a good opportunity for creative and artistic work. The day will also be favorable for family excursions made primarily for the benefit of children. You will have better luck if you are trying to get closer to members of the younger generation. Accidental encounters with influential or important people can produce interesting results. But it is important not to impose on such people as they are likely to value their privacy.

25. MONDAY. Deceptive. Don't take any risks with your money today, or any time. This day warns against taking gambles of any kind. Try to avoid people who bring out the reckless and live-for-the-moment side of your nature. You will probably find that you operate best when dealing with people older than yourself. If you get involved in any sort of speculation, you and your bank account are most likely to wind up the losers. Deals with people in the entertainment or theatrical business are likely to fall through. This is not a day for branching out in an entirely new direction, as far as your career is concerned. There will be less time for furthering hobbies and artistic endeavors. But as long as you don't abandon them you can go back to them later.

26. TUESDAY. Favorable. The next couple of days look promising. Be sure that you make the most of the excellent opportunities that are likely to present themselves. This is the beginning of a particularly favorable few days for routine work and occupational affairs. The self-employed Aries person may be in a position to make an important breakthrough. You might be able to win a lucrative contract that makes you more self-sufficient. Superiors could grant a promotion out of the blue. Personal problems that have been hanging you up are likely to resolve themselves in a most surprising manner. Physical ailments may disappear. But don't risk going without a checkup.

27. WEDNESDAY. Important. Use this as a follow-up day. Carry on with whatever projects you began yesterday. It will be far easier to win the support of influential people who are in a position to offer you financial backing. Do all that you can to bring your natural talents to the notice of the boss. Family members may win substantial pay raises. This will certainly mean that you will not feel as responsible for others as has been the case. Loved ones who have been going through a rough stretch will be better able to stand on their own two feet. Aries themselves may be able to finish heavy workloads ahead of schedule. You will have more driving force. It looks as though romance will be much more promising, too. It might be a good time for delving into the esoteric or occult.

28. THURSDAY. Excellent. This would appear to be another first-class day. You should be very well pleased with the progress that you have made. You may now be in a position to settle a long-outstanding debt. It has been hanging over your head for some considerable time. You will be relieved to get rid of account work. Write any letters that are overdue to friends or family who are living abroad. The day will be good for shopping expeditions and for bulk buying. It will also be favorable for buying new pets; good, too, for attending routine medical checkups. Take advantage of the day to do all work that requires attention to minor details and special concentration.

29. FRIDAY. Difficult. It looks as though you have been having things fairly much your own way for the past two or three days. But all that is likely to change now. The difficult conditions that you are likely to encounter today will account for it. Watch your step at your place of employment. Although you mean well, suggestions that you make to colleagues as to how work should be handled could be considered as interfering. Aries may be forced to compromise against their will. There will be less latitude for implementing personal plans. Legal problems, if left unattended, can develop into something serious. It may be necessary to introduce tighter discipline into domestic and home affairs.

30. SATURDAY. Worrisome. Expect another worrying day. There seems to be so much that you want to handle before the week and the month come to a close. However, this is a period when more haste would definitely mean less speed. Do not be in too much of a hurry when attending to accounts and the payment of bills. Errors made now could prove to be most costly at a later date. Brushes with the authorities should be avoided if at all possible. Aries may be held responsible for actions of which they are innocent. Or, they did not know such actions to be controversial or against the law. Official permission for new business ventures may be refused. This is not a favorable day for instituting litigation proceedings. Wait until next week.

OCTOBER

1. SUNDAY. Demanding. Do not try to pressure other members of the family. Take more of a live-and-let-live attitude toward life. Loved ones will have very set ideas about the way they wish to spend their leisure time today. These may not coincide with your own plans. You may find yourself mixing more with friends than with relatives. You could have reason to believe that certain household members are not telling you the truth about recent happenings. Even if such people are being obviously dishonest it is best not to question their integrity. Marital and partnership affairs need handling with tact and discretion. Arguments can easily develop into long-lasting quarrels. The best solution would be to avoid arguing.

2. MONDAY. Difficult. The atmosphere within your own four walls will continue to be very sensitive. Arguments will erupt over minor matters. This is a better day for employment affairs than it is for attempts to sort out the more personal issues. Secretly conducted investigations can yield interesting results. Family members may receive tax rebates which will help toward maintaining domestic funds. See what you can do to put more money to one side to meet the heavier winter bills that will be coming in very shortly. Influential people will be difficult and uncooperative. They can be even more unpleasant if they appear to offer assistance, but are merely bluffing. Try to avoid such people.

3. TUESDAY. Exciting. It looks as though you will be taking a much more optimistic attitude toward life. There will be opportunities for making money by resorting to activities that have nothing to do with your regular job. Friends may come up with some useful ideas for putting more money in your pocket. You may have the chance to make use of talents that not many people know about. Today will be favorable for getting people to reveal their feelings rather than your beating about the bush with questions. This is a good day to find out if a new romance has the chance of becoming something permanent and meaningful. Aries' personal magnetism can be especially strong. It can work in ways that will be a surprise even to you. Try it out in different situations.

4. WEDNESDAY. Mixed. This is an important day for discussing future employment affairs with superiors. But it is advisable not to be too pushy with your boss. Influential people may be a little bit vague just now. They may not have all the answers to the questions that you are putting to them. The day is also first-class for getting on closer terms with co-workers. Do what you can do speed up routine affairs by promoting team effort. But such cooperation is only likely to work with day-to-day jobs. It will not necessarily be so successful when attempts are made to make progress with artistic endeavors. It could be a pleasant evening for socializing. The company you will be mixing in will be more exciting than your usual group. They may be from out of town.

5. THURSDAY. Easygoing. You will have a chance to take a breather today. Make use of the opportunity that the quiet conditions offer you today to assess your chances of promotion at your place of employment. You will have the chance to go back over routine work. You may not have been entirely happy with it when it was done. Now you can make good any errors before your work comes to the notice of superiors. The day is excellent for all letter writing, as well as attention to accounts. You will have more chances to attend to personal issues. You may even be able to take some time off from your job to do a bit of travel. It might be in connection with the affairs of older relatives. It is important to rise above petty emotional and practical difficulties.

6. FRIDAY. Tricky. Communicating with people at a distance can lead to problems. Aries need to concentrate on one thing at a time. It is essential if they are going to produce the sort of results of which they are capable. Do not set out on trips to see influential people on chance. This is a day when you need to plan your activities every step of the way. It is necessary if you are going to make any progress at all. This is not a particularly favorable day for making journeys to straighten out personal issues, either. You might be better off attending to matters nearer to home. Problems can arise in the handling of new office machinery. Important advance planning would be best postponed, at least until you can ascertain some basic facts.

7. SATURDAY. Difficult.   This has not been an easy week during which to start the month. And this will not be the day you will be likely to see any great improvement in your fortunes. There seem to be a number of problems connected with your personal life that you have not been able to resolve satisfactorily. You must be sure that you do not allow difficulties connected with romance to affect your performance at your place of employment. Influential people may have noticed a change in your attitude and your attention span. It could be far more than you may realize. Nothing should be done that might endanger business reputations. It is best to avoid mixing with people of dubious repute. Family members should not be neglected or taken for granted.

8. SUNDAY. Important.   You will feel that some heavy burden has been lifted from your shoulders. You will be much more optimistic about the future and what it holds for you and yours. The chances are that you will find a way out of a personal difficulty that has been taking up a lot of your time. This is the right day to lay your cards on the table and speak your mind. Talk to the person who has been putting a drain and a strain on your emotions. Trips in the locality will be helpful for Aries. They may be able to pick up some useful information that will be a help to them when it comes to promoting artistic endeavors. This should be a good day for discussing career and professional matters with the well-informed. Don't pass up any opportunity.

9. MONDAY. Rewarding.   You are in for what would appear to be a promising couple of days. You should be sure to make the best of the opportunities that present themselves. You should be feeling much more confident and determined about the future now. It looks as if you were able to iron out one or two important issues over the weekend. This is a first-class day for Aries who are taking up positions with overseas firms. Any new challenges that arise will be exciting and stimulating. Today will be favorable for attempts to boost business profits. It would be a good time, too, for making an effort to reduce unnecessary overheads. Put more exertion into furthering humanitarian or philanthropic ventures. Interest friends and business colleagues in joining organizations to help with office work.

10. TUESDAY. Enjoyable. The morning can be particularly favorable for the handling of legal matters. Influential people will be more cooperative and willing to give advice. This is quite a good day for asking the boss to grant favors. You may well have some important issues that you wish to straighten out with a lawyer or accountant. If so, you should be able to get some time off during a slack period at the office or store. It's good for obtaining official clearance for business financial ventures. Friends may be able to provide valuable introductions to people in positions of power and authority. Evening will bring some unexpected but pleasant surprises. There may be an unexpected invitation, or an old friend might come to see you.

11. WEDNESDAY. Manageable. This should be a pleasant enough day. But you will not, perhaps, have the opportunity to make quite as much progress as you would have liked to. You were able to keep up much more during the first three days of this week. Try to get ahead at a calm and steady pace. This is not the sort of a day when you are likely to achieve spectacular results. Favorable for resorting to more indirect and subtle methods in the handling of routine business and career affairs. Do not ask the boss for favors outright. Just drop one or two hints about what your hopes are for the future. Discretion can be all-important. If you spread news around of your good fortune, it will probably come to an abrupt end.

12. THURSDAY. Demanding. You may receive a letter or telephone call early on in the day. Either one could be a little upsetting for you. You may get the feeling that you are being pressured. This is something that the Ram certainly does not take kindly to. When dealing with new jobs at work, it is best not to rush them. Be sure that you follow any instructions given to you by superiors to the letter. If you don't, you will be hard pressed to find good excuses for the errors that you are likely to make. Aries can benefit from some extra time spent in comparative privacy and seclusion. Reviewing the recent past may help you spot major errors. You would thus avoid repeating the same mistakes in the future.

13. FRIDAY. Disconcerting. Don't allow feelings of superstition to depress you too much. Although this is a day that many consider unlucky, you are not likely to find that any great ill luck befalls you. More time should be given to straightening out day-to-day jobs. Try to catch up with routine matters that you do not want to have hanging over your head during the weekend. Partners can make a show of force in any confrontations. You may find that you have to spend rather more time dealing with sensitive domestic issues than you had bargained for. This is not a day for banging your head against a brick wall. Knowing when to admit defeat can be the equivalent of wisdom.

14. SATURDAY. Tricky. Health may not be up to par. This will be an upsetting day for Aries. They were hoping to involve themselves in sporting or any other energetic activities in which they would have to use quite a lot of physical strength. They will probably feel it wise to withdraw from team events. Do not go against your intuition today, especially where your health is concerned. It would not make sense to jeopardize it for the sake of some strenuous activities. However, the day is favorable for forming new romantic liaisons. Routine business transactions should be handled with more care than usual as there is a greater risk of deception. Brushes with the law can have unfortunate consequences. The police are most unlikely to bend the rules.

15. SUNDAY. Enjoyable. Some excellent progress can be made with painting and decorating jobs in and around the home. You will have good opportunities to save money today. Be more of the handyman. Attempts that you make to promote teamwork will be more successful than has been the case recently. You and your mate or partner are likely to be able to reach agreement faster on matters of mutual concern. This has been a stumbling block over the past few days. Do all that you can to strengthen relationships that mean a lot to you. There should be a good chance for getting out of the domestic environment sometime during the day. You could visit relatives and old acquaintances who live within reasonable distances.

16. MONDAY. Easygoing. There will be an easygoing start to the working week. You are not likely to find that any new pressure is exerted on you. This applies to your home as well as your place of work or business. Your relationship with your opposite number is likely to be pleasant. Now is the time to sit down with other interested parties and work out a budget. Your goal is one that will enable you to make extra savings. Although it is still quite a few weeks away, you should be attempting to put more money aside for Christmas. Aries should be able to handle affairs at their own pace without being rushed or pressured. The Ram should try not to become too materialistic in his or her attitude. This is something that would be very easy to do.

17. TUESDAY. Difficult. New contacts would be particularly useful to you. You appear to have run out of ideas for promoting your artistic talents. It would be a good idea to try new people. You should not allow yourself to get in too much of a rut. Friends may be able to put you in touch with professional people who would undoubtedly be very enthusiastic about your creative abilities. The important thing is that you do not stand still. This is a good time for outings with partners and loved ones. Give your opposite number a special treat. It should not be necessary to spend a lot of money in order to have a good time today. Signing of formal agreements will be successful. But it will be difficult for you to reach agreement with older relatives over future plans. You may find some difficulty in nodding off to sleep.

18. WEDNESDAY. Misleading. You need to be on the alert today. Someone may be out to pull the wool over your eyes. Do not part with money to back ventures that you have not had the opportunity to look into thoroughly yet. This is a favorable day for getting out and about more in connection with your work. Those of you with show-business connections should make more of an effort to be seen in the right places with the right people. Collaboration over major projects can produce particularly good and rapid results. But people can be keener to conceal their intentions. If Aries resort to guesswork, they may well make some fundamental errors. Why risk putting yourself on the line? Don't go out on a limb for no good reason.

19. THURSDAY. Disappointing. You may be a little disappointed that you have not really made the amount of progress that you had been hoping for this week. Do not allow yourself to get too down in the dumps. Be more practical and realistic. Think in terms of what it is possible to achieve; don't be such a daydreamer. You must not allow your personal life to infringe on your work. Influential people will not grant favors if they feel that you have not been giving one hundred percent. Professional activities are likely to take up a lot of this day and may not earn you very much money. Property affairs can be complicated by major setbacks or delays. It is wise, however, to iron out all the details to everyone's satisfaction before committing yourself.

20. FRIDAY. Satisfactory. Valuable objects should be kept in places where they cannot be damaged. If you are assuming responsibility for other people's possessions, it might be wise to take out some insurance on these, just to be on the safe side. The day will favor making bold attempts to further joint financial ventures. Do what you can to reach agreement with people with whom you are involved in any kind of partnership deals. Handling property on behalf of others should produce good results. Readers who are in the real estate business should be able to increase profits to a considerable degree. Introductions to people who come from a distance could lead to the forming of new romantic attractions. Some of these could even lead to a more permanent relationship.

21. SATURDAY. Disturbing. Aries may be forced to do what they dislike doing most. They know very well that no personal benefit is likely to come from it. You are probably going to have to give a good deal of your time over to catering to the whims and fancies of others. Older relatives may be making extra demands on your time. You find, of course, that it is extremely difficult to refuse. You may feel that you have little choice as to how you fill in your leisure time. Youngsters will also be making demands on the Aries parent. It will be difficult to control your temper. Nerves are likely to become frayed and on edge. This will be a difficult day, with personal morale and incentive both low.

22. SUNDAY. Happy. It is well worth your while to make a determined effort to overcome problems. Specifically, these are connected with creative or artistic pursuits. You should devote more time to promoting your natural talents. You may have the chance to show your best side in a favorable light to influential people whom you meet socially. The rewards of your endeavors are likely to be well worth the extra effort involved. Today will be favorable for dreaming up late vacation plans with loved ones. It will be good for making arrangements to get a bit of sun before Christmas. This is also the right time for attempts to get closer to youngsters. This will be a pleasant day for romance. Your love life looks more interesting now than has been the case in recent weeks.

23. MONDAY. Challenging. At last you will feel that the shackles are off you. You will have greater opportunities to work out a plan of campaign that appeals to you. Influential people will not be laying down the law quite so frequently. Knuckle down to some serious work. It may be possible to be more artistic with projects that have become a little routine. You will find that the possibility of increasing your earnings by a considerable degree will be an added incentive for working overtime. Superiors will be watching your progress very carefully. This makes it particularly important for you to maintain a high standard of efficiency. Go all-out to do an impressive job. Prove that you are a reliable and dedicated worker who wants to achieve.

24. TUESDAY. Important. Influential people will make reassuring comments regarding future employment prospects and economic security. Today will be good for research projects. This is also an important day for any Aries who are taking examinations shortly. You will find it much easier to concentrate and retain important knowledge. This is a favorable day, too, for handing over certain responsibilities to trustworthy employees. Bosses born under your sign should be able to give themselves more time to deal with whatever they consider essential. Perseverance in routine work affairs can lead steadily toward almost inevitable promotion for Aries workers. Keep this in mind, especially if you wonder sometimes how you are doing.

25. WEDNESDAY. Mixed. You may have to slow down a bit for awhile. Think it over before you make any moves that would entail your dipping into your reserves. Don't be in too great a hurry to back speculative ventures. You will regret it if you throw your hard-earned money around. The urge to gamble will be strong, but it would best be resisted. Personal health, or that of loved ones, may not be all that it should. Your physical condition could be somewhat below par. It might be a good idea to call in on your doctor for a checkup before minor ailments turn into something more serious. Aries people may have less time to devote to their pastimes. You are likely to resent this because you enjoy doing what gives you peace of mind.

26. THURSDAY. Frustrating. Influential people may not live up to the promises made to you yesterday. You should not build your hopes around agreements that have only been reached casually. New contracts may not be signed on time. In many ways you will find this is a somewhat frustrating day. It may be necessary to treat loved ones with almost exaggerated respect in order to avoid wounding their feelings. In teamwork or cooperative endeavors, it may be necessary to change course in midstream. It is impossible to plan too far ahead. Overexcitement can lead to impaired reflexes. You must try to be calm and not give way to sudden outbursts. Do not take on anything that might be too taxing.

27. FRIDAY. Disturbing. It is best to end legal problems as fast as you can. Letting them drift along in the hope that they will straighten themselves out of their own accord is not realistic. You should make more of an effort to face up to your responsibilities. If you allow matters to drift on they would probably develop into something more serious. People who live with you or are in the same building as Aries may act foolishly or irresponsibly. It may be they are objecting to a raise in rent and are unwilling to pay their share. This could leave you responsible and liable for legal action. You will have to move fast and find a new roommate or pay a lot more money. Do not be intimidated; stand your ground.

28. SATURDAY. Mixed. It may be necessary to commit an act of faith. You do not particularly like this role one bit. But you may have to let others take responsibility for you in some way or other, at least temporarily. Perhaps you have rather a lot more to do than usual. It may be necessary to make a journey in connection with your work. Other people at your place of regular employment can insist on taking the initiative and having things their way. Resistance or complaints are likely to be futile. This would appear to be a more promising period for Aries who are able to deal with home and family affairs. They can remain on the spot rather than having to go out to earn a living. This will be a good day for shoppers and bargain hunters as well as favorable for bulk buying.

29. SUNDAY. Important. You should have better opportunities for taking control of your own destiny. People generally will not be so pushy or demanding. Loved ones will show a greater willingness to fall in with any schemes that you have for making changes in and around the home. It will be a good day for decorating and for being more of a handyman in general. Youngsters will be a source of joy to the Aries parent. You should be able to get closer to members of the younger generation for whom you have some responsibility. Today is favorable for drawing together the results of research work. You compiled this for submission to influential people after the weekend is over.

30. MONDAY. Lucky. Negotiations should go well for you upon return to work. This is the right time to make overtures to large business corporations. Projects that you have been working on for some time have a greater chance of becoming successful. Act with confidence. You have every reason to be more optimistic about the future now. The day is good for backup investigations into current business transactions. Your thinking can be sharp. Its ability to reach the heart of the matter is most astonishing. Favorable for discussing joint financial matters with other interested parties. Look for ways to make economies that will leave you more money in your bank account. Desk jobs and letter writing, together with minor accounting chores, are all favored today.

31. TUESDAY. Quiet. This will be just the sort of day that you want to end the month on. You will not have any new pressures to contend with. This is not a day when you should be attempting to make any new starts. Artistic projects that you have been working hard on should be left in abeyance until the month of November. You will be feeling more optimistic about the future after what has taken place over the last couple of days. Recent doubts and fears should be disappearing. Aries should be clearer about just where they stand and where they are heading. It will be good for drawing up tentative plans for the next few weeks and months. Attempts at increasing work efficiency through the introduction of time-saving devices will have favorable results.

NOVEMBER

1. WEDNESDAY. Rewarding. With plenty of energy at your disposal now, you will be keen to get ahead with money-making plans. You will certainly wish to make a concerted effort to boost your income, knowing about all the additional expenses that winter brings. Remember, too, that Christmas is only just around the corner. For those of you with children in the house, you are going to have quite a large additional outlay. This is a favorable period for taking your time to develop new interests. It would also be good for drawing up tentative plans for the future. Influential people can be particularly helpful. This will be especially true with regard to business or joint financial affairs. It will be easier to arrange loans for a long-term period with a comparatively low interest rate.

2. THURSDAY. Lucky. This is still another promising day. You should certainly be feeling pleased about the way the new month has started for you. Self-improvement or academic pursuits can lead to the forming of new romantic attractions. Aries people who are at a university or some other institution for further education should find that work and pleasure mix together rather well. You will have no difficulty in retaining knowledge that will be of value to you when your time comes for taking examinations. It will be good for putting more exertion into furthering cooperative and teamwork endeavors. Legal problems will be more easily overcome. They were probably of relatively minor importance in the first place.

3. FRIDAY. Productive. Nothing of any great importance is apt to go wrong for you today. In fact, this Friday is likely to prove itself a rather anticlimactic day. You may not be able to continue making the same progress you have made on the first two days. Your self-improvement endeavors are likely to suffer a severe setback. Today is good for presenting the results of work that you completed last week, though. Superiors may have one or two reservations. But, in the main, they will like what you have been doing. It's favorable for initiating negotiations about acquisitions with heads of large business firms or companies. But routine affairs can be delayed through errors and miscalculations.

4. SATURDAY. Slow. Not much of importance will be taking place today. You will be pleased that you have greater control over your actions. Go over any accounts that still need to be brought up to date from October. It is essential that you get an exact picture of your financial standing. Bills that you know will be coming in for heating, etc., are likely to be higher than the last quarter's. You should therefore budget accordingly. Aries who are keen to further or to implement personal schemes are likely to be disappointed. The necessary impetus for getting major new ventures off the ground is likely to be lacking. Without it, don't waste valuable time trying. It would be akin to pushing water uphill.

5. SUNDAY. Manageable. Friends can be a downright nuisance! This is one of those Sundays when you would prefer to spend more time with family members. This pertains especially if you have been giving rather a lot of attention to your career over the last few days. Unexpected callers to your home are likely to disrupt the peace and quiet. People will not take hints. You may have to be somewhat curt if you want to get your message across. It is simply that you want to be left alone with your nearest and dearest. You feel that it is a nerve when people try to abuse intimacy. This is a day when Aries will be more perceptive and discriminating than ever. It will also be a good day for attending to minor routine matters.

6. MONDAY. Difficult. There will probably be some rush jobs that you suddenly, and quite unexpectedly, have to give your attention to. Routine matters will have to take a backseat during the morning period. Superiors will be unpredictable and will seem to have very little regard for all that you have achieved. You will have to be alert and on your toes at all times. All in all, this is likely to be rather a difficult beginning to the working week. It will be unfortunate for you if you rub influential people the wrong way. The hope of getting any special favors granted by employers appears to be a distant dream at the moment. Try to come up with some unusual way to speed up routine jobs. If you can save time and money, you will get attention.

7. TUESDAY. Changeable.   Mixed trends are indicated for today. This will be a period when you can make certain progress on the job. However, spectacular results would not appear to be within your reach. Do what you can to promote team effort. Try to get the support of your colleagues for speeding up the handling of daily duties. These do not offer the possibility of earning you any extra money. It will be a good time for unearthing plots and dealing openly with troublemakers. You may be able to get to the bottom of who has been spreading nasty rumors about you. Later on, it will be favorable for deepening and strengthening current romantic relationships. This should give you a lot of pleasure.

8. WEDNESDAY. Satisfactory.   As long as you avoid confrontation with people in authority, you are not likely to have any major problems to deal with. But power struggles with people who have power over you, in some way, will be doomed from the start. This is a good day for the use of secrecy and diplomacy in all affairs, both private and public. A more subtle approach to people will be especially effective. Today would be good for furthering property transactions. If you have been thinking of moving, this is an opportune day for putting your house on the market. Major financial negotiations would be best postponed. Unless you have full confidence of their total success, back off for now.

9. THURSDAY. Tricky.   You will be strangely restless today. No sooner will you have settled down to a job than you will find that your mind is wandering. This is especially true for those Aries-born readers who have desk work to attend to. Be sure that you do not allow your mind to wander when going over accounts. Mistakes that you make now will not be easy to rectify at a later date. It will be easy to act in a way that alienates other people. Rams should try harder to moderate the brash side of their nature. They should do nothing to offend other people's sensitivities. They can do it easily and without having the least idea that they are.

10. FRIDAY. Mixed. Romantic affairs seem to be going through a difficult period. Aries-born who have been going steady for some time may come to a crossroads. You may have to make a decision about the future. Loved ones may be forcing you to take a definite stance. It is best not to strain the credulity of people. They may challenge the integrity of Aries at an embarrassing and sensitive moment. All business and professional transactions should be kept well documented and aboveboard. Be sure that you keep a clear record of where other people's money has gone. You have had some sort of responsibility for this recently. Bankers will be helpful with the advice that they give. If you can, try to act on it.

11. SATURDAY. Productive. The past week does not appear to have been a particularly inspirational kind. You should be able to get going now that it is coming to a close. You can probably achieve quite a lot of what you have been forced to hold back on. The most important factor about today's activities is the fact that you will have a better chance of getting teamwork off the launching pad. Associates at your place of employment will agree with much of what you want to do. You can unexpectedly catch up on jobs that you thought you might have to leave until after the weekend. This can be a particularly favorable day for major breakthroughs. This will be good news.

12. SUNDAY. Fair. This should be a good day for devising shortcuts to reduce the time that you normally spend on dealing with domestic duties. This is an important period for doing what you can to strengthen personal ties and relationships. It will be a favorable day for romance. You and your mate or partner will be able to have some frank discussions. These will make life a lot easier for both of you. It will be possible to voice openly doubts and fears that you have been keeping to yourself. Aries-born who are without a steady date at the moment may have the opportunity to form new and exciting attractions. Loved ones will show considerable insight into the professional or career affairs of the Ram.

13. MONDAY. Difficult. You will have to be very careful about making any changes in the way you deal with routine matters today. You may have devised some shortcuts for handling tasks that have become rather boring and commonplace. But you had better explain them to your boss before you put them into practice. Anything that you do strictly on your own is not likely to have a successful outcome. Do not overstep the authority that has been entrusted to you. Aries people will need to keep a clear head today. A vague or impractical attitude to finances can spell major troubles ahead. There is a greater risk of deception than usual in business, as well as in public affairs.

14. TUESDAY. Disturbing. Old enemies may resort to underhand methods in attempts to get even. You want to be more careful than ever about whom you trust or confide in. Health needs protecting. You may not be feeling up to snuff. Be sure that your diet is giving you all the nutrients that your mind and body need. It might be a good idea to pay a visit to your doctor if minor ailments have not been clearing up of their own accord. Major property moves or real estate transactions are best postponed. There are too many unknown factors to make it wise or safe to continue negotiations. Problems can arise in connection with home or accommodations for those who do not own the home in which they live.

15. WEDNESDAY. Disconcerting. You are likely to be brought down to earth with a mighty bump today. Perhaps you had been pinning your hopes on some promise about money that had been made to you verbally. People are likely to forget conveniently about giving their word to you. You could find yourself short of cash as a result. You may be in an embarrassing position about the payment of a bill. Perhaps you will have to borrow from Peter to pay Paul. Aries business people may have to reopen old cases, getting behind schedule as a result. This is another sensitive day for property and home affairs. Unexpected developments can complicate the most seemingly simple projects.

16. THURSDAY. Mixed. Aries can have a stroke of good luck today. It will assist them in affairs related to home and property. Be more of a handyman. Do odd jobs yourself. You should be able to cut down on expenses considerably by making some effort to deal with the easier ones yourself. You should be able to rely on the support and backing of your nearest and dearest when it comes to making major changes in the home. But at your place of employment, other people can be slow off the mark, possibly frustratingly so. Bankers may be helpful in arranging a loan that will ease your immediate financial problems. This will be a sensitive day for romance.

17. FRIDAY. Rewarding. This would be an opportune day for starting a course of keeping-fit classes. You may have been putting on a bit of weight of late. But you should find now that you have the necessary discipline to take yourself in hand and do something realistic about it. This is a promising day for those Rams who are involved in buying and selling. This might be a good day for trips to see influential people and to win them over. You should be more successful today if you are appealing to your boss for any kind of assistance. Entertaining at home is recommended for the evening. It will be favorable, too, for joint financial negotiations and transactions.

18. SATURDAY. Demanding.   Bring any insurance policies up to date. Make sure that you are covered where it counts. You may have to dip into your reserves to pay regular bills. But you must not put off till tomorrow what you know you should be dealing with right now. Aries may have their all too few hours of rest and relaxation rudely interrupted. Pleasure and entertainment plans can be turned upside down. Children may become quite a handful. This is not a day for taking gambles of any kind: financial, romantic or otherwise. Creative and artistic work will require a lot more patience. You are probably distracted, so cannot focus necessary attention on what you're doing.

19. SUNDAY. Manageable.   This will be a pleasant enough day as long as you are not expecting too much. Do not aim your sights too high. More time should be spent nearer home than in galavanting around. If you are seeking pleasure and entertainment, they could cause you to dig deep into your pocket. Get ahead with home improvement and extension of space schemes. Use your leisure time as constructively as possible. Do all that you can to put an end to silly family feuds. Try harder to rise above silly squabbles. Today would be good for pursuing secret investigations. Later in the day, you should keep more aware of what your children or others' are doing.

20. MONDAY. Useful.   This can be an excellent day for all routine matters. Housewives and mothers among you should be able to catch up with household chores and duties. There will not be a great deal happening within the home. So you will be quite pleased to have a bit of time on your own to do as you wish. Readers who have to go out to earn a living will not have any major problems to contend with, either. Ambitious Aries people may seize an opportunity to discuss the possibility of promotion with their boss. Their goal would be sometime early in the New Year. You may have some trouble following instructions for the operation of machinery and other equipment.

21. TUESDAY. Important.   With plenty of energy at your disposal, you have a good opportunity to make real progress in your career. Aries-born people will have the chance to take the lead. It will give you a good opportunity for getting team effort going. Other people at your place of employment will show a greater willingness to sit up and listen to what you have to say. This will be a fairly pleasant day. You will, in all likelihood, be able to please yourself as to how you fill in your time. There will be time for Aries readers to search the shops for things at reduced prices. Even mundane and repetitious chores will be more pleasure to perform. Promote a more attractive public image.

22. WEDNESDAY. Mixed.   There will be a good chance of your obtaining professional advice or assistance. If you have been worrying about the threat of legal action, you should seek some advice from a lawyer. You may discover that the people who have been making a lot of noise about taking you to court would not have a leg to stand on in the eyes of the law. You must do more to protect yourself and your reputation, however. Do not take defeat lying down. In litigation proceedings it is advisable to be well represented. Obtaining official clearance for partnership affairs would be a good bet today. Business colleagues may fail to report any misunderstandings relating to important instructions.

23. THURSDAY. Uncertain.   There will be a good opportunity for communicating with people at a distance. Valuable information can be obtained. This is not a particularly good day for undertaking long journeys in person. It might be smarter to make better use of the telephone and express mail service. Or, alternatively, you could send a representative on your behalf. Any trips that are made from your place of employment would be best left to colleagues or partners. The day is favorable for reading and for catching up on your studies. You are not likely to have to rush any of your duties. Scandal or gossip should be avoided, as this could affect your reputation adversely.

24. FRIDAY. Inactive.   This is likely to be a fairly inactive and undemanding day. Neither will you be apt to find yourself put under any additional pressure, either at home or at your place of work or business. Your relationship with the people with whom you have to spend quite a lot of time with should be greatly improved. But Aries will have fewer opportunities of getting their own way or furthering their own interests. Compromises may be called for when dealing with older relatives. This may be necessary to maintain the peace and a semblance, at least, of goodwill. It is important to understand the feelings of partners and not neglect them. If you work together, show concern for their cares.

25. SATURDAY. Fortunate. Today winds up an excellent week that you should be able to look back upon with a certain amount of satisfaction. You certainly seem to have achieved much of what you set out to accomplish. There will be good opportunities to round off outstanding jobs. You will also have a chance to devote more time to the desires of your nearest and dearest. This is a favorable period for exploring new opportunities for expansion and self-development. Aries may derive considerable pleasure, as well as success, from trying their hand at something unusual and possibly conventional. Conditions within your own home will be more positive in general.

26. SUNDAY. Uncertain. This can be a rough-and-tumble day. The Aries-born may have to defend themselves against challenges from the most unlikely of quarters. People may try to outwit you at your own game. This is not a time when you should be taking risks of any sort, but most especially not with money. Keep a check on your finances. You should be seeking ways to put more cash to one side for Christmas. Power struggles within the family can turn out to be more serious than they first appear. You and your opposite number will have difficulty in seeing eye-to-eye on any number of issues. But genuine love and affection can overcome obstacles.

27. MONDAY. Demanding. The chances are that you will be lacking energy. You do not appear to have the necessary driving force to get anything new going at your place of employment. Aries-born people with very young children are likely to be driven to distraction by the demands that are made. All in all, this will be a somewhat disconcerting period for the Ram. Power struggles that have been brewing under the surface for some time are now likely to reach their peak. Other people may try stealing from Aries' own armory in order to equip and defend themselves. Joint financial problems should not be minimized, but it is also important not to overreact. The day is favorable for bulk buying.

28. TUESDAY. Exciting. There is likely to be a complete reversal of yesterday's somewhat dismal trends. A letter or telephone call that you receive will cheer you up considerably. This is an excellent period for Aries who are involved in the arts in any way. Your natural talents are likely to be much in demand. You should be able to demand quite a high price in order to exhibit them. All in all, your outlook on life will be more optimistic. Teachers can praise the endeavors of the Aries student. Success in examinations is more than likely. Publishers will be particularly helpful and will be more receptive than usual to accepting manuscripts. You may be able to benefit from their assistance.

29. WEDNESDAY. Easygoing. Children and their problems should not be neglected. It will pay you to exert extra effort to win the confidence of a child. But do not assume that because tears are stopped the problem, whatever it is, is resolved. Old patterns are likely to repeat themselves. It is a good day for broadening personal outlooks and tolerances. This will bring greater understanding and contentment. The day favors taking up new interests, possibly of an academic nature. In-laws can be helpful and may assist you in overcoming a marital problem. There will be a good chance for making inquiries about necessary visas for travel to distant places. This information may be for your own benefit.

30. THURSDAY. Disturbing. Do a lot more to build up your estate. Get involved in a savings or investment plan encompassing land or buildings. Do not allow money to lie idly in the bank. Make it work harder for you. Routine business transactions may have been going through a stormy time, with sudden, possibly alarming, fluctuations in success and financial returns. Any financial moves aimed at long-term returns require great caution. You may not be as bright as you think in assessing situations. It is a day when the more deliberate and plodding Aries person is quite likely to come up with the right answers. Do not carry more money than you need. It will only burn a hole in your wallet.

DECEMBER

1. FRIDAY. Important. The final month of the year gets off to an excellent start for you people born under the sign of the Ram. You will be in an up-and-at-'em mood. Nothing is likely to be too much trouble for you. Aries who are involved in public relations will have an opportunity to catch the eye of superiors. Today is good for getting on the right side of the press. You may be able to land one or two scoops. This is a favorable period for putting some extra exertion into furthering routine business affairs. Get your accounts in better order. There will be a favorable opportunity for handling your affairs. You could get a jump on next year's.

2. SATURDAY. Slow. It is worth your investigating even apparently irrelevant matters or those of questionable relevance, if you feel they merit the effort. Knowledge can mean power and the more you broaden your scope, the better off you will be. Leave no stone unturned in your quest for recognition and promotion. You do not have to project your image too forcefully, though. There will be opportunities to make your presence felt by ticking quietly along in the background. This will not be a particularly important day for creative work. It would be best for you to deal with more mundane chores. Renew the business affairs and transactions of last week. It should be a good day for property matters.

3. SUNDAY. Mixed. Friends or close acquaintances may make possible particularly favorable introductions for you. These would be to people holding positions of power and authority who could help you. Do what you can to get on friendly terms with anyone who can assist you in your quest to get to the top of your chosen profession. Business and pleasure will mix in rather well on this day of rest. You may have some difficulty, however, in getting loved ones to go along with your plans. Arguments in the home could become rather heated. Your mate or partner may not understand your motives for taking the stand you have chosen. Lack of funds may interfere with secret hopes and dreams.

4. MONDAY. Important. With more energy than usual at your disposal, there is no reason why you should not achieve most of your ambitions for today. A single-minded approach is what is called for from you now. This is a starred period for delicate business negotiations. You should be able to get most of what you are asking for if you are discussing new contracts. Any natural talents you have should be exploited to the full. You may be in the fortunate position of having one or two choice offers to consider. People at or from a distance can be particularly helpful in providing interesting information. Group gatherings, later on in the day, will meet with favorable response.

5. TUESDAY. Satisfactory. This can be a good day for doing what you can to assist those people who are less fortunate than yourself. Charity work should be high on your agenda today. If you are not a member of an organization which works for the underprivileged, you may want to investigate various ones. Choose carefully before promising your time. You may feel that is more precious to you than money. The advice of friends is likely to prove reliable and worth serious consideration. The best results, as far as business is concerned, will be obtained by being diplomatic.

There can be happy reunions with people whom you have known in the past, but had lost track of over the years.

6. WEDNESDAY. Mixed.   This could be a good day for pinning down people who are usually very evasive. You may have the chance to discuss matters that you have been wanting to talk over for some time on a one-to-one basis. This will be useful, as it will prevent the persons from whom you want answers from passing the buck. Wriggling out of responsibilities has long been their style. Now, definite commitments can be extracted. This might be a good day for getting in some early shopping for the holiday season. You still have quite some time before the Christmas rush really takes hold, however. Straightforward, out-of-court legal or financial settlements can save many complications and expense.

7. THURSDAY. Disconcerting.   Life seems to have been running fairly smoothly for you so far this month. Unfortunately, the peace and calm are likely to be shattered at this juncture. This is not a time for attempts to grab the limelight. You could be sorely tempted to push your luck with influential people, but this would be an extremely unwise move. Superiors will take more than just offense at demonstrations of unusual or unconventional behavior. They will be angry. Family or household members are likely to act foolishly or irresponsibly. You will become annoyed at how extravagant people can be at this time of the year.

8. FRIDAY. Sensitive.   There will be more and better opportunities to put to rights what went wrong for you yesterday. Have a serious conversation with your mate or partner. You must be able to get them to see reason and make the cutbacks that you consider to be so important. Try to get a clearer idea of exactly where you stand with superiors. If your boss is noncommittal, you may have to take the initiative yourself. Once this is done, others are likely to show less reluctance and hesitation. But the day will probably lack the impetus needed to get major projects off the ground. It may be that you are devoting too much time to matters.

9. SATURDAY. Lucky.   This will be an important day. On the whole, you seem to have had a fairly successful week. But you should push yourself just a little bit harder to conclude a number of deals. These are ones that you have been patiently pecking away at. There may also be some new financial opportunities and propositions presenting themselves today. They will doubtless be particularly worthwhile. Today should be good for the handling and furthering of property affairs and transactions. The Aries-born who have to rely on other members of the family for money should find they are less stingy. Land or house owners may reduce rents or propose somewhat more favorable conditions.

10. SUNDAY. Demanding. Perhaps you will find conditions a little boring. You will probably have to give more of your time over to the call of domestic duty. There are lots of little odd jobs that you should come to grips with in and around the home. This is not a day for speculating with joint funds or resources. In fact, you should be making a concerted effort to make cutbacks in expenditures. Personal funds need protecting and conserving. Thinking tends to be erratic. No important decisions should be made about the future on this day of rest. Aries can severely overestimate the case of getting their own way. Stop and ponder your own actions as they may be seen from others' viewpoint.

11. MONDAY. Satisfactory. You will be able to get on with many of the jobs that you were not able to come to grips with over the weekend. This may possibly have been due to getting out and about more. Many Aries, in particular, will be pleased that they are able to catch up with domestic chores. There are likely to be fewer interruptions than usual. It should be a good day too for attending to desk jobs. Go over your accounts and try to work out just how much money you will have to spend over Christmas. All in all, this will be a fairly relaxed start to the working week. Conserve energy and channel it into constructive activities.

12. TUESDAY. Confusing. Too much running about today would be pointless. Do not set out on journeys unless you are absolutely sure that you have definite appointments. Arrangements that you made last week may have been postponed. People frequently forget the courtesy of telling others anything about their change of plans. Correspondence or telephone calls will probably be just as effective. Even trips in your immediate locality can be subject to frustrating delays. They could even prove to be a complete waste of time and money. This is certainly a period when you should be making more of an effort to conserve your money.

13. WEDNESDAY. Mixed. An early start would be helpful. You would do well to come to grips with all matters of a routine nature as early in the day as possible. As time goes by, you are likely to find that you have to make one or two unscheduled calls. Influential people will be friendly enough, but they will also be fairly definite as to exactly how they want jobs carried out. There will not be much room for inventiveness. But this is a good day for furthering plans in connection with setting up your home in a distant place. Some of you who have been keen to change your locality may be able to do just that now. Remember that lack of attention to detail in doing paperwork can lead to serious errors.

14. THURSDAY. Happy.   This will undoubtedly be one of the best days of the week for attending to accounts. You are holding these in conjunction with other people. The morning can be particularly good for attempts to close joint financial affairs and transactions. You may be able to put the finishing touches on negotiations that seem to have been dragging on for far too long. The day will be favorable for submitting the results of such ventures to clients. Property investors will have more opportunity for gain. It will also be a good day for dealing with the practical and financial aspects of family life. You will have an opportunity to enjoy a good time this evening. Play your cards right.

15. FRIDAY. Tricky.   This is one of those tricky days you occasionally experience. You should place more trust in yourself and your own judgment than that of outsiders. Friends and associates will mean well, but the advice they may offer you will be way off the mark. Romantic affairs could also be somewhat difficult to handle. As far as love affairs are concerned, there are likely to be setbacks and complications. Aries may feel unsure of precisely where they stand with their romantic partner. Their actions, as well as their thoughts, are likely to be confused. Friends may insist on maintaining relationships on a strictly platonic level.

16. SATURDAY. Disturbing.   Problems that you may have been brushing under the carpet all week are likely to come home to roost today. You may have some fairly awkward questions to answer today. This is also going to be a very tight period for readily available money. A check that you had been expecting for some work or service that you recently completed is not likely to come through. Pleasure and entertainment plans for the day or the weekend may have to be canceled. Romantic involvements can lead to power struggles. Speculation or gambling should be avoided as they would only lead to heavy losses.

17. SUNDAY. Changeable.   This is an extremely sensitive day for financial affairs. Your reserves certainly appear to have taken quite a heavy pounding recently. The important thing now is to go over your Christmas plans. Try to see where it might be possible to make some savings. Try, also, to get loved ones to go along with your schemes to cut back. You will certainly be more successful if you can get relatives to join you in a concerted team effort. The temptation to overspend must be resisted. Later on, the day can be good for putting some extra time into furthering routine work and performing necessary chores. But leave yourself some time to have a change of pace. Meet with friends for an impromptu party.

18. MONDAY. Lucky. This is an important day. You will not have many more chances before you take a Christmas break to add to your income. But there are likely to be excellent opportunities to supplement your earnings. These will come at a time when some extra cash would certainly come in very handy. This can be a memorable day for employment affairs. Promotion may be forthcoming. Even just a hint dropped by superiors can be enough to give the Ram more confidence. Their future employment prospects and financial security appear secure. It will be a favorable day for extending the contracts of dependable employees.

19. TUESDAY. Disconcerting. Employers and other influential people can be annoyingly noncommittal. Promises that were made to you verbally last week are likely to be forgotten, conveniently. You may be left with the feeling that your hopes of some early promotion are slipping away. The best way for you to deal with this is to shrug your shoulders and to be philosophical about it. Get on with any routine work that is at hand. This will help take your mind off depressing thoughts and feelings. You may, however, be forced to tackle certain jobs for which you feel a natural revulsion. One way or another, you may get the feeling that you cannot win. Put such thoughts out of your mind.

20. WEDNESDAY. Mixed. Extra workloads and responsibilities may be imposed on you. Although you are likely to be feeling the strain, you may also have the chance to earn more money. You could certainly do with some additional cash. This time of the year is always an extra-expensive one. Teachers may express disappointment at the progress of certain Aries students. Perhaps you have been neglecting your studies. You will certainly have to pull your socks up if you wish to achieve the results and the qualifications that you desire. But this is a favorable day for getting on closer terms with friends. It is also a particularly good day for making marriage plans and for all marital affairs.

21. THURSDAY. Difficult. Perhaps you are feeling the pressure of work as well as private problems? With the buildup to Christmas well under way, you are not likely to have much respite.

Loved ones will be demanding and could be quite a drain on your resources. It will be very difficult for you to keep to any budget that you may have set for yourself. Children will be pestering you to buy them gifts. You do not feel you can really afford any more than you have. Closer liaison with business colleagues and partners is essential in order to guard against misunderstandings. This would also preclude duplication of efforts. Relatives' curiosity can create some impatience.

22. FRIDAY. Satisfactory. This will probably not be a particularly exciting day. But you will at least have the opportunity to get caught up on matters that you have been having trouble coping with. It will be a good day for getting in last-minute Christmas shopping. It must be said, however, that the crowds in the big department stores will test your patience. There are likely to be long lines at all cashiers. Try to find gifts for people who always remember you at this time of the year. Bankers will be helpful if you require short-term loans. Other people in the business world will also be cooperative. But romantic partners will be quick to take offense, particularly over financial issues.

23. SATURDAY. Sensitive. It looks as though you will be rushed off your feet today. There are so many jobs to do you might wonder if you will be able to get through them all in time. Your best bet would be to try to leave matters connected with home and family affairs until Sunday. Then you will be better able to cope with them and to come to grips with outside matters. Handle whatever work you do not want to have to cope with during the holiday break. Many Aries people are likely to have their hands full with shopping. It might be possible to get younger members of the family to lend a helping hand in this area. Aries who handle money on behalf of others must be very careful.

24. SUNDAY. Exciting. This will be a pleasant day for trips and outings. You will enjoy meeting with various people whom you will not have the chance to see on Christmas Day. Loved ones will be easier to get along with. There will not be such a tense or emotionally charged atmosphere at home. This will be a good time for making the last-minute Christmas preparations. Youngsters will bring special joy to the heart of the Aries parent. There will be plenty to keep you occupied without your having to strain yourself. You might have the chance to further business negotiations and transactions. You want to get these off your chest before tomorrow when you intend to have a complete break.

25. MONDAY. MERRY CHRISTMAS! This can be one of the best and most exciting Christmas that Aries have ever had. Older Rams may experience the thrill and feelings of eager anticipation they have not felt since they were children. Everyone around you will be in good spirits. The atmosphere within your own home will be warm and generous. You should be able to spend much of your time with people who mean a great deal to you. Travel undertaken on the spur of the moment may prove to be especially enjoyable. You will have the chance to spring a surprise on an old pal whom you have not seen for quite awhile.

26. TUESDAY. Happy. You are likely to continue your celebrating today. Loved ones will continue to be warm and affectionate. You may feel like taking in a Christmas show or getting involved in some other form of outside entertainment. All in all, this will be an interesting as well as unusual day. There will be a good chance for spending more time in the company of people who live at or come from a distance. It could be favorable for taking up with a new interest that may have been spurred on by a present that you received. Today will be good for reading and study. This time of the year makes it particularly easy to rise above petty, emotional difficulties, as well as practical ones.

27. WEDNESDAY. Confusing. You may have to exert quite a lot of discipline over yourself today. Perhaps you have been overindulging. Try to cut back. Check your weight. You could well have put on quite a few unwanted pounds. This will be a difficult day for Aries-born people who have to go back to work. Conditions at the office or a store will seem to be cold and uninviting. You will have to give quite a lot of your time to checking up on your concerns and interests, holidays notwithstanding. Professional emergencies can compel you to neglect your family temporarily. But the day is favorable for new romantic attractions. Don't be shy about making the first move.

28. THURSDAY. Deceptive. You may be in the mood to spend, spend, spend. It would be a good idea to check up on the state of your accounts first. Some of the post-Christmas sales may have started and there are likely to be many tempting bargains in the shops. You would like to spend money on clothes and household goods very much. They are real bargains, but you would be well advised to remember the regular bills that will soon be pouring in. This can be a rather confusing day. Aries people will find it difficult to correctly gauge the sincerity of other people's words and actions. There is a genuine risk of deception in business and professional affairs. Check out all deals carefully.

29. FRIDAY. Demanding. This can be a good day for furthering business negotiations that came to a halt with the holiday break. Discussions that you have with colleagues should augur well for the New Year. It would not be in your interests, however, to agree to anything that you have not had the chance to examine in detail. Do not sign contracts that would tie you down far into the future; not until you are absolutely positive that you have obtained the best possible financial arrangements for yourself. Today would be good, too, for the handling of official correspondence. But Aries need to keep their minds on what they are doing. Otherwise, there is a greater risk of making some serious errors. You don't want to start 1990 on a sour note.

30. SATURDAY. Exciting. Attempts to make yourself a better person will be under favorable influences. But where willpower is involved, you may feel a little weaker. You may be inclined to make excuses about why you should give in. There will doubtless be lots of tempting foodstuffs around the house. Those will make it difficult to be strict about starting a new diet. Perhaps you should wait until the New Year before you really try to take off any extra pounds. You have put on more weight than you care to admit, but you can at least make some cutbacks with eating and drinking. This is a particularly favorable time for romance and romantic affairs. It will also be good for spending more time with friends.

31. SUNDAY. Quiet. Aries may find that this will be a rather quiet ending to the passing year. But you are not likely to have any objections on that score. You are apt to be feeling the fast pace of the week that has just come to an end. You will be grateful that you have the chance to relax and put your feet up. Get involved in a good book or tune in to some favorite TV program. This is a pleasant opportunity for spending time in the congenial company of friends and acquaintances. It will also be good for attending the traditional end-of-the-year festivities and parties. But it would be best to keep such activities at a relaxed and informal level and dispense with the more expensive frills. Say goodbye to the '80s and greet 1990!

OCTOBER—DECEMBER 1988

OCTOBER

1. SATURDAY. Sensitive. If you feel that certain specific problems on your home front are getting you down, you might ask a trusted relative to come over and lend you a hand. If others have not offered to lend a helping hand before, it may be that they did not want to risk being accused of interference. You will be glad to know that parents and other family members are willing to help. It makes you more aware of the fact they have your best interests at heart. A short trip could be very effective in furthering partnership affairs and teamwork efforts. It will be a favorable day for Aries who are getting married or becoming engaged. More attention should be paid to existing in-laws.

2. SUNDAY. Upsetting. It will be difficult to get to the root of your problems. A family member may be hiding something from you, or may even attempt emotional blackmail. Do not allow yourself to be scared off or threatened into agreeing to any demands. Stand up for what you know is right. Feelings about the past may be misleading. Do not try to get in touch with an old flame just because you are hit by a wave of emotional memories. It would definitely be a bad idea to try to rekindle the spark that was extinguished a very long time ago. Memories play odd tricks and people tend to forget the heartaches, while recalling only the romance and good times.

3. MONDAY. Disquieting. This will be an unsettled day. There appear to have been many problems that you had hoped to straighten out over the weekend. But they seem to have been left hanging in midair. There will be an uneasy atmosphere at home for reasons unknown to you. So you will be quite pleased to get away from the domestic environment. Correspondence or telephone messages may go astray. Check to be sure that mail you posted some days ago has arrived safely. This is a time when you should leave nothing to chance. Bring old work up to date with the latest information and news that is available to you. This will involve research to make certain you have current information.

4. TUESDAY. Exciting.   Expect this to be the best day of the month, so far. You will have more energy and drive than usual. You will now be able to throw yourself wholeheartedly into tasks that you have been staying away from. It will be favorable, too, for all artistic and creative work. Make the most of your natural talents. Show samples of your work to influential people for their approval. You are not likely to be disappointed with their reactions. You will be able to express your feelings and your ideas through the mediums of art or music. Results could be spectacular. This reaction should show you clearly that you should concentrate efforts on developing your talent.

5. WEDNESDAY. Easygoing.   This will be a good period for quiet reflection. Review events of the past few weeks and try to determine where and why you made whatever mistakes you did. Only then can you take preventive measures against their repetition. Go over all accounts in detail. Find ways to cut back on unnecessary and wasteful spending. This will not be an important day from a money-making angle. You can still achieve a great deal, however, if you are prepared to deal with jobs that require a lot of attention to detail. Relax and take things easy in your leisure time. You may have become absorbed in a speculative proposition earlier on. But conditions are not favorable for taking action.

6. THURSDAY. Exciting.   You will find yourself raring to go right from the start. The day will be favorable for distant travel. You will enjoy yourself most if you can keep on the move. Romance will be uppermost in your mind. Love affairs are likely to take on a more serious overtone quite unexpectedly. The Ram may feel that now is the right time to consider making a close relationship permanent. Long-term, practical considerations point to marriage rather than keeping involvements on a purely casual basis. Your love of adventure and your curiosity could lead you to some interesting, unique places of entertainment. Be on guard against smart operators who may see you as an easy mark.

7. FRIDAY. Successful.   You could find that routine affairs are not as boring today as they usually are. There may be more leeway to use your imagination and to be more original in the handling of your daily jobs. The atmosphere in your work environment will be pleasant and free of discord. This aura of pleasant relationships will be conducive to your giving free rein to natural talents. You can find new ways to streamline jobs that have begun to pall from tedium. You enjoy the challenge of this as well as the relief from boredom. This is a banner day for all work that calls for some degree of expertise and imagination.

8. SATURDAY. Productive. No particularly exciting or even difficult developments are likely to arise today. It will be unnecessary for you to take any important action as far as your career is concerned. It should be an opportune day for dropping in to visit with neighbors. But do not bother to travel very far out of your immediate vicinity. The results of any long trips you might take will probably be more than disappointing. Those who find themselves facing housework and such dull chores should try to catch up with them today. At least their completion will give you a sense of satisfaction. You can always make efforts to find ways to improve your health without going to extremes or taking a crash course in exercise.

9. SUNDAY. Demanding. Play it straight with loved ones right from the start. Aries people must be very careful about getting involved in secret love affairs. They could easily jeopardize everything that you have worked so hard to achieve. Pay more attention to the needs of your mate or partner. Youngsters will also require more than routine attention. Arguments may flare up within the home that will not be easy to resolve. You may feel that you are being pulled in two different directions at the moment. It will not be easy or satisfactory for you to cope. But harsh words can be quickly forgotten if forgiveness is asked and granted. Compromise is usually the key to fights and disagreements.

10. MONDAY. Fortunate. Start this working week as you mean to finish it. Go all-out to make a good impression on your boss. Now is the time to use all the energy at your disposal to persuade superiors to give your original ideas a fair hearing. Professional people who are experts can provide you with valuable legal advice. You may need it in regard to the drawing up of contracts. These could relate to a proposal you made some weeks ago. Today will be helpful for trying new approaches in teamwork and all cooperative endeavors. You should get the full support of your associates and superiors. Loved ones will be more understanding of the practical needs and basic requirements of Aries people. This will create harmony on the home front.

11. TUESDAY. Successful. Professional people and experts can provide valuable legal advice, if needed. Someone may be threatening to take you to court. It would be a good idea to check out just where you stand in this matter. You might find that you have nothing to fear. Those people may have been bluffing and talking so much hot air. It will be a favorable day for striking up partnerships with people at or from a distance. New starts that you embark on today are likely to turn out to be wholly successful. They could well bring you in handsome profits in the future. Discussions can be particularly valuable for clarifying difficult matters that have been unsettled for too long.

12. WEDNESDAY. Fair. A partnership's financial affairs may become critical if Aries allow their spending to get out of hand. You must try harder to keep control of the extravagant side of you nature. All will be well today, as long as you do not dip into savings to support pleasure-seeking. Don't allow so-called friends to sponge off you. Remember that you have worked hard for your money and you don't want to act foolishly now. It will be a good day for career affairs. Large companies and corporations will respond favorably to unusual and imaginative propositions. This positive sign will bring encouragement and relief to you.

13. THURSDAY. Easygoing. Self-employed Aries should find this a particularly pleasant and enjoyable day. You will not have to deal with a whole lot of jobs just to earn good money. Your services will probably be in great demand so that you will be able to pick and choose the kind of job you want. It will be an important day for the Ram who earns a living as a writer. Serious interruptions will be few and far between. All in all, this will not be a particularly active or demanding day. You can go over accounts and get caught up on any backlog of correspondence. Review recent spending. You may find ways you had not thought of for cutting costs. Confer with family members for their ideas.

14. FRIDAY. Mixed. Long journeys that you undertake today are unlikely to produce the results you wish. Trips made in an effort to improve business affairs will probably turn out to have been a complete waste of time. It would really be best for you to stick to your regular place of employment. The best way to gain information from people in other cities or towns is to write letters and to make more use of the telephone. The Aries person will find it hard to concentrate. He or she may also start to lose interest in studying and self-improvement programs. You should try to stay with such interests for your own sake. It will be a favorable day for deepening romantic ties.

15. SATURDAY. Special. This will be one of the best days that you have experienced in quite a few weeks. You will be in a much more optimistic frame of mind. Problems you have been fretting about will no longer get you down. Your approach now to difficult situations will be more dynamic. You should be able to find ways to boost your income to make up for any losses you have recently incurred. You will also find it possible to rise above any petty emotional and practical issues that have tended to cramp your style. Those of you who are prepared to paint on a broader canvas will find that this will be a banner day. Just make up your mind that you can do anything you really want to!

16. SUNDAY. Frustrating. The well-being of people who live at a distance from you is likely to be a cause of much concern. Someone for whom you care very deeply may be in some sort of trouble. This will tend to make the day extremely frustrating for you. You will feel powerless to do anything to help a friend whose interests and welfare you hold close to your heart. Various study courses you are taking seem to make quite unreasonable demands on the spare time of the Ram. You will find that concentration for very long periods is rather difficult. Impetuous or erratic actions can endanger good names. Think carefully before you speak unkindly about anyone. Are you in a position to know the facts?

17. MONDAY. Uncertain. It might be a little difficult to get into high gear early in the day. But by midafternoon, you should find that you have caught up with most of the jobs you had wished to handle. This would be a good time to do some background research into current business transactions. Find out exactly what has led up to the present stages. Rapport with your associates may not be particularly effective. It will be best to rely on yourself as much as possible now. Your associates appear to be vague and difficult to pin down. Misunderstandings can easily flare up. The Ram will not be above resorting to flattery and charm when the possibility of promotion or a pay hike arises.

18. TUESDAY. Upsetting. Influential people may decide on some business deal in favor of the opposition. This will cause you great disappointment. It looks as though your competitors have the upper hand over the Aries-born, at least for the time being. You will just have to bide your time and see what develops in coming weeks. There seems to be little you can do to change the minds of those who have some authority over you. Friends will easily be won over to your side by the infectious enthusiasm of the Ram. Their encouragement and support will go a long way toward restoring faith in yourself. Some conventional people may turn out to have surprisingly unconventional interests.

19. WEDNESDAY. Productive.   It will be a good day for getting on with important business matters. See what you can do to upgrade profits. Perhaps you have been getting into too much of a rut lately. You should be on the lookout to see how newer methods could be employed. You will find that superiors will be more amenable to your plans for change and progress. Valuable new agreements could be obtained. But bankers may not be willing to loan you sufficient funds to enable you to progress with your own projects. Influential people will not be as helpful as you may have thought they would be. Do not allow friends to try to influence you, even if they have your best interests at heart.

20. THURSDAY. Special.   Influential people in good standing are likely to side with Aries in legal matters. You will be pleased to realize you can rely on the support of superiors. There seems to have been a problem that has been hanging over your head for some time. It concerns a matter that could take you into court. But you feel now that this contretemps could probably be settled privately, and at a lesser cost. It will be easier to concentrate on your work today. Interruptions will be few and far between. Friends and acquaintances may provide valuable contacts and introductions. It should be favorable for taking decisive action to assure the repayment of debts.

21. FRIDAY. Important.   This should be an excellent day for coming to grips with the kinds of jobs that stimulate you. They allow you the opportunity to give free rein to your natural, inborn talents. It will be better for working away from the public today. Close scrutiny by others can hamper your style. It is also favorable for appealing to the true emotions of superiors. You may be able to make an important breakthrough in your career. Opinions can easily be swayed with the correct logic. Your powers of persuasion will be at a high pitch which will carry great influence. Swearing associates to complete secrecy may be the best way to handle even the most routine of business matters.

22. SATURDAY. Worrisome.   Aries people may be having misgivings about the future. Perhaps you are unsure about your prospects in staying on in your present employ. Superiors may have made promises about promotion that you do not feel sure they can or will fulfill. But it would be best for you to take your time before making any life-changing decisions. Your perspective may be out of whack today just because you are feeling down-in-the-mouth. Unexpected and promising developments may be just around the corner. Today would be good for tracking down people who are always virtually unavailable. Do not keep feelings of anger and resentment bottled up inside you at any time. They can get out of hand too quickly and you will suffer.

23. SUNDAY. Confusing. Young Aries-born people may grossly miscalculate the impression they make on others. If you are invited to some social affair where there will be many strangers, try to restrain your natural boisterousness. Don't be too pushy, either, especially with people older than yourself. Your sense of humor may not be appreciated as much as you like to think. Causing embarrassment for family and friends will hurt them and yourself. In the area of business matters, inaccurate appraisals of public opinion can result in a considerable amount of wasted time. But set aside a large portion of this day for some special entertainment. You should get away from anything connected with business and enjoy yourself.

24. MONDAY. Mixed. Don't hold back; get right into high gear. Make every effort to catch up with routine matters that were left over from last week, right at the start. Once you settle down into the regular routine, you should not find it too difficult to make fast progress. The Aries-born should now be able to assess business conditions reasonably far enough ahead to make long-term plans. On the other hand, superiors will be rather difficult. You may even feel that your boss is being obstructive and you will find it hard to figure out why. Those even higher up may impose severe restrictions with regard to absences and lateness. This would be a good period to try and do some serious reading, either for pleasure or a course you're taking. If it's for a course, find a quiet nook.

25. TUESDAY. Variable. A mixture of diplomacy and round-about methods can be the best way to make routine business dealings more lucrative. It will be a good time for having discussions with people behind the scenes. You may be able to find out somehow what your competitors intend to charge for their products in the future. If you succeed, you should then find a way to undercut those so that you will get more orders. This is a better day for the self-employed Ram than it is for those who have to take orders from above. Keeping your plans for future moves secret can be a major key to their success. Wrangling with partners over joint financial ventures is a pointless waste of time, money and energy.

26. WEDNESDAY. Fortunate. This should be a happy and enjoyable day. If you can work in more flexibility in handling routine work and normal business affairs, you will see increased earnings as a result. Do not limit yourself to the old ways of performing your work. It is also quite likely that changes will be forced upon you, and you should not try to block them. Monies earned by your spouse or other family members can help swell the financial coffers. Be sure that whatever savings accounts you have are earning the best possible interest. But you might have to go about recovering bad debts by the threat of legal action, or even by resorting to it. But try to avoid that if you possibly can.

27. THURSDAY. Quiet. This will be a useful day for pausing and assessing your personal affairs. You could try to get caught up with any backlog of correspondence, for instance. Keeping in touch with good friends is very important, especially if you are now separated by great distances. The telephone is another way of keeping in touch without having to resort to making a trip. And there are probably other areas of your life that require attention from time to time. There could be income tax matters, either a car registration or your driver's license to renew, and the inevitable bills to pay. Or you may just want to wander around the neighborhood and catch up on the gossip.

28. FRIDAY. Worrisome. Your spouse or loved ones may try to coerce you into taking on extra responsibilities and certain commitments. You will have to take a firm stand with the people who seem bent on throwing your money around. Arguments may develop, naturally, but you must take a stand and stick to your guns. You do not want to see your future security jeopardized for the want of determined action on your part. The quarrelsome behavior of romantic partners is probably only temporary. It may be due to simple fatigue or to ill-health. Disconcerting news may arrive from people who live at a distance later in the day. It might force you into taking an unexpected trip.

29. SATURDAY. Mixed. Some form of official permission that you have been waiting for might finally come through today. This may have to do with some household repairs that you cannot make without proper clearance because of building regulations. Or you may perhaps be adding onto an existing building. Whatever it is, you must adhere to building codes. You would be wise to seek professional help with the actual building which must be planned carefully down to the last detail. You don't want to find yourself spending more than is necessary for its construction. Romantic affairs can take on the state of a tug-of-war. Arguments and general friction may make the Aries-born doubt themselves.

30. SUNDAY. Sensitive. Aries and their mates or spouses may find themselves in bitter disputes over domestic and/or property affairs. The arguments not only will heat up but they will get you nowhere. The only way to take the wind out of your partner's sails is to stick to facts alone. Do not let yourself get drawn into a shouting match. It may be that the only way you can settle disputes is to declare a truce. Then, at least, you can get some rest and relaxation on this so-called day of rest. You may wish to give your favorite charity a helping hand by getting in touch with friends and persuading them to help out. Try to do something you cannot on work days, even if it's only a picnic or a long walk.

31. MONDAY. Important. Today will be a most fortunate ending to the month. Many of the worst problems that have been plaguing you, causing you sleepless nights frequently, can be resolved. You and your family will be able to come to decisions on the best ways to launch a new budget. This is an excellent time of year to try and increase your savings. The bills in winter are normally heavier than summer's, and there will be extra expenses over the holidays. Summon your inner resources of strength and determination. Help your associates to improve their work output. In doing so, you will doubtlessly improve your own. This will be a much happier day for romance than you have known for some time. Make the most of it and enjoy yourself.

NOVEMBER

1. TUESDAY. Manageable. Do not try to lay down the law with loved ones. If you try to be too bossy, serious fights could erupt within your home. Take a more relaxed form of live-and-let-live attitude toward your loved ones. You should be able to solve your own problems rather than attacking others. Using forcefulness will only produce even stronger opposition. It is not a day for taking speculative risks. If and when you have any money to spare, you should put it aside for use in paying bills. This should be a starred day for romance. It will also be lucky for engagement and marriage plans.

2. WEDNESDAY. Exciting. This will be an important day for you. Challenges should be met head-on. Aries people will have more confidence than usual and will be in the mood to take on exciting new ventures. Your superiors will be helpful and will encourage you to go further. Talk over vacation plans with loved ones later. You may be planning or hoping to go away over Christmas. Resorts and transportation are extremely popular and in demand for holiday travelers. This is a good period for reaching a better understanding with your spouse or partner over the best way to handle children of mixed age groups.

3. THURSDAY. Mixed-up. An overly casual or disrespectful attitude at work could seriously jeopardize your relationship with your boss. Do not take people in authority for granted. Just because they may have been friendly toward you recently does not indicate that you are buddies. Be sure that you do not neglect your routine duties. No matter how dull they may seem, they must be completed. Dawdling and gossiping on the job will get you nowhere, fast. Aries people should keep in mind that any promises or commitments they make today must be lived up to at a later time. If you remember that, you may be less likely to go overboard when you commit to something.

4. FRIDAY. Difficult. A personal problem you had thought you solved is likely to come up again today. You may not be able to give the amount of time and attention to your work that you were hoping for. It will be quite difficult for you not to fall behind schedule. You might even have to work overtime to get it finished. Bankers or local officials may force Aries people into a difficult situation. Tensions and disagreements that have remained beneath the surface may come bubbling to a head. Alimony settlements could be particularly unfavorable. Some may be forced to pay out far more than they can afford.

5. SATURDAY. Mixed. It would be unrealistic to be pleased with the start made so far this month. It has not been easy for you to get along with other people. This is true both at home and at your place of employment. This will be a better day for dealing on your own with any jobs that arise unexpectedly. But you should guard against fatigue which can lead eventually to ill-health. Be alert to the danger of accidents, especially if you sometimes work in an unsafe area. Falls or a blow could lead to serious injury. But your partner or spouse will be helpful, cheerful and optimistic, without any complaints or nagging.

6. SUNDAY. Enjoyable. This will be a pleasant and peaceful day for you and your immediate family. The more time that you can spend with them, the more likely you will be able to solve any irritating problems you have been unable to shake off during the week past. You might also try to make some hard and fast decisions about money. First, you want to increase savings meaningfully. It almost goes without saying that expenses will rise rapidly with the approach of several big holidays. You do not want to be caught short at such a crucial time. But take some time out just to relax and forget your troubles for a few hours.

7. MONDAY. Rewarding. Those Aries people who live alone may sometimes feel a bit lonely. They should actively seek others with interests similar to their own and share their knowledge. If you take a positive outlook on life you will get much more out of it. If you are someone whose career has suddenly come to a standstill, it will be very much up to you to alter the situation. The day will be favorable for all partnership ventures and transactions. Teamwork can assure lasting and lucrative results for deals it helped to get launched. Loved ones may come up with some sound, sensible ideas about the future.

8. TUESDAY. Good. This will be a first-class day. You should now be able to visualize the very real prospect of turning your hobby into an ongoing business concern. You have always tended to consider it as little more than a side interest. An influential person may take some special interest in your natural talents. You will feel encouraged to try some experimenting. Routine jobs will present no problems for you today. You are in the right frame of mind to race through them at top speed. If you have any interest in the occult, this would be a good time for investigations. Or some special sale might lure you to do shopping, instead.

9. WEDNESDAY. Fortunate. This is the third in a cycle of especially good days. Take all the opportunities that are open to you to increase your earnings. At the same time, try to improve your position before the year comes to an end. People with influence at your work place will be impressed if they see you are going all-out to get ahead. They are likely to give you a helping hand and encourage you to greater efforts. You should review your pension and retirement plans to be sure they are up to date. You must be on the alert to guard your future economic security.

10. THURSDAY. Changeable. Try to plan ahead as much as possible. This should be a good period for attempts to implement plans made earlier. You may have been considering forming new business partnerships. If so, you should arrange for meetings to see what would be the most propitious way to raise capital. You will need that if you hope to launch projects in the future. Aries people should also ponder ways in which they could speed up schedules. Time wasted is money lost, plus the risk of losing future orders. It may become necessary for you to travel for a face-to-face meeting with someone at a distance.

11. FRIDAY. Good.   This will be a very important day. Professional advice should be obtained in connection with marital affairs. Your relationship with your opposite number may be going through a very rough period. Try as you may, you are unable to come up with any solutions to these difficulties. So it would be a good idea to get in touch with a person who has marriage counseling experience. He or she can look at the situation more objectively than those directly involved. The day is good for healing rifts with in-laws. It should also be favorable for commencing study or self-improvement programs together with a loved one.

12. SATURDAY. Disquieting.   Any interruptions will be most irritating. You will have trouble dealing with desk jobs, especially if you are attempting to do so from your home base. Children will be something of a problem for the Aries parent. They are likely to demand a lot of attention. Unexpected developments can interfere with distant business interests. You may have great trouble in finding out precisely what is going on. The search for new horizons can take on an entirely new aspect. But the inability to control emotions can damage reputations. The person who cannot keep a check on his own is surely unable to boss others.

13. SUNDAY. Sensitive.   You may be feeling very uptight after a hectic week. But do not resort to panic measures. On this so-called day of rest, you should try to slow down a bit and get extra rest. Do not mix with high-strung and emotional people. Try simply to relax; do nothing if that suits you. The morning will be a particularly helpful one for professional artists. Aries, in general, are likely to realize that they can no longer afford to keep sitting on the fence. Shilly-shallying will only waste their own time, to say nothing of that of others. Have confidence in yourself and your creative talents. The day will be favorable for visiting relatives.

14. MONDAY. Rewarding.   People with a good deal of influence will be willing to put themselves out to help you. You should be able to make excellent progress with this assistance from authoritative figures. This will pertain especially if you have to deal with public or governmental departments. Large transactions can be satisfactorily closed. Bonus payments may be offered in return for extra hours of work. This financial reward will make it well worth your while to spend additional time working. But later on, financial discussions may result in Aries having to take on other commitments. And these will come at a time when you least want them. You will have to make up your mind to compromise.

15. TUESDAY. Mixed. Your personal affairs will require more attention than usual. You must devote more time and energy to them, at least for now. Loved ones may be feeling neglected. As they see it, you seem to be giving more time to your work and less to your home and family life. The irony is that what you are achieving in your career is for the good of all in the long run. However, you must not ignore the emotional needs of your family. The Aries-born will find it easier to express themselves at this time. Also, they will do so with greater clarity and decisiveness than usual. But you must leave your work at the office.

16. WEDNESDAY. Uncertain. Any attempt to address a large group of crowds could prove disastrous today. Aries people may have made an error in judging public opinion. It would therefore be best to keep your opinions to yourself. Today is favorable for reaching an amicable understanding with associates. You can settle matters relating to business financial affairs and division of profits. You might even come up with a fairer way of distributing dividends. People of influence may stand in the way of your realizing a secret hope or dream. Tax experts and accountants could increase their fees.

17. THURSDAY. Encouraging. The week looks as if it is starting to improve in many ways and will from here on. You should be very pleased at the way an artistic venture is going. You will receive every kind of praise. This may make you feel that you are on the verge of an extremely important breakthrough. It will be a good day for attending auditions and interviews. Secret maneuvering can prove to be the key to success in career and public transactions. Aries business people should not think themselves above beating others at their own game. Retired people can be especially helpful with the advice they can give you. Listen carefully; their experience is priceless.

18. FRIDAY. Good. This should be an even better day than yesterday for all creative jobs. You should be able to increase your income by making more of your specialist talents. It will also be favorable for attempts to settle legal disputes out of court. A mutually acceptable agreement can probably be reached. This is a good time for gaining sponsorship and public support for worthwhile charitable causes. Among other things, it will also be good for conducting negotiations behind closed doors. It is also the right time for signing secret or confidential documents. Later on, you may be able to catch influential people in a relaxed and informal mood.

19. SATURDAY. Useful. You may be feeling somewhat jaded this morning as a result of your late-night partying. But this must not stop you from making good use of any excellent business opportunities that may arise. Some good news may come in through the mails this morning. This might be money that has been owed to you for special work you completed some time ago. Aries-born people may have found others willing to sponsor their personal projects. This could be of great help as it is not easy to come up with large amounts of cash on short notice. But Aries must guard against being excessively outspoken.

20. SUNDAY. Easygoing. Any action on the business front is going to be decidedly limited. This is as it should be on the one day you have to rest up. Instead of concentrating on your career, try devoting more time to your home and family. There are lots of ways you can show them how fond you are of them all. A heart-to-heart talk with loved ones would go a long way to clearing the air. Understanding another's problems is half the battle. And knowing that someone is listening, and caring, will bring you closer together. They, too, have personal desires and goals. Make time to work on your favorite hobby.

21. MONDAY. Important. The morning is probably going to be the best period of the day. In the first place, you will have a clearer idea of what you want. You should be able to go a long way toward getting this if you make the right approach to influential people. Debts that have been owed to you for some time should be repaid. You may even have to remind friends of the money they borrowed from you. It would appear they have conveniently forgotten about their debt. Long-term schemes, that were expected to yield profits over a considerable period of time, can start producing quicker returns than were hoped for.

22. TUESDAY. Promising. Take care of your minor financial matters first. Get your accounts in good order and review them.

Consult with accountants on matters you feel unsure of. You may not have any idea of what you should do to make more interest on money you have stashed away. They may come up with ideas that you know nothing of. Romantic and marital affairs will take a sudden turn for the better. In fact, the future looks decidedly more promising in all areas having to do with someone who means a great deal to you. Influential people may not be available for interviews at just the time you most want to talk with them.

23. WEDNESDAY. Satisfactory. Publicity drives and advertising campaigns can yield substantial profits. Those of you involved in commercial affairs such as these will not have any complaints. You will find yourself treated fairly by the people in authority. The firm you work for may be offered an extremely lucrative contract, despite its having faced some very stiff competition. You will find some ideal ways for expanding operations faster than planned. Place any spare cash you may have in good, solid investments that will bring you high profits. Speculation sometimes works to your advantage, but it is risky.

24. THURSDAY. Important. There will be nothing that will be too much trouble for you today. You will possess qualities that will naturally draw others to you. Show off those of leadership. If you are involved in a business involving buying and selling, the new contracts you land could lead to a promotion. But be careful that you do not neglect your loved ones in your zeal to get to the top of the heap. It will be a favorable period for romantic involvements with people in age groups different from your own. But such relationships will tend not to be meaningfully emotional. They could be compared with ships that pass in the night.

25. FRIDAY. Upsetting. Self-employed Aries may become alarmed to realize that new contracts are not coming in as fast as you would like. This is the time of year when business usually picks up, not drops off. Your cash flow could be jeopardized, leading to serious shortages. This would not be a good day for requesting a loan from a bank official. It would be better to wait a bit if you can. You should not have much trouble in dealing with day-to-day affairs, however. You might find them fairly dreary and unchallenging, of course. Travel is not recommended as far as business is concerned. It is not likely to produce any results.

26. SATURDAY. Important. You will find that this is just the kind of day you were hoping for! The first part, including midday, should be devoted to business affairs. Try your best to wind up the loose ends of work contracts and agreements. After that, the time will be very much your own. It will be a kind of helpful day all around for you. You can concentrate on future planning without interruption. People of influence will respond to enthusiasm to Aries' proposals. They may even offer valuable assistance and full support. On the home front, this would be a good time to plan how to increase its value.

27. SUNDAY. Enjoyable.   This would appear to be another good day for you. Combining its better aspects with yesterday's will result in an excellent weekend for you. There will be next to no pressures to contend with. Your loved ones will be especially happy if you can devote the major part of your day to them. There is much to be straightened out in the way of home and family affairs. Acting as a team, you and your mate will find it easier to work out any differences. Your hobbies and other creative endeavors should receive some attention. Young children and teenagers will enjoy an outing.

28. MONDAY. Sensitive.   Today may be largely taken up with disciplining children. You cannot afford to let them walk all over you, so it is up to you to show who is boss. When they realize this, their attitude will become more respectful. Your business affairs will probably not give you much cause for worry. You might even be able to finish your work early and use the time off for yourself. If you are taking any courses, it might be an opportune time for some extra study. Or you might feel more like spending an hour in the gym exercising moderately. It's not too early to think about Christmas and whatever shopping you have to do.

29. TUESDAY. Uneventful.   There will be no need for Aries to put themselves out today any more than absolutely necessary. This may be just as well because they are probably feeling rather drained after yesterday. Straightening out emotional problems for others always takes a lot out of one. Superiors at your work place will undoubtedly be willing to allow you to attend just to routine matters. They will not appear to want to burden you with anything extra. You will appreciate this and realize that they are considerate. Later on, you might want to continue roughing out holiday plans and making notes of gift ideas.

30. WEDNESDAY. Productive.   There will be plenty going on today to keep you fully occupied. Unfortunately, the only jobs you will have to contend with are unlikely to be creatively stimulating. This will not apply to your personal plans. Study and other self-improvement programs will be better than ever for you. At home, you will probably find that proposed vacations have been made final. So the time has come for making firm reservations for travel and hotels. Your advance planning for daring projects will win the cooperation and support of others. This is no time for idle gossip. Even though someone else starts it, you need not reply.

DECEMBER

1. THURSDAY. Important.   This should be an important and active month for the Ram. Start it off well by pushing as hard as you can to reach your objectives. And your goal to do so is before the end of the year. Greater concern over your future economic security may provide the necessary incentive. Another ingredient is the added exertion you must put into routine work and other business matters. Take a fresh look at the old, familiar problems that have not been solved by using regular methods. There have to be other ways of doing almost anything. It's up to you to figure them out. Just use your usual ingenuity and common sense.

2. FRIDAY. Changeable.   Do not let the pressure of work and personal affairs make you forgetful. Check your appointment book daily so as not to miss important engagements. If you fail to keep a date with someone, whether they are important or not, you will be in the doghouse. If the appointment was a business one, you may lose out on a contract. This is a good time to buy pets. An animal can become the focus of love and affection, especially if there are children. But they should be taught how to give it proper care and not tease it. If you happen to be an Aries boss, this would be a good time to give your staff a pay raise.

3. SATURDAY. Difficult.   You may think that you have more time to take care of your regular job than you actually do. You may try goofing off during the morning, so that you will run into great difficulty in keeping up to your schedule. Take greater pains in trying to resolve problems that have sprung up in the relationship between you and your partner. Control your urge to justify yourself and try to prove that you are right all the time. If you can't adopt a give-and-take attitude, you may doom your relationship. Do something special this evening to show your affection and sincerity. Try asking your partner what they prefer to do.

4. SUNDAY. Sensitive. Tread softly today. One word of criticism could really cause a major blowup within your household. You may be feeling the strain of the past week and be overly critical. Take your mind off problems by concentrating on hobbies and other creative pursuits. Or get out of the house and take a long walk to calm yourself. Later, you may find you can show interest in family affairs and become part of the group again. You could even offer to help out with some of the routine chores. Find ways of enjoying yourselves as a group, even if it's only looking at old family albums.

5. MONDAY. Lucky. Your work and other employment affairs must take priority over personal ones. For one thing, you need to increase your income insofar as possible. There will be more than the normal number of bills coming due by the end of the year. And the holidays always mean extra spending for entertainment and presents. Long-term research projects can be advanced, particularly those involving large numbers of statistics and other data. And don't stop experimenting with new ideas. You can never tell when you might just hit the jackpot.

6. TUESDAY. Demanding. Joint resources could become the cause of extra concern and anxiety. Loved ones have ideas of their own about how to handle these. They may be unwilling, too, to try and reach a compromise solution. Your health may require attention. You should see a doctor at the first sign of a bad cold and nip it in the bud. If you let it get really bad, you could be sick over the holidays and ruin your fun. Aries should learn to tone down their tendency to speak to others in an abrupt way. They should show the same respect toward them as they expect to get themselves. Otherwise, you will find yourself being left out.

7. WEDNESDAY. Upsetting. If you go over your accounts, you may discover that you are not as well off as you thought you were. Aries may invite the wrath of partners by their excessive spending and extravagance. Just plain carelessness in handling financial matters could lead to unnecessary expenses. Be on guard against letting your bank balance get into the red. That would be bad news indeed, especially at this time of year. If you handle tools or machinery today, be extra careful. Safety guards should be used at all times. They are there to protect you, not annoy you. Do not dramatize a personal crisis.

8. THURSDAY. Buoyant. This will be a tip-top day, the opposite of yesterday. Superiors may drop hints of a pay raise and promotion in the coming year. This will wipe out the dismal events of yesterday and give you a charge. Use your initiative in drawing up plans for the future. You have a vivid imagination and you should not let it go idle. You can afford to strike out against well-known precedents and set your own guidelines. If you have difficult people to deal with, take a no-nonsense attitude toward them. Otherwise, you will find your authority jeopardized. It is not too early to go on a shopping expedition, with Christmas drawing near.

9. FRIDAY. Important. If you are a gambler, this is quite likely to be your lucky day. You may very well receive a financial windfall. A project that you invested in a long time ago, and had just about written off as a dud, may suddenly show profits. This would be an excellent time to get together all information you can about courses in higher education. You might have to enroll quite early in the most useful ones. If you're aiming for a higher niche, you could probably improve your chances by learning about its makeup. You might also get help from experts in the field who could advise you what to study.

10. SATURDAY. Disconcerting. Do not jump to hasty conclusions about your associates at your place of business. People may have been spreading rumors that are totally unjustified. Wait until you can get all the facts together before pointing any fingers. Some Aries have a tendency for deception in the field of public affairs. Still others may deliberately conceal their motives. But nobody should be reprimanded for being allowed to have their say unless they are lying. Since this is the start of a weekend, make plans for fun and entertainment in advance. Put all thoughts of business affairs right out of your mind. Worry doesn't help, anyway.

11. SUNDAY. Good. Today should be favorable for deepening your existing romantic involvements. Most relationships can be made more secure. Loved ones will be willing to lend you a hand in your business and career affairs. Much progress can be made in discussions about your financial affairs with a spouse or partner. Your thoughts may also turn to Christmas and whatever plans you are making. If you are preparing to go away for several days, you might have to confirm certain reservations. You could probably do some shopping today since many large stores are open at this time of year, even though it is Sunday.

12. MONDAY. Special. Go all-out today to try and earn more money, even if it means you must work overtime. Expenses are always higher than anticipated, especially at this season. The day will be good for business transactions as a whole and for financial affairs. You might be able to make use of group or club functions to air your personal views and ideas. Your audience will be comprised of many with your sort of background and tastes. This will ensure rapport and understanding of some people, even if they are not in total agreement. Friends may also be actively helpful which will give you a boost.

13. TUESDAY. Mixed. An important letter or telephone call you were hoping to receive will not arrive. This will be upsetting because the matter is one of money that is owed to you. But today would be good for getting in touch with government officials or similarly influential types in connection with affairs overseas. They are frequently able to cut red tape in connection with business dealings. This might be a good day for you to join a club or society with interests that you wish to study. Loved ones may disturb Aries by making financial demands that you will find excessive and unreasonable. But you sill still find it difficult to know where to draw the line.

14. WEDNESDAY. Productive. Today will be somewhat mixed, but not a total waste. It would be well to get rid of any routine jobs that you always find boring early in the day. You might not have enough determination later on. It will be favorable for pinning down people who are usually evasive and even somewhat devious. Get them into a situation they can't back out of, for once. You might even be able to extract a firm commitment for something. Behind-the-scenes actions can be especially helpful in furthering your career and business affairs. Original and unusual business propositions may prove to be particularly worthwhile.

15. THURSDAY. Successful. Any dispute in which you are involved, whether legal or personal, would be best settled as quickly as possible. Taking such cases to court can be an unnecessary waste of time and money. There are only ten days left till Christmas which means it is now or never for mailing your cards. Aries should practice using tact and diplomacy in their dealings, rather than their normal aggressive tactics. As the old saying goes, honey catches more flies than vinegar. You might want to find out some rather personal information about someone you are thinking of employing. If so, private investigations are favored.

16. FRIDAY. Sensitive. New financial propositions you receive from peculiar or unlikely sources can turn out to be especially lucrative. Your secret contacts, as well as those who work away from usual business setups, can bring Aries good luck. Your personal likes and dislikes can sometimes interfere with your good judgment. This is a failing many Aries have, one which should be suppressed. Your words should be chosen carefully, especially if you have negative feelings. If children have come back into your household for the Christmas holidays, do not lose your temper with them. They have naturally high spirits.

17. SATURDAY. Tricky. Any shopping you try to do today will probably be made more difficult than usual by crowds of Christmas shoppers. Almost any other day or evening would be less frantic. The day could be useful for Aries who want to get new projects started. If you need the help of others, however, you must be very careful of the danger of stepping on people's toes. Your directness is sometimes considered rude or even offensive. You are apt to make others feel threatened in some way. Trying too hard will often produce negative results rather than those you were aiming for. Save some of your energy for having fun this evening.

18. SUNDAY. Fortunate. An undercurrent of excitement will be felt by all in the household. Everyone will getting into the spirit of the holidays. Young people do not have to worry about school for the next two weeks and can enjoy themselves. You may find that in-laws can provide you with valuable introductions to certain key people in positions of authority. The upshot might be a boost for your career or access to even more influential officials. Learning as much as you can about your profession can be extremely beneficial. Try to get some advice from an expert as to what courses of study would be the most useful to you.

19. MONDAY. Upsetting. This will not be a good day for your financial affairs in general. You may get word of higher taxes in the coming year, as well as a rise in insurance fees. The cost of borrowing money could also be in for an increase, as well as the charges made by your accountants. All of these will have a direct effect on your personal funds for daily expenses, as well as your reserves. You may have to work out a new budget before the end of the year. Don't let such worries affect the quality of your work. You have established yourself as a steady, dependable person, with good rapport with those in authority.

20. TUESDAY. Mixed. This should be an auspicious day for financial transactions. Fresh proposals made by your colleagues could be especially worthwhile. Great care must be exercised when contracts or agreements are being drawn up for business deals. Be on guard against loopholes and ambiguities which could cause financial losses to Aries people in the future. You may receive some money today without having had to work for it. It might be a commission due to you for some time that you had forgotten about. As an unexpected windfall, it could not have come at a better time.

21. WEDNESDAY. Enjoyable. You will find that business affairs and pleasure will mix well today. If the office party takes place some time, you will have a chance to socialize at all levels. This would also be a good opportunity to take a more active role in your community affairs. There are usually many opportunities to volunteer your help for. Fund-raising is an important role, to say nothing of talking neighbors into helping out. If you don't have time to talk face-to-face with someone, you could telephone or write a brief outline of what is needed. The day will also be favorable for putting more exertion into your creative projects, or catching up with reading.

22. THURSDAY. Difficult. You are going to have to keep a tight rein on your feelings today. For some obscure reason, you seem to want to alienate those with whom you hope to work closely in the future. You appear to be in an argumentative mood, willing to get into any kind of heated discussion with almost everybody. People in authority may opt for radical changes or unconventional ideas. If the changes favor Aries, they will last for only a short time. You must make every effort to keep your extravagant tendencies in check. A major upheaval in your business career could necessitate similar changes in your home and family life.

23. FRIDAY. Tricky. Regular business affairs may turn out to be confusing and potentially deceptive today. Do not assume anything, no matter how normal it might seem, nor should you take anything for granted. At the same time, the day will be good for signing contracts or agreements with large firms. You could find that prior discussions with a bank official are enormously helpful in clearing up any misconceptions. If you feel that someone in your firm is withholding information that could help you, bypass the person and go straight to the top. Assistants sometimes assume they know more than their superiors and could mislead you.

24. SATURDAY. Sensitive. You may be feeling the need for some good advice today. So do not ignore what people in authority tell you about the future of your career. Try to exercise greater tolerance when dealing with others. Any personal criticism of yourself may contain more than a grain of truth; think about it carefully before dismissing it. You are not always able to judge the effect that your attitude sometimes has on others. Even short trips will prove ineffective if Aries tries to cover too many bases in too little time. The generosity of family members is quite exceptional. This is your absolute last chance to buy Christmas presents!

25. MERRY CHRISTMAS! There should be no pressures on you to mar the day. You can relax and enjoy some good times, and forget your worries. There may be some family reunions with those who live in other parts of the country. It might also be possible to patch up an old feud with a family member. Forget the past differences and start building a new and happier future. Even if there is little excitement or activity within the household, you can still enjoy the best part of the day at home.

26. MONDAY. Satisfactory. This may feel like the lull after the storm, or perhaps a bit of a letdown following the excitement. Certainly today will be more dynamic than yesterday, with plenty of action. You might want to give children some special treat. But you will have to watch your budget carefully, with entertainment costs on the rise. The same goes for any special ideas you might have connected with romance. You may find yourself planning ahead for possible moves you will make in your career early in the coming year. That is a mere five days away, so it is not a bit too early to give it thought.

27. TUESDAY. Mixed. This is definitely not the day to gamble. Follow this piece of advice and you won't have to worry on that score. You certainly have paid out a lot of money during the Christmas season, but it would be stupid to think you could win it back. Children may become overly excited and tend to break their possessions or those of other people. But far worse will be the tendency of your romantic partner to break his or her word. The person you probably felt very sure of has probably just been playing with your emotions. Turn to your creative or artistic pursuits. Your originality and inventiveness will occupy your mind.

28. WEDNESDAY. Manageable. Some of you may be returning to work for the first time since last week. If so, you could be faced with completing the routine sort of work you should have done before the holiday. You could enhance your business reputation by handling unusual and out-of-the-way matters. Craftsmanship and technical skills can earn anyone the respect of other workers and employers. Unfortunately, your work could conflict with romance today which will cause quarrels. But you must realize that your work has to come before pleasure now and stick to it. A loved one may be trying to coerce you into changing your job.

29. THURSDAY. Challenging. Today will be favorable for getting new contracts signed. The agreements you are able to consummate today should make you feel far more secure about your future. Be sure you get the best possible terms without sacrificing anything. Making allowances for inflation rates should have been taken into consideration. The Aries alertness and quick thinking will attract the attention of those who have some measure of control over you. Not only could a promotion result, but you may also earn a substantial end-of-the-year bonus. Even a self-employed Aries can secure a valuable contract.

30. FRIDAY. Demanding. Even though you may have worked out a busy schedule for today, you might have to rearrange and streamline it. Your health could be the deciding factor, requiring you to concentrate on personal matters. At the same time, loved ones may nag you to take on more responsibility for domestic problems. Legal proceedings may take a disconcerting turn with unexpected devlopments. You simply cannot count on a favorable outcome now. Quarrels between partners can lead to sudden separations and then to breakups. And it will undoubtedly be the Aries people who have to pick up the pieces and bear the burden.

31. SATURDAY. Mixed. New information that has been provided will prove particularly helpful to you. It will enable you to forumulate your business plans that you are so keen to launch in the New Year. Aries may find ways to increase their net incomes, but it is important to keep receipts for spending outlays. They will enable you to take tax deductions on certain items. It would be a good idea to review all your personal financial affairs at this time. You find that certain people in positions of authority are unreliable and unlikely to keep their word. Forget them and concentrate on having a happy New Year's Eve!